General Editor's Introduction

Asbury Theological Seminary Series in World Christian Revitalization Movements

This volume is published in collaboration with the Center for the Study of World Christian Revitalization Movements, a cooperative initiative of Asbury Theological Seminary faculty. Building on the work of the previous Wesleyan/Holiness Studies Center at the Seminary, the Center provides a focus for research in the Wesleyan Holiness and other related Christian renewal movements, including Pietism and Pentecostal movements, which have had a world impact. The research seeks to develop analytical models of these movements, including their biblical and theological assessment. Using an interdisciplinary approach, the Center bridges relevant discourses in several areas in order to gain insights for effective Christian mission globally. It recognizes the need for conducting research that combines insights from the history of evangelical renewal and revival movements with anthropological and religious studies literature on revitalization movements. It also networks with similar or related research and study centers around the world, in addition to sponsoring its own research projects.

This project helps give definition to the decisive trend in the current trajectory of world Christianity by focusing on the shape of global renewal in the context of religious pluralism, on the one side, and the mandate given by the Great Commission, on the other. Its authors provide substance to the discussion with their special foci on a wide spectrum of expressions of Christian renewal. The discussion also is consistent with the concerns of this project in assessing world Christian revitalization movements. As such, we commend the work to scholars and practitioners of Christian revitalization, as well as students of this timely theme.

J. Steven O'Malley, Director
Center for the Study of World Christian Revitalization Movements
Asbury Theological Seminary

Sub-Series Foreword

The Pentecostal and Charismatic Sub-Series

Of all the renewal traditions that have engaged the theological landscape, the Pentecostal Movement has undoubtedly made the most significant impact since it emerged at the turn of the twentieth century. Starting as a revival in a small African-American congregation on Azusa Street in Los Angeles, California, the movement soon swept the world, establishing itself in more than forty countries in the first three years. One hundred years later Pentecostalism has grown to an estimated 500 million global adherents or approximately twenty-five percent of all of Christendom. In the same manner that Wesleyanism burst beyond the bounds of Methodism to embrace an interdenominational holiness movement following the American Civil War in the nineteenth century, Pentecostalism transcended denominational lines in the form of the Charismatic Movement during the second half of the twentieth century.

This sub-series is designed to explore the historical, theological and intercultural dimensions of these twin twentieth-century Restorationists traditions from a global perspective. In this volume Clifton Clarke and Amos Yong have edited essays that address the theological task of how an evangelistic theological tradition engages in authentic dialogue with non-Christian religions. Originally presented at a symposium held at Regent University, this volume breaks new ground as many of the leading global Pentecostal/Charismatic scholars addressing this issue were brought together to reflect upon this question. The results that emerge offer exciting possible trajectories as these persons join forces with scholars of other Christian traditions to engage in this significant dialogue of our time.

D. William Faupel
Sub-series Editor

Global Renewal, Religious Pluralism, and The Great Commission

Towards a Renewal Theology of Mission and Interreligious Encounter

Amos Yong
&
Clifton Clarke,
Editors

The Asbury Theological Seminary Series in World Christian Revitalization Movements in Pentecostal/Charismatic Studies, No. 4

EMETH PRESS
www.emethpress.com

Global Renewal, Religious Pluralism, and the Great Commission:
Towards a Renewal Theology of Mission and Interreligious Encounter

Library of Congress Cataloging-in-Publication Data

Global renewal, religious pluralism, and the Great Commission : towards a renewal theology of mission and interreligious encounter / edited by Clifton Clarke & Amos Yong.
    p. cm. -- (Asbury Theological Seminary series in Christian revitalization. Pentecostal/charismatic section)
 Includes bibliographical references (p.   ) index.
 ISBN 978-0-9819582-8-6 (alk. paper)
 1. Missions--Theory. 2. Pentecostalism. 3. Christianity and other religions. 4. Theology of religions (Christian theology). I. Clarke, Clifton. II. Yong, Amos.
 BV2063.G563 2011
 266.001--dc22
                        2010044672

To

Allan Anderson

Doktorvater, colleague, friend

Table of Contents

Acknowledgments

This book arose out of the idea to host a colloquium on the theme, which was instigated by Clifton Clarke joining Amos Yong and the Regent University School of Divinity faculty as associate professor of global missions and world Christianity in the fall of 2008. We are grateful to Divinity deans Michael Palmer, Don Tucker, Randall Pannell, and, especially, Joy Brathwaite, dean of business and administration, for their support in making this event happen. We are grateful also to the following for their various contributions to the symposium which was held in February of 2010:

- Veli-Matti Kärkkäinen, Kirsteen Kim, Cephas Omenyo, Tony Richie, and Steven Studebaker for responding to our initial invitation to participate in this project, for writing such fine essays for inclusion in this volume, and for being timely with their final revisions;
- Antipas Harris, Skip Horton-Parker, Bramwell Osula, Rich Danzeizen, Dan Backens, Katy Attanasi, and Diane Chandler for participating in the symposium, responding to the papers in various ways, and providing important critical questions that have shaped the revisions and final outcome of what is now seen in this volume;
- Joy Brathwaite, Christie Davie, Ella Thompson, Charles Eichmann, Marc Santom, Paula Finch, Kathy Shultz, Jason Wermuth, Timothy Lim Teck Ngern, Amanda Rinker, Sara Orszulak, and Christopher Springer (we hope we have not forgotten anyone!), all of whom contributed to the symposium to make it possible.

Thanks to Bill Faupel, Larry Wood, and J. Stephen O'Malley for a swift and ringing endorsement in response to our proposal to publish the symposium papers in the Asbury Theological Seminary Series in Christian Revitalization—Pentecostal/Charismatic section. Bill carefully read the manuscript and saved us from numerous blunders, not to mention helped ensure that the book was more consistently formatted in terms of its style. Timothy Lim Teck Ngern, Amos' graduate assistant at the School of Divinity, helped out with formatting and indexing the volume, and Samantha Van Saun, Clifton's graduate assistant, produced the first draft of the index – we are thankful to both.

We dedicate this book to Allan Anderson. Allan was *doktorvater* to Clifton at the University of Birmingham, and has been a long time friend to and dialogue partner with Amos on matters related to the topics of this volume. He has established himself as one of the consummate scholars of global renewal and of the history and theology of mission. We are both in your debt, Allan—thank you for your life's work in the Spirit!

Preface

Three theological themes intersect in the pages of this book: theology of religions, theology of interreligious relations, and theology of mission. The first asks questions about how to understand the diversity of religions in relationship to God; the second explores how Christians should approach and interact with people of other faiths; and the last concerns missiology, the discipline that studies the character, purpose, and methods of the church's missionary work in the world. Together, these themes combine as the threefold cord around which this book is woven. In a word, the task at hand resolves to query the nature of the Christian mission in a religiously plural world.

However, this undertaking is being carried out particularly in light of the explosion of renewal Christianity in the global South. The tensions are exacerbated precisely because renewal Christians—coming from pentecostal, charismatic, and related movements—are uncompromisingly evangelistic and missionary in their self-understanding and practices, and because, by and large, they have neglected reflecting theologically on the fact of religious plurality. In short, the authors of this book all seek to address the urgent theological and missiological questions confronting renewal Christianity in a pluralistic world.

Part I includes three more theoretically oriented chapters. Clifton Clarke covers a good deal of the theology of religions and theology of interreligious encounters terrain in a helpful way that sets up the other chapters of the book. Simultaneously, he also proposes that contemporary renewal theologies of interreligious dialogue can be furthered by engaging with non-Western epistemologies and indigenous traditions. This in itself will be suggestive for a renewal theology of mission in a pluralistic world.

Steve Studebaker goes to the heart of the theological issues that are at play in recent pentecostal and charismatic proposals regarding a pneumatological, or Spirit-driven, approach to theology of religions: the relationship between the doctrines of creation and redemption, the meaning of Pentecost, and the nature of the work or economy of the Spirit vis-à-vis that of the Father and the Son. Thus he hopes to expand on the pneumatological theologies of religions and missions toward a more fully trinitarian vision, one that sees the religions as potentially caught up in the Spirit's activity inaugurated on the Day of Pentecost. While theoretically dense, Studebaker's chapter is important in highlighting how missiological issues are intricately bound up even in what some may consider abstruse discussions about the inner-trinitarian life of God.

The second chapter by Tony Richie brings renewal theologies of religions and missions into dialogue with Roman Catholic perspectives, particularly that of the ecumenical theologian, Yves Congar. The latter helps renewal theologians articulate a more inclusivistic—rather than exclusivistic—approach to theology of religions that does not neglect the missionary witness of the church in a pluralistic world. At the same time, the vibrant pneumatology characteristic of renewal theology invigorates Congar's more classically formulated theology of the Holy Spirit.

The three authors in part II focus more concretely on the intersection of renewal Christianity and other religions in Asia and Africa. Veli-Matti Kärkkäinen is a theologian with missionary experience in Thailand, which informs his discussion. He suggests that in the Theravadan Buddhist Thai context, renewal theology is challenged to think more deeply about the nature of suffering. Yet in response, the centrality of the affections in renewal spirituality and theology in turn challenges the fundamental Theravadan Buddhist concept of *apatheia*, inviting us to consider instead the notion of *passio* or *pathos*—both human and divine—as central to the Christian message in the South East Asian context.

Kirsteen Kim's chapter is focused on Hindu India, building on her previous work on Indian Christianity and its theological developments. She suggests that while the pneumatological motifs of renewal theology of religions enable dialogical engagement with indigenous Indian and Hindu theological systems, perhaps more important are the liberationist strands of Dalit theology. The point is that the renewal emphasis on conversion is consonant with Dalit theologies of liberation: both stand to gain from dialogical interaction not just at the theological level but in terms of the plight of the masses, especially untouchables, on the Indian continent.

The final chapter in this part of the book focuses on the encounter—some might say, "clash"—between renewal Christianity and Islam in sub-Saharan Africa. Cephas Omenyo, a Ghanaian Presbyterian (which has been largely charismatized) and expert on the forces of renewal in West Africa, provides historical, demographic, and socio-political perspective on the challenges confronting especially renewalists. If mainline Christians in Nigeria (where the most serious conflicts between Christians and Muslims have occurred) and Ghana can learn from renewal spirituality and piety, renewalists can in turn gain perspective on evangelistic and missionary methods from the wisdom of their elder Christian brothers and sisters.

The concluding chapter by Amos Yong overviews the missiological issues confronting the global renewal movement, particularly as present in its rhetoric of demonization of the "other," and attempts to adjudicate some of the urgent questions related to this matter by correlating the contributions in this volume with a fresh reading of relevant passages in the book of Acts.

This collection of essays attempts to discern and chart the way forward toward viable theological views regarding the religions in the twenty-first century, especially as these might enable the renewal and re-invigoration of mission in the present pluralistic age. The goal is to suggest how renewal Christianity can continue to engage in the missionary task in a religiously plural world but do so in a manner that neither compromises its core theological convictions and spiritual practices on the one hand nor that undermines the gospel's capacity to bear witness in a world of many faiths on the other. If we are successful, then the questions will no longer be *if* we should formulate a theology of religions or a theology of interreligious encounter but *what kind of* theological perspective will be most helpful for our time. This will be measured by the ongoing vitality of the Christian witness, albeit one that, paradoxically, builds up rather than tears down religious others who have been created in the image of God in Christ, and to whom the Spirit may yet be mysteriously present and also actively at work.

Part I

Renewal Christianity,

Interreligious Encounter,

& Theology of Religions

Chapter 1

Dialogue or Diatribe:
Toward a Renewal Approach to
Interreligious Conversation

Clifton Clarke

Introduction:
Interreligious Dialogue and the Postmodern Context

Today's major world religions no longer exist separated by geographical and cultural boundaries. World religious traditions that were once seemingly "worlds apart" now flourish nearby to one another. In the old order Hinduism was located in the Indian subcontinent, Buddhism in East and Southeast Asia, and Islam in the Middle East and North Africa primarily. But the great migrations of the twenty-first century are bringing together a complex tapestry of religious diversity changing irreversibly the global religious kaleidoscope.[1] In the USA, these changes have been brought about in part by the 1965 law which allowed for previously restricted groups to immigrate on the same basis as Europeans before then. According to Diana Eck, there are now an estimated 5.5 million Muslims in the United States, 1.3 million Hindus, and about six hundred thousand Buddhists.[2] Fluid immigration patterns have brought people of many religious backgrounds together in the places where we live and work. Ethnic, cultural, and particularly religious diversity are the hallmark of modern urban life. Francis Clooney thus notes that diversity not only envelops us, it works on us, and gets inside us.[3]

The emergence of a multicultural, multiethnic, and multireligious world makes cooperation and dialogue among religions essential for building a harmonious and civil society. Interreligious dialogue is also central for creating a genuinely free and just society that fosters mutual tolerance and respect.[4] A healthy dialogical relationship with Muslims, for example, can engage issues such as the legitimation of racism in the name of the Bible in South Africa and in the Middle East. In a similar vein the Muslim-Christian dialogue will provide opportunities to question Muslim radicalism and extremism as well as advocate for the rights of women. Christianity's historical encounter with Hinduism has also sharply challenged the very basis on which traditional Hindu society was organized, which contributed to the reform and renewal of Hinduism in the nineteenth and twentieth centuries.[5] Other examples could be cited but the point made is that dialogue—among other things—is instrumental in creating the environment and establishing the relationships that allow hard questions to be asked.

This past century has perhaps been the cruelest in human history. In the light of this century of conflicts and brutality Jacques Dupuis highlights the need for a purification of memory and theological language if we are to enable authentic and sincere encounters between the various religious traditions.[6] An example he cites which epitomizes this healing of memory concerns the response to the inhumane massacre of millions of Jews during World War II:

> Purification of memory is not at all easy. People and religious communities cannot be asked to forget how much they have suffered, even at the hand of Christianity, if not in the extermination of their population, often in any case to the point of the destruction of their cultural and religious heritage. For them forgetting would tantamount to betrayal. The personal identity of a human group is built up from a concrete historic past that in any case cannot be annulled even if there were a will to do so. But even while not forgetting, memory can be healed and purified through a shared determination to begin new constructive mutual relations of dialogue and collaboration, of encounter.[7]

Along with the purification of memory, Dupuis also advocates for the purification of theological language. He notes that pejorative classification of people as "pagans," "infidels," or even "non-believers" is offensive and polarizes religious communities. Today's multiethnic, multicultural, and multireligious world requires from all a qualitative leap proportional to that launched by the forces of global communication and integration. I argue that if we are to have open and positive mutual relation between peoples, cultures, and religions of the world in the future, dialogue and collaboration is vital.

In the Western world this convergence of religious traditions coincides with an emerging postmodern context which rejects objective truth and any global narrative.[8] This egalitarian mindset has brought about a widespread change in attitudes towards other religious traditions and their right to religious space and to their own views on "truth." The once esoteric teachings and religious virtues of non-Western religious traditions are now banal. This openness is indicative in the ease of access to the tenants and teaching of the major world faiths. For example, it is not unusual to see translations of the Bhagavad Gita, the Dao De Ching, and the Dhammapada alongside of the Bible in book stores.[9] It is also common to find a Qur'an conveniently located beside the Gideon's Bible in some hotel rooms. The appetite for greater openness to and knowledge of other religious traditions is further reflected in increased airing of the depths of religions on public television, and in the rise of interest in world religion courses on college campuses which often attract more students than courses in Christian theology.

The horrors of World Wars I and II, along with more recent devastating events such as 9-11, have hastened the quest for greater openness and mutual acceptance. This atmosphere of parity and equality as it relates to the Christian message of salvation through Christ presents serious challenges for Christianity. Arnulf Camps, the Dutch Franciscan priest and a former Consultor to the Vatican Secretariat for Non-Christians, suggests the causes of this changing outlook between Christianity and other religions are extra-ecclesial and intra-ecclesial. He identifies four extra-ecclesial factors:

1. Religions in the past were separated geographically which is no longer the case as our world has become more pluriform in the religious realm.
2. Within the various world religions we can detect a growing mission-mindedness. The collapse of the colonial system has led to a revival of the old religions and cultures and to the demise of Christianity's feeling of superiority.
3. There is a greater awareness of human need in terms of health provision and famine relief.
4. Developing nations of the world are incorporating indigenous religious values and cultural and religious theologies and philosophies to aid their economical and political development.[10]

The intra-ecclesial factors are traced to the shift to a greater openness towards other religions which began in the Catholic Church after Vatican II. Both Dupuis and Camps view Vatican II as a watershed with regard to the greater openness and dialogue toward different religious traditions.

In the midst of these rapid changes in the West is the burgeoning of the Renewal movement, most of whose adherents espouse a conservative Evangelical faith. I suggest that the Renewal movement within Christianity needs to find new expressions and approaches to interreligious dialogue beyond the language of what has become known as the threefold paradigm of exclusivism, inclusivism and pluralism.[11] While this typology has been helpful in delineating broad positions adopted by various traditions and theological perspectives, it now appears to have run its course. As Gavin D'Costa points out, employed heuristically or pedagogically, the typology has its uses; nevertheless, the fact remains that it is basically a simplification of a highly complex issue, "forcing diverse materials into easily controlled locations."[12] The premise on which this typology is based primarily serves the pluralist agenda and places inclusivism and exclusivism into rigid categories unpalatable for the postmodern mindset.

The issue of interreligious dialogue and the theology of religious pluralism is perhaps one of the greatest challenges demanding a concerted response from those in the Renewal movement. The questions still linger: Is interreligious dialogue of any value to Renewal Christians who hold to a non-negotiable Christ-centered salvation? Is the only appropriate posture one of proclamation and proselytization? In a world which is witnessing increased religious tension and conflicts should Renewal Christians adopt a more amenable and conciliatory attitude to other religions? Or are other religious traditions essentially "demonic" and should they therefore be exorcised and denounced as "false religions"? As the Renewal movement continues to burgeon across the world the issue of its approach to other religious traditions is unavoidable.

This chapter does not seek to carve out a Renewal approach to a theology of religions *per se,* but rather it seeks to explore "interreligious dialogue" from a Renewal perspective,[13] particularly one that is premised upon a non-Western and non-enlightenment approach. I will be arguing that the pneumatological insights into interreligious dialogue provide fresh opportunities for input particularly from a non-Western perspective. My approach is to first, revisit some of the key developments and challenges of interreligious dialogue within the Catholic and Protestant traditions, along with the Evangelical entrance; second, briefly describe the nature of interreligious dialogue; third, assess emerging Renewal contributions to the debate on interreligious dialogue, particularly the works of Amos Yong; and last, postulate what I consider to be non-enlightenment contributions from an African context. A key question that undergirds this essay is: "is it possible to move from diatribe to dialogue as the predominant interreligious posture?" The goal of this chapter is thus two-fold: to provide an orientation to the issues that are the subject of the essays in this volume as a whole, and to answer our key question affirmatively by drawing upon resources from within the Renewal tradition and scholarship, as well as from non-Western epistemological perspectives.

Interreligious Dialogue in the Twentieth Century

Christianity's dialogue with other religious faiths is as old as Christianity itself. The history of the development of religious dialogue has been well documented and does not need to be rehearsed in detail here.[14] Still, in order to contextualize and introduce the Renewal contribution, it is necessary to highlight some of the major developments leading to current discussions. I will thus present aspects of the Catholic developments through the activities carried by Vatican II and by the

Secretariat for Non-Christians in the Vatican (renamed the Pontifical Council for Interreligious Dialogue in 1988), review initiatives in the International Missionary Council and the Division for Dialogue of the World Council of Churches (WCC) in Geneva, and lastly comment on the Evangelical entrance to this arena.

Catholic Developments

The official Catholic view with regards to other religions was characterized by the formula "outside the church there is no salvation."[15] It was not until Vatican II (1962-1965) that fundamental changes began to emerge. The Catholic Secretariat for Non-Christians was established in 1964 with the specific goal of broadening interreligious discourse. Under the leadership of Paolo Cadinal Marella the Secretariat focused on scholarly publication from different parts of the world. Examples of these deliberations are found in its *Bulletin* which delineates different views concerning dialogue. Later innovative guidelines were written on how dialogue between different religions might proceed.

One of the most influential scholars and churchman during this period who made an impression at Vatican II was Karl Rahner, architect of the theory of the "anonymous Christian." Rahner promulgated the view that under certain conditions, devout Hindus or Buddhists could be regarded as "anonymous" or "implicit" Christians, and thus have access to salvation even though they have never heard the Good News of Jesus Christ or come in contact with the visible church.[16] After Vatican II Catholic theologians struggled to reconcile the idea of "no salvation outside of the Church" with the doctrine of Christ being normative for the salvation for all persons.[17] On one level there was still a sense in which the church was indispensible for salvation. *Lumen Gentium*, the "Dogmatic Constitution of the Church," stated, "Basing itself upon scripture and tradition, this Council teaches that the Church, a pilgrim now on earth, is necessary for salvation: the one Christ is mediator and the ways of salvation; he is present to us in his body which is the Church."[18] Given the supreme position Christ still occupied and the necessity (in some sense) of the Church for salvation, the council strongly affirmed in *Ad Gentes,* the "Decree on the Church's Missionary Activity," that the church still had a vital role to play in human salvation. Yet the council also underscored a much more optimistic and constructive way of looking at other religions. *Lumen Gentium* §16 for example states:

> Those who, through no fault of their own, do not know the Gospel of Christ or his Church, but who nevertheless seek God with a sincere heart, and moved by grace, try in their actions to do his will as they know it through the dictates of their conscience—those too may achieve eternal salvation. Nor shall divine providence deny the assistance necessary for salvation to those who, without any fault of theirs, have not yet arrived at an explicit knowledge of God, and who, not without grace, strive to lead a good life. Whatever good or truth is found amongst them is considered by the Church to be preparation for

the Gospel and given by him who enlightens all men that they many at length have life.[19]

Paul Knitter, a well known Catholic theologian and leading advocate of interreligious dialogue and religious pluralism, and Jacques Dupuis, a Catholic theologian and veteran officer within the WCC, interpret the documents of Vatican II as affirming that the non-Christian religions can provide avenues to salvation.[20] Catholic inclusivism found expression within the creative tension between the normative value of Christ and the Church on the one hand and the possibility of salvation and truth within other religions on the other hand. Theologians such as Heinz Schlette, Joseph Neuner, Karl Rahner, and Hans Kung, just to name a few, have been major players in constructing an inclusive interpretation of Catholic theology of religions.[21]

Protestant Developments

Protestants have grappled with interreligious issues much longer than Catholics. Questions of an interfaith nature began to surface in tangible forms during the first meeting of the International Missionary Council (IMC) in Edinburgh in 1910. At the outset of the debate views varied between those who saw dialogue as leading to compromise and syncretism and others who saw dialogue as a means to foster healthy relationship between people of different faiths. In spite of reservations there have been a plethora of meetings which have engaged questions of interfaith dialogue by the earlier IMC to the present-day Division of Dialogue of the World Council of Churches (Geneva). It is beyond the scope of this chapter to discuss all the different congresses that have taken place here but I will highlight some of the more significant ones.

To begin with it is important to recognize that the history of such congresses goes back to the World's Parliament of Religions, which was held in Chicago in 1893. Representatives from virtually all of the major world religions attended. Although the congress was heavily weighted towards a more theologically liberal agenda and was vastly overrepresented by Christians, the voices of various religious traditions were nonetheless heard. An influential voice within the congress was Ernst Troeltsch, who presented a relativized understanding of the absolute claims of Christianity via a more historical conception of the religions.[22] This congress later gave birth to the World Missionary Conference which held its first meeting in Edinburgh in 1910 under the theme, "Carry the Gospel to All the Non-Christian World." This was followed by other major conferences at Jerusalem (1928) and Tambaram (1938).

It was in preparation for the Tambaram conference that Hendrik Kraemer was asked by the council to conduct a study on Christianity and the other world religions. The result was his best-known and controversial book entitled *The Christian Message in a Non-Christian World*.[23] The book was published in German, English, French, and Swedish and had a major influence in subsequent decades of missiological thinking. In the book Kraemer threw down the gauntlet and drew a clear line in the sand between Christianity and other religions. He declared that other religions were merely human works, however great they might be on that level, and that they were efforts at self-deliverance. Over and against them, but also over and against Christianity as an institutional religion, was the Christian faith with its demand to renounce everything. The book marked a critical juncture and received varying responses and reviews. Not surprisingly Kraemer was opposed from those outside of the Christian tradition who felt his views nullified devotion to their own sacred traditions. However, the argument was warmly received among some European theologians, especially those who were influenced by the neo-orthodox theology of Karl Barth and Emile Brunner which argued for a discontinuity between Christian faith based on divine revelation and human religiosity derived from natural revelation.[24]

Another significant organization deserving mention here is the Temple of Understanding, which held its first spiritual summit conference in Calcutta in 1968. The conference included representatives Hindus, Christians, Buddhists, Muslims, Jews, Sikhs, Bahaists, and followers of Confucius and Zoroaster. The allotted theme was the "relevance of religions for the problems of the modern world." Each religious representative sought to provide insights from the vantage point of his or her faith. The second conference of the Temple of Understanding was held in Geneva in 1970. Once again participants gathered in convocation to find solution to the world's woes. There were discussions and deliberations on mutual understanding, peace, justice, and brotherhood. In addition to this were other organizations, including the World Conference of Religions and Peace in 1961, which led to the International Conference of Religions for Peace in Kyoto, Japan, in 1970 and again in 1974. A full presentation of the various interreligious conferences and organization goes beyond my allotted space here. Suffice it to say that particularly in the last century the issue of interreligious dialogue and cooperation has been an important project for both Catholics and Protestants.

In the meanwhile, the most recent developments have included reactions to Kraemer's exclusivism, resulting in the emergence of a more pluralist paradigm. Recognizing the seismic shift this pluralist approach would require from the whole of "Christendom," John Hick termed it the "Copernican Revolution." Hick compares his pluralistic theology of religions to Copernicus's astronomical model. God, the Ultimate Truth, is the center of all religions around which they revolve in the way of planets:

> And the needed Copernican revolution in theology involves an equally radical transformation in our conception of the universe of faiths the place of our own religion within it. It involves a shift from the dogma that Christianity is at the center to the realization that it is God who is at the center, and that all the religions of mankind, including our own, serve and revolve around him.[25]

This revolution, Hick contends, removes Christianity from the center of the universe of faiths and replaces it with "the Real" or "Ultimate Reality."[26] Hick notes: "And we have to realize that the universe of faiths centers upon God, and not upon Christianity or upon any other religion. He is the sun, the originative source of life and light, whom all the religions reflect in their won different ways."[27]

In several places, including his books *The Myth of God Incarnate* and *The Metaphor of God Incarnate*, Hick proposes a reinterpretation of traditional Christology, particularly the doctrine of the Incarnation.[28] He argues that, the historical Jesus of Nazareth did not teach or apparently believe that he was God, or God the Son, Second Person of a Holy Trinity, incarnate, or the son of God in a unique sense. Hick argues for a paradigm shift in Christian self-understanding.[29]

Following Hick's Copernican revolution which departed from the traditional Christological view, the floodgate of pluralism burst wide open. Even Roman Catholic scholars such as Paul Knitter and Raimundo Panikkar have taken the baton and have been forceful advocates of the pluralist approach to the theology of religions.[30] In spite of the prominence of these pluralist voices, many within the Catholic Church question the plausibility of this approach. The inclusivist Catholic Gavin D'Costa, for example, asserts:

> Against a pluralist theocentrism, it must also be stressed that "whatever is said of the Father is said of the Son." We cannot, as Christians speak of the Father without the story of Jesus. The Father cannot be conjured up through speculation or abstraction, but is revealed in the particularities of history, in the story of the Son, understood and interpreted through the illumination of the Spirit.[31]

In a substantive review of the various positions held by different traditions in regard to a theology of religious pluralism, Veli-Matti Kärkkäinen notes that in reality it is probably D'Costa's inclusive position that better represents current Catholic opinion as opposed to the pluralistic approach by Hick, Knitter, and others in the pluralist camp.[32]

Evangelicals and the Interreligious Encounter

Evangelicals are somewhat late comers to the debate on interreligious dialogue. The preponderance of a more liberal agenda and representation at the various congresses on interreligious dialogue precluded the participation of most Evangelicals. As Gerald McDermott points out, Evangelicals, unlike their liberal and postliberal counterparts, reject liberalism's faith in human experience as a final norm for truth and morality.[33] Against the homogenizing tendency of liberal theology, which would postulate an underlying religiosity common to all faiths, Evangelicals emphasize the particularity of Christian revelation and the uniqueness of Christian Spirituality. This Evangelical commitment would have been perceived as compromised by its church leaders and umbrella associations if its members or theologians were seen dialoguing with people of other faiths in tandem with liberal scholars and ecclesiarchs. This has led to a dearth in critical reflection on issues of interreligious relations from an Evangelical perspective. This late entrance to the debate means that by default Evangelicals allowed others to define the category of exclusivism—with all its pejorative associations—as well as their stance on religious pluralism. Although the traditional taxonomy of exclusivism, inclusivism, and pluralism has come under fire,[34] exclusivism still very much broadly defines the Evangelical position. In the early eighties Neal Punt and Norman Anderson were the first to engage the issues.[35] More recently the inclusivism of Clark Pinnock, John Sanders, and Stanley Grenz has drawn Evangelicals into a more nuanced and less cut-and-dry discourse.[36]

When Evangelicals have considered the world religions, for the most part they have focused on the questions of truth (do all religions teach the same essential truths? Is truth propositional or ineffable?) and salvation (can non-Christians be saved?), not revelation (is there divine revelations in the religions?). The Evangelical problem with postliberalism is that it tends to reduce truth to a matter of internal consistency, which has a very difficult time addressing questions such as "why be a Christian and not a Buddhist?" The issue of how truthful one religion is over the other is therefore central to the Evangelical inquiry into interreligious discourse. This matter of ultimate truth and salvation therefore becomes a point of impasse, with exclusivists (or particularists) insisting on a singularity of truth and salvation and pluralists on the diversity of truths and salvation. The task of moving the debate beyond this impasse has provided Renewal scholars an opportunity to make a significant contribution. Their contribution is not only crucial for the theology of religious pluralism but even more so for refreshing the whole debate surrounding the merits of interreligious dialogue.

In sum, interreligious dialogue within both Catholic and Protestant traditions have undergone developments on which current and future work must build. There are perhaps three things that stand out in regards to this history. First, there is still no consensus as to what constitutes "dialogue." Perhaps one should speak of levels of dialogue. Notto Thelle suggests four levels of dialogue: 1) dialogue at the level of theology and philosophy, often conducted by scholars of religion; 2) various types of spirituality dialogue, often less interested in theoretical exchange than in the sharing of spiritual practices such as prayer and meditation; 3) dialogue aiming at cooperation about common concerns, such as poverty, discrimination, injustice, conflict, militarism, the environment, etc.; and 4) the everyday dialogue between neighbors of diverse faiths.[37] Thelle's levels of dialogue are helpful in directing interreligious dialogue theorists to the right context. Second, dialogue goes beyond multifaith symposia, colloquia, and convocations; it extends to the whole life of the faith community. Third, the question of a dialogue about salvation has not been resolved and the issue of truth continues to be a sticking point for many, particularly those in the Evangelical camp. In this next section I will be narrowing the focus to briefly examine nature of dialogue and its role in interreligious conversation.

The Nature of Interreligious Dialogue

The work of Wilfred Cantwell Smith on the nature of religion is helpful for thinking about the nature of interreligious dialogue. Smith insists that interreligious dialogue and understanding is fundamentally the concern of religious persons.[38] Smith's person-centered perspective is critical of any approach to religious understanding that transmutes religion into a static system or limits religious life to its historic forms within particular religious traditions. Religion in the contemporary sense of the word is for Smith the product of both identity politics and apologetics:

> One's own "religion" may be piety and faith, obedience, worship, and a vision of God. An alien "religion" is a system of beliefs or rituals, an abstract and impersonal pattern of observables. A dialectic ensues, however. If one's own "religion" is attacked, by unbelievers who necessarily conceptualize it schematically, or all religion is, by the indifferent, one tends to leap to the defence of what is attacked, so that presently participants of a faith—especially those most involved in argument—are using the term in the same externalist and theoretical sense as their opponents. Religion as a systematic entity, as it emerged in the seventeenth and eighteenth centuries, is a concept of polemics and apologetics.[39]

Smith's approach to religion seeks to unhinge the religious individuals from fixed hegemonies of dogma and history into a more dynamic and "personalistic" lived experience. In order to accomplish this more fluid understanding he suggests the elimination of the single concept, "religion" and the substitution of two concepts, "faith" and "tradition," what he calls the "cumulative tradition." By faith Smith means an "inner religious experience or involvement of a particular person," and by tradition he means the "cumulative mass of overt objective data that constitutes the historic deposit...of the past religious life of the community in question."[40] Smith's position has been criticized for not clearly distinguishing between the categories of faith and tradition and for not explaining how one can separate the language of faith and the inner experience of the religious person.[41] But Smith's approach to interreligious dialogue has great appeal in its emphasis on religion as a way of life rather than as a static system. In fact, his understanding of the essence of religion as the "life of personal faith" has much to teach the Western enlightenment approach that reduces faith to dogma.

Protocol for interreligious dialogue has been an important feature of the discussion about the nature of interreligious dialogue, and various models have been proposed.[42] In a 1984 document by the Secretariat for Non-Christians entitled "Dialogue and Mission," several principle types are presented. Dialogue includes following: 1) witness; 2) the concrete commitment to the service of humankind and all forms of activity for social development and for the struggle against poverty and the structure which produce it; 3) liturgical life, prayer and contemplation; 4) the dialogue in which Christians meet the followers of other religious traditions in order to walk together towards truth and to work together in projects of common concern; finally, 5) announcing the kergyma and catechesis.[43] The totality of Christian mission involves all these elements. Together, however, all these types and forms of dialogue are, for Christians, different ways of working for the Evangelical transformation of cultures, and for sharing with others the values of the gospel.[44]

Interreligious Dialogue and Renewal

I have taken the time to give a brief sketch of some of the developments of interfaith dialogue because any discussion of interfaith dialogue and the theologies of religious pluralism from a Renewal vantage point should build on these past and current developments. We now shift to review the Renewal contributions to the theology of interreligious dialogue. I will do this by giving an overview of the traditional Renewal posture towards the other religions and interreligious dialogue, and assessing the contributions of Renewal scholarship to this topic. The latter sub-section, the longest of this chapter, shall involve conversation with Amos Yong and other Renewal scholars working in this area. Our goal will be to draw out what I perceive to be the most significant aspects of these contributions toward interreligious dialogue and cooperation.

Reasoning with the Devil and Interreligious Dialogue: Renewal Postures

During the early periods of the Renewal movement in North America the idea of Pentecostal Christians dialoguing with the historic Christian traditions, such as Catholicism, Methodism, Presbyterians, Baptist churches, and the rest, would have been like pouring new wine into old wine skins. Many Pentecostals even doubted the authenticity of the salvation claimed by people in these traditions, many of whom—it was believed—had sold out to a more liberal agenda. As a step child of North American fundamentalism and adopted cousin of conservative Evangelicalism, Pentecostals promulgated a literalistic reading of Scripture which sought to return to the basics of differentiating between light and darkness; between God and the Devil; heaven and hell; and the saved and the unsaved. The task of distancing itself from the liberal trends of the day, which included the ecumenical movement and a soft approach to other religions, in part defined this new renewal movement and what it stood for. It is of little wonder therefore that the idea of dialogue with people from other religions was nowhere on the radar. Spurred on by the Great Commission, the eminent premillennial second coming of Christ, and what Steven Land calls "passion for the Kingdom,"[45] Pentecostals sought to win a lost world to Christ and chief among sinners were those in other religions.

During the middle of the twentieth century some early signs of nuance were registered. Within the Church of God (Cleveland, Tennessee)—the denomination in which I am a minister—there were interesting developments worth noting. First, the Church of God's Pathway Press published a denominational guide to the religions,[46] reflecting a very significant shift in attitude. In addition *Church of God Evangel* reported on a number of features indicative of a desire for dialogue with other religions from this classical Pentecostal denomination.[47] The sentiments expressed in these publications were a part of a broader recognition stirring among Pentecostal and Charismatics that a blanket dismissal of other religions as "devilish" and as being of no ethical or moral value was gradually being reassessed.

To fast forward slightly, the move from an austere exclusivism to a more sympathetic exclusivism within the classical Pentecostals—urged on by the growing Evangelical inclusivism championed more recently by Clark Pinnock and others—marked a point of departure for Renewal theology of religions. Along with this was an increasing participation of Pentecostals within ecumenical endeavors such as the Roman Catholic and Pentecostal dialogue and the Oneness Pentecostal and Muslim dialogue. It is this background that has given rise to some of the most innovative and groundbreaking contributions to theology of religious pluralism from a Renewal perspective, particularly from the vantage point of pneumatology.

Renewal Pneumatological insights

The turn to pneumatology to stimulate fresh insights into interreligious dialogue could arguably be traced to three sources. First is George Khodr's address to the Central committee of the World Council of Churches (WCC) entitled "Christianity in a Pluralistic World—The Economy of the Holy Spirit," delivered at Addis Ababa in 1971.[48] This thought provoking speech challenged its hearers to begin to look at the Spirit as a point of entry for an understanding of other faiths. Second, it is well known that the second Vatican Council's constitution *Gaudium et Spes* took note of the universal activity of the Spirit of God amidst the aspirations of all humankind. Third, the presence and universal action of the Spirit of God among the "other" and in their religious traditions was suggested by John Paul II and may have been his most important contribution to the theological foundations of interreligious dialogue. In *Redemptor Hominis* §6 the Pope notes that the "firm belief" of the followers of other religions is "an effect of the Spirit of truth operating outside the visible confines of the Mystical Body."

From an Evangelical standpoint Clark Pinnock, the Canadian charismatic theologian, wrote a systematic pneumatology, *Flame of Love: A Theology of the Holy Spirit.* This book was probably the point of entry for Pentecostal pneumatological reflections on religions. Pinnock pointedly challenged Renewals for not having a "spirit-oriented theology of mission and world religions," in spite of their sensitivity to the Spirit, their openness to religious experience, and their prevalence among the oppressed of the Third World where they have experienced most growth.[49] The gauntlet thrown down by Pinnock has been taken up by Renewal scholars. In the context of this discussion of interreligious dialogue in general and in further response to Clark Pinnock's challenge I wish to explore some of these Pentecostal contributions. I will do this by interacting with Amos Yong's pneumatological theology of interreligious dialogue as well as referencing other Pentecostal scholars on this issue.

Yong's contributions as a Pentecostal to theology of interreligious dialogue should not be surprising given his origins in the pluralistic world of Asia (he was born in the multifaith nation of Malaysia). Pentecostalism itself as a global movement emerged from a vicissitude of ecumenical, intercultural, and international vantages. It has derived from a multiplicity of other centers apart from that of Europe and America. For example, in the late 1900s, Pandita Sarasvati Ramabai led a powerful revival movement in India. Ramabai, a converted Brahmin, was instrumental in the origins of Pentecostalism and in the acceptance of its phenomena among the wider Indian Christian community.[50] In Africa, Pentecostalism also has a unique historiography emanating from various indigenous movements which include African prophetism, African indigenous churches, and African traditional religion.[51] This variegated movement of the Spirit is borne out of an ability to interlace and dialogue with cultures, traditions, religions, institutions, and so forth as its spirituality and vitality inculturates and incarnates throughout the world. The Holy Spirit is therefore in many respects a dialogical Spirit which negotiates, convicts, inspires, rebuke, and discerns as it leads the community into *all* truth (John 16:13). There is a prospect here, as Johannes Nissen rightly observes, of coming into a new understanding beyond what the community has already reached.[52] This understanding of the Spirit is reflected in John 3:8: the Spirit blows wherever it pleases. In reflecting on this passage Amos Yong wonders, if the Spirit blows where it chooses, why would the Spirit blow "outside" the church but not at all in the religions, especially if the religions themselves are socially, politically and cultural laden?[53]

My colleague and co-editor of this volume, Amos Yong, is the J. Rodman William Professor of Systematic Theology at Regent University and possibly the most innovative and productive Pentecostal scholar addressing the issues of interreligious dialogue and theology of religious pluralism today.[54] My purpose here, once again, is not to do a full review of Yong's works but to highlight its contribution to interreligious dialogue as I develop my own thoughts. Perhaps the best place to begin is with Yong's groundbreaking PhD dissertation, *Discerning the Spirit(s)*.

While a forceful pneumatological contribution to the theology of religious pluralism debate, *Discerning the Spirit(s)* is also a valuable sourcebook which carefully documents the historical developments of the various theologies of the religions. Yong concludes from his thorough and careful review that Christian theology of religions is at an impasse under the constraints imposed by Christology. According to Yong, the question posed by Jesus Christ as he travelled with his disciples to the villages of Caesarea Philippi, "Who do men say that I am" (Mark 8:27), continues to be a stumbling block for interreligious conversations. Yong, echoing the challenge posed by Pinnock, urges Renewalists to take up this quest for a theology of religious pluralism and to participate in the interreligious dialogue.

Without in any way trying to undermine or side step the very important place of Christ within the interreligious discourse, Yong posits a pneumatological approach to interreligious dialogue as a way forward beyond the current Christological impasse. The basis of this pneumatological approach is what he calls *foundational pneumatology*. Here he builds upon the pneumatology of charismatic Catholic theologian Donald Gelpi, but takes as a point of departure Gelpi's notion of conversion and posits instead a "pneumatological imagination." For Gelpi foundational theology assesses the conversion experience as being essential for religious traditions. Yong suggests that a better strategy for foundational pneumatology is to focus on the entirety of the epistemological and experiential spectrum of the human being-in-the-world rather than on the methodological or functional role of specific experiences, including that of Christian conversion.[55] This more encompassing or holistic approach which he calls a pneumatological imagination suggests a way of seeing God, self, and world that is inspired by the Pentecostal/Charismatic experience of the Spirit.[56] This pneumatological approach to the religions advances the idea of the Holy Spirit as a cosmic divine presence whose work extends beyond the ecclesiastical boundaries of the visible church, perhaps into even that of other religious traditions.[57] Yong systematically develops this pneumatological outlook by laying the biblical foundation and establishing a Trinitarian balance.

Yong's pneumatological focus on the economy of the Spirit as opposed to the traditional economy of the Son has attracted accusations of dichotomizing the ontology and functions of the Christ and the Holy Spirit in a way that blurs their inseparability and mutual dependence.[58] Although it is understandable that the very appearance of dichotomization or isolation of the economies of the Son and the Spirit will attract the attention of Trinitarian theologians, the silence in the face of the historical dominance of Christology is deafening. One wonders whether the cautionary red flags waved by those warning against a rigorous pneumatological approach to interreligious dialogue stems from concerns about the Trinity or from the perennial strain towards Western conceptual and rational Christology within the enlightenment tradition. Allan Anderson notes that the difficulty with some Western approaches to theology is a dualistic rationalization that does not adequately understand a holistic worldview uniting the physical, the spiritual, the personal, and the social.[59]

Another very important reason for a pneumatological approach to interreligious dialogue is the prevalence and resurgence of traditional religions around the world, particularly in the global South.[60] A predilection to pneumatology often generates dialogue between religions that transcends classical theological verbiage and historical rivalry. Anderson insightfully notes that the Pentecostal churches have made possible a dialogue between autochthonous worldviews, religions, and Christianity at an existential level.[61] A pneumatological approach to religions allows interreligious dialogue to take place on the existential level where the presence and activity of God can be seen operating in the religious other through acts of love, kindness, and love, virtues that find their origins in the ultimate source of all things which we call Good (Luke 18:19).

In his book *Hospitality and the Other*, Yong sets forth his pneumatological theology in very practical terms. Responding to charges of theological abstraction, he attempts to "show that in a postmodern and pluralistic world of interreligious war and violence, there are glimmers of hope manifested in various acts of interreligious hospitality."[62] He proposes a theology of hospitality as the basis for interacting with people of non-Christian faiths. We need new ways of relating to people of other faiths in light of the violence, oppression, and injustice manifest on the contemporary interreligious scene: the civil war in Sri Lanka that had been intensified by the convergence of the Sinhalese Buddhists with the Sinhalese Nationalists, the ongoing Muslim-Christian conflict in Nigeria, and the multicultural and multireligious democracy of the United States. Yong argues that today's global village has led to an increase in multicultural and multireligious communities resulting in a need for a multifaceted Christian theology of religions and interreligious engagement.

Yong's pneumatological theology of hospitality views the "many tongues and many practices of the Spirit of God" as "the means through which divine hospitality is extended through the church to the world, including the worlds of the religions."[63] It is "through such hospitable interactions that the church in turn experiences the redemptive work of God in anticipation of the coming kingdom."[64] In other words, the tongues and practices of the Spirit are the means by which we extend and receive God's hospitality.

In an earlier book, *Beyond the Impasse*—which in many ways is a refinement and a sharpening of his pneumatological approach—Yong lays out how a pneumatological approach to religions might reinvigorate interreligious dialogue.[65] Yong's acknowledgement that the Spirit of God is possibly at work in other religions comes with a very important caveat. As a Pentecostal scholar and minister, Yong knows too well the potential pitfalls of this position and goes to great length in advancing a pneumatological Spirit of discernment as a corrective. This theology of discernment, though central to Yong's pneumatology of religions, is sometimes overlooked.[66] Idiomatically speaking Yong's theology of discernment is designed to not throw out the interreligious dialogical "baby" with the potential demonic "bathwater." He notes: "I am convinced that the Achilles' heel of any pneumatological approach to theology of religions will be its failure to develop a criteriology of discernment adequate for dynamic complexity of lived human experience."[67] Yong argues that a robust sense of discernment is therefore needed in order to engage the various dimensions of human experience in all their interconnectedness and complexity.[68] Accordingly, a pneumatological theology of religions needs to reengage not only the academic study of religions but also the discipline of comparative religions and theology[69]: "Discerning the Spirit(s) in the world's religions has to begin with the empirical actuality of these traditions and therefore requires an interdisciplinary methodology designed to engage that multidimensional phenomenon."[70] This interdisciplinary approach should include both the practitioners such as missionaries as well as those involved in the academic study of religions.[71] In addition to this interdisciplinary approach to the comparative study of religions, the assessments of other religious traditions should be reflective of an insider's perspective.

So far in this essay I have overviewed the growing religious, cultural, and ethnic diversity which is a hallmark of modern life, especially in the Western world. I have outlined developments in the area of interreligious dialogue and in theology of religious pluralism within both Catholic and Protestant traditions. While advances have been made, the conversation has been stuck because of a Christological impasse. The entrance of the Evangelicals into the discourse has brought about further developments, especially scholars such as Clark Pinnock who have turned to pneumatology for further insights while challenging Renewalists to expand their pneumatology to include a theology of interreligious dialogue. I have suggested how Amos Yong's pneumatological insights can inform interreligious dialogue from a distinctly Pentecostal or Charismatic vantage point. One of the appeals of this pneumatological approach to interreligious dialogue is the degree in which it resonates with indigenous worldviews and spiritualities. The foregrounding of the "Spirit" as a fresh lens through which to see "inter-religiously" provides indigenous spiritualities a more conducive medium for interfaith dialogue. In this last section I would like to suggest ways in which this non-Western epistemology might aid the interfaith conversation.

Interreligious Dialogue and the *Missio Dei:* Non-Western Epistemological Perspectives

It is important to keep in mind that at the heart of this discussion and of the various theologies of religions is a desire to interpret the *Missio Dei* to humanity. The Catholic Secretariat for Non-Christians sought to broaden the debate on God's mission to include dialogue with those from outside of the Christian religion. *Nostra Aetate, Lumen Gentium, Ad Gentes*, and the various documents, in spite of their various interpretations and application, in essence sought to enlarge the *oikoumene* beyond the visible and institutional manifestations of the church. The various commissions within the International Missionary Council and the present-day Commission for World Mission and Evangelization of the World Council of Churches have grappled with the ultimate question of the *Missio Dei*, namely making sense of God's mission to the world in the light of the other. The Evangelical and Renewal effort as we have seen through the works of Pinnock and Yong also embraces this ultimate concern.

But as a missiologist and theologian who has spent many years living outside of the Western context I am struck by the degree in which the discourse has been shaped and informed by Western thought forms and epistemology. The interreligious debate surrounding Christology, for example, is preloaded with the Western presuppositions that have precipitated the ensuing impasse. Christology has been historically shaped and expressed through the vortex of the Western enlightenment tradition. So part of the stumbling block that has resulted in the impasse within interreligious dialogue is not Christ per se but the Western cerebral conceptualization of him. I would like to suggest that the turn to pneumatology as a means of opening up fresh avenues is ostensibly a move away from the Western rationalization that suffocates and hinders interreligious conversation. One of the challenges that faces the turn to pneumatology, well articulated by Pinnock, Yong, and others in this volume, is the danger of shrouding the discussions with the same rationalistic framework that was indicative of Christology. In such case one can foresee the turn to pneumatology will also lead to a pneumatological impasse, thus begging next for (re)turn to God the Father for further advances.

What I am trying to articulate here is that the turn to pneumatology must resist the hegemony of Western epistemologies in the interreligious conversation and dialogue. This becomes even more urgent with the growth of Renewal Christianity in the global South wherein interreligious dialogue is becoming more and more necessary in the face of the rising conflicts and clashes between cultures and faith traditions. I would like to suggest three possible ways in which the turn to pneumatology in interreligious conversation may tap into alternative non-Western epistemologies and modes of thought. Particularly from the West African context, I propose that a contextual pneumatology which draws upon integrated worldviews, communicative symbolism, and discursive orality might provide effective avenues for interreligious learning and dialogue.

Interreligious Dialogue, Holistic Epistemology, and Integrated Worldviews

In many languages throughout the world there is no word for "religion" as a noun. The Akans of Ghana, for example, have no word or vocabulary for "religion."[72] For them religion is not a body of ideas but an act, namely serving God (*Onyamesom*). This is also true of Islam and Buddhism, each of which is not merely a body of knowledge but a way of life. The difficulty with some Western approaches to theology is a dualistic rationalizing that does not adequately understand a holistic worldview uniting physical and spiritual, and personal and social, where there is a presumed inter penetrating of both."[73] The interreligious dialogical conversation—even as it pertains to pneumatology— often involves a clash of worldviews.

In the Western world the classical basis of epistemology is perception, memory, consciousness, and reason. This list has been simplified under the heading of "experience and reason."[74] The dominance of this reductionist dichotomization of reason and experience in which the history of Western epistemology has been premised and exported has contributed to the "suffocation" of other sources of knowledge, particularly those of traditional societies. There is therefore a need for what David Bosch calls "an epistemological break"[75] in which interreligious dialogue can be liberated from the stranglehold of Western rationalist modes of thought. In this regard interreligious dialogue must go beyond discursive propositions to conversations of how respective religious traditions inhabit cultural identity, traditional values, and worldviews.

In the Western world the existing knowledge systems reflect a certain way of understanding and interacting with the world. But such may not necessarily be conducive to African peoples, for example, the vast majority of whom still live in rural communities and do not express themselves through literary modes. Elleni Tedla elucidates this point:

> A model of living arises from a particular cosmological framework—a framework that "shapes the mind or informs knowledge and understanding." When we turn to Africa, we find that approximately seventy to ninety percent (depending on their location) of African people follow the traditional mode of living. This means that their relationship with each other, and with the rest of life is determined by the way they interpret the world. In other words, their understanding of cosmic life is the basis of their political, economic and educational activities.[76]

Historically African people have expressed their understanding of the world and the universe which they inhabit in different ways to those in the Western world. For them it has been through song, dance, proverbs, story, rituals, symbols, and a host of other means. These are the treasures that should be cultivated in our quest to understand and dialogue with different religious traditions. The holistic and integrated worldview of African societies (and other traditional societies) has a strong affinity with the pneumatological approach to religion. This affinity is due to the multidimensional activity of the Spirit which mediates between the invisible realms and concrete realities of life.

The holistic epistemological approach to interreligious dialogue maintains that since the creation of the world God's invisible attributes are clearly seen, being understood by the things that are made, even His eternal power and Godhead (Rom. 1:20). Although God has decisively revealed God-self through God's Son, Jesus, the divine attributes still permeate the atmosphere drawing people of all faiths to love, justice, grace, and truth which I affirm find their ultimate expression in the Christ event. It is within this dimension that the language of symbolism becomes a means of communication.

The Epistemic Use of Symbols in Interreligious Dialogue

Attention to symbolism, especially its religious functions, is essential for interreligious dialogue. In his discussion of African symbols and proverbs as sources of knowledge and truth, N. K. Dzobo shows that in Ghanaian culture, symbols are classified in to six major groups with unavoidable overlapping: adinkra symbols, stool symbols, linguistic staff symbols, religious symbols, ritual symbols, and oral literary symbols.[77] I ponder the potentiality of these sources for fruitful and productive interreligious conversations. For the purpose of this section I would like to highlight the epistemic use of symbols as possible tools for interreligious dialogue. Paul Ricoeur has a celebrated dictum, *Le symbole donne à penser*—the symbol gives data, or stimulus, or both, for thinking.[78] The implication here is that symbols are not merely consciously elaborate rhetorical devices designed to make communication more vivid or successful, but something without which thought would not be possible. Symbols then are used to communicate complex knowledge, abstract truths, and ideas about life and its meaning, which makes for good interreligious mutual learning. This symbolic perception of reality is very conducive for interreligious dialogue. It implies that meaning is attached to words and objects beyond themselves and relates to the whole drama of existence that expresses relationship between human beings and the invisible realities. Symbolic language is therefore based upon consensus of meaning that connects the visible and invisible entities of reality.

This is the level of meaning and reality which the Western cerebral outlook has failed to connect with inter-religiously. For example, though there are no official symbols in Islam, several symbols and images have special place in Islam. Islamic symbols are non-textual and non-verbal, visual symbols that have been used, or are used, to express identification with Islam or a particular tradition within Islam, to evoke feelings of joy, sadness, devotion, happiness, and so forth. Some symbols such as the color green have been associated with Islam for a long time and in many areas; others are more limited duration and extent. Muslims often use symbols to represent complex ideas. The star and crescent is the best-known symbol used to represent Islam and features prominently on the flags of many countries in the Islamic world, notably Turkey and Pakistan.[79] It seems to me that interreligious conversations between Muslims and Christians on the level of symbolism might be mutually more rewarding in that symbolism speaks, beyond the cerebral cortex, to the intuitive and sensual part of our human existence. Religious figures and spiritual authorities form a vast complex of symbols: the gods, saviors, redeemers, heroes, avatars (incarnations), Ishvaras (manifestations, in Hinduism), lawgivers, saints, and reformers of the great religions all function symbolically. The biblical prophets, apostles, and evangelists and the Christian saints are characterized by a very complicated system of symbols. Theologians, mystics, and contemplatives may also be symbolically and pictorially represented.

The pervasiveness of symbolism means that human beings find ways to talk about what is beyond their experience. Thus the use of metaphor, for example, helps us speak of the One who exists beyond words. What Father Placide Tempels says of the Bantu articulates this point well: "They cannot conceive a man as an individual existing by himself, unrelated to the animate and inanimate forces surrounding him. It is not sufficient to say he is a social being; he feels himself a vital force in actual intimate and permanent rapport with other forces—vital force both influenced by and influencing them."[80] This foregrounding of the subliminal world, which underlines much of the consciousness of the major religious traditions, is fertile ground for interreligious learning and dialogue. It is in this realm where religions meet beyond words or philosophical truth claims. Christian theology must guard against what William Placher calls "the domestication of transcendence"[81] and always retain a sense of the ineffability of God who exists beyond human intellectual grasp. Placher writes: "We can know the transcendent God not as an object within our intellectual grasp but only as a self-revealing subject and even our knowledge of divine self-revelation must itself be God's doing."[82]

I believe that these are the kind of discourses that a pneumatological imagination, to use Yong's term, opens up to. It is the idea of the Spirit blowing beyond the boundary of the visual church that makes this kind of dialogue possible. The turn to pneumatology then plumbs the well-springs for interreligious dialogue on the level of symbolism, metaphor, intuition, and the language of the "spirit." It is by connecting with this traditional pneumacentric universe, which is the realm that many non-Western cultures use to talk about God and live out their faith meaningfully, that academic theologians are reintroduced to the world of symbolism and metaphor. Restoring the treasures of symbolic discourse into the arena of interreligious dialogue will make it possible to speak about the revelation of God in the language of proverbs, song, dance, silence, art, sermon, and other such forms of religious communication. It is here I believe non-Western and traditional societies can make meaningful contribution to interreligious understanding.

Interreligious Dialogue and Oral Discourse

Finally the turn to pneumatology makes possible and lends legitimacy to oral discourse as a means of interreligious exchange. The issue of orality is usually associated with oral tradition which can be defined in various ways. Here I employ the definition of Theodorson and Theodorson: oral tradition can be understood as the "culture that is transmitted from one generation to the next by word of mouth rather than through written account."[83] Further, oral tradition according to Vansina, is described as constituting "historical sources of a special nature, which is derived from the fact that they are unwritten sources couched in a form suitable for oral transmission."[84] Orality stems from a living, singing, dancing, narrating, nurturing, cultivating way of being. It points to the vibrant and dynamic modality of human experience most clearly manifest in our aesthetic and rhetorical interrelationships.

Orality in interreligious dialogue encounters God through the matrix of a religio-cultural universe. The starting point of this orality is not the message or the form in which the oral tradition exists, which could be narrative, song, proverb, etc., but rather the invisible domain or dimension from out of which it emerges. My usage of the term "orality" therefore will not be limited to "oral communication" but will also include the wider framework that gives these forms meaning. The oral universe upon which the tenants of faiths are held together, such as myths, legends, narrative, folklores, creations stories, sayings, revelations, prophecies, wisdom traditions, etc., are the grounds for mutual sharing and comparisons among religious faiths. The oral traditions of the Old and New Testament; the Hadith literature, the Sutras (lessons) of Buddhism, the Hindu Vedas, the sayings or proverbs of the ancestors in traditional religion, just to name a few, provide various points of entry into the interreligious dialogue. Once again it is the pneumatic imagination that heightens our sensibilities to this realm. Yong notes that such "an experiential vision is a holistic one which is integrative and transformative not only for individuals but also for whole communities."[85]

The turn to a pneumatological approach to religious pluralism provides the scope and the creativity to go where Western rationalism has no logic and where positivistic propositions have little meaning. By this I mean taking us beyond the Western rationalistic approach to a more transcendental and holistic apprehension of the religious other. In John 6.63 Jesus says to his disciples that the words that he speaks to them are spirit and life. The tension between "word" and "spirit" has been an ongoing one with "word" (propositional or cerebral theology) taking the high ground in the Western theological tradition. Interreligious dialogue afforded by a pneumatological imagination provides a significant entry point for interreligious learning, particularly for religious traditions in the global South.

Conclusion

In this chapter I have sought to highlight some of the trajectories of interreligious dialogue that have developed in Christian tradition. I consider the pneumatological entry as a fresh and insightful possibility that opens up all kinds of venues for interreligious learning that have the potential to take us beyond the Western discursive and propositional approach. The holistic, symbolic, and oral approaches I have outlined above are some of the directions a pneumatological theology of interreligious encounter makes possible. These are not meant to be definitive in any way but to highlight some of the raw materials upon which interreligious conversation might ensue.

Globalization—the growing integration of economies and societies around the world—has been one of the most hotly-debated topics over the past few years. It has forced cultures to relate to each other in ways that were previously unthinkable. In this global context Renewal Christianity has arguably emerged as the dominant global expression of the Christian faith. The global impact of Renewal Christianity necessitates a dialogical approach to the religious other. This task becomes more urgent in the global South where Pentecostal and Charismatic types of movements are growing the fastest. It is also the global South where we see much of the tension and conflicts among religions. It is encouraging to see that Renewal theologians are finding their voice within the global Christian community. A few of them will be echoed in the rest of this volume.

Notes

1. Harold Netland, *Encountering Religious Pluralism: The Challenge to Christian faith and Mission* (Downers Grove: InterVarsity Press, 2001), 9.
2. Diana Eck, "America's New Religious Landscape," in *Religion and Ethics Newsweekly: Viewer's* Guide (New York Thirteen - WNET, 1998), 2.
3. Frank Clooney, *Comparative Theology: Deep learning Across Religious Borders* (Malden: Wiley-Blackwell, 2010), 4.
4. Michael Nazir Ali, *Frontiers in Muslim-Christian Encounter* (Oxford: Regnum Books, 1987), 105.
5. Ibid., 114.
6. Jacques Dupuis, *Christianity and the Religions: From Confrontation to Dialogue* (Maryknoll: Orbis Books), 5-7.
7. Dupuis, *Christianity and the Religions*, 5.
8. For a fruitful discussion on the impact of the postmodern condition in America see Darrell L. Guder, ed., *Missional Church: A Vision for the Sending of the Church in North America* (Grand Rapids and Cambridge, UK: William B. Eerdmans Publishing Company, 1998).
9. Paul Knitter, *Theologies of Religions* (Maryknoll: Orbis Books, 2008), 5.
10. Arnulf Camps, *Partners in Dialogue* (Maryknoll: Orbis Books, 1983), ch. 2.
11. Broadly speaking exclusivism privileges one's own tradition against others; inclusivism recognizes some merits in other religions but recognizes that in and of themselves these traditions fall short; and pluralism argues for the relativising of all traditions, including one's own.
12. Gavin D'Costa, "The Theology of Religions," in David Ford, ed., *The Modern Theologians* (Oxford: Blackwell, 1997), 637.
13. The global renewal movement is broader than the Pentecostal/Charismatic tradition; in this chapter I shall be using "renewal" predominantly, and my references to "Pentecostal" or "Charismatic" should always be understood within this wider framework.
14. E.g., Viggo Mortensen, ed., *Theology and the Religions: A Dialogue* (Grand Rapids and Cambridge, UK: William B. Eerdmans Publishing Company, 2003), and Chester Gills, *Pluralism: A New paradigm for Theology* (Grand Rapids: Eerdmans, 1993).
15. This phrase was coined by St. Cyprian following Augustine. It was not written in reference to non-believers but rather directed towards schematic or heretical Christians.
16. See Karl Rahner, "Christianity and the Non-Christian Religions," in *Theological Interpretations* (Baltimore: Helicon, 1966), 5:115-34, and "Anonymous Christianity and the Missionary Task of the Church," in *Theological Investigations* (New York: Seabury, 1974), 12:161-78. For discussions of Rahner's position, see Gavin D'Costa, *Theology and Religious Pluralism: The Challenge of Other Religions* (Oxford: Blackwell, 1986), chs. 4-5, and Amos Yong, *Discerning the Spirit(s): A Pentecostal-Charismatic Contribution to Christian Theology of Religions* (Sheffield: Sheffield Academic Press, 2000), ch. 2.
17. In the "Declaration on the Relation of the Church to Non-Christian Religions," it is "in Christ, in whom God reconciled all things to himself (2 Cor. 5:18-19)." See *Nostra Aetate*, in A. P. Flannery, ed., *Documents of Vatican II* (Grand Rapids: William B. Eerdmans Publishing Company, 1975), 739.
18. Flannery, *Documents of Vatican II*, 365-66.
19. Ibid., 367-68.

20. Knitter, "Roman Catholic Approaches to Other Religions," *International Bulletin of Missionary Research* 8 (1984), 50; Dupuis, *Towards a Christian Theology of Religious Pluralism* (Maryknoll: Orbis Books, 1999), 161-70.

21. Heinz Schlette *Die Religionen als Thema der Theologie* (Freiburg: Herder, 1963); Joseph Neuner, "The Place of World Religion in Theology," *The Clergy Monthly* (March 1984): 102-15; also Neuner, *Christian Revelation and World religions* (London: Burns & Oates, 1967); Hans Küng "The World Religion in God's Plan of Salvation," *Indian Ecclesiastical Studies* 4 (1965): 182-222.

22. For a clear and succinct portrayal of Troeltsch position see Yong, *Discerning the Spirit(s)*, 40.

23. Hendrick Kraemer, *The Christian Message in a Non-Christian World* (London: International Missionary Council, 1938).

24. Yong, *Discerning the Spirit(s)*, 41.

25. John Hick, *The Second Christianity* (London: SCM Press, 1983), 82.

26. Hick asserts that he had previously opted for the terms the Transcendent, the Divine, and the Eternal One, but notes that these descriptors were too theistically colored. He reflects that on balance the most suitable term is the Real. See Hick *An Interpretation of Religion* (New Haven: Yale University Press, 1989), 10-11.

27. John Hick, *God Has Many Names: Britain's New Religious Pluralism* (London: Macmillan, 1980), 52.

28. See John Hick, ed., *The Myth of God Incarnate* (1977; 2nd ed., London: SCM, 1983), ch. 9, and *Jesus the Metaphor of God* (London: SCM, 1993), ch. 10.

29. See John Hick, "Jesus and the World Religions," in John Hick, ed., *The Myth of God Incarnate* (Philadelphia: Westminster Press, 1977), ch. 9.

30. Knitter articulates his position in his *No Other Name? A Critical Survey of Christian Attitudes towards the World Religions* (Maryknoll: Orbis Books, 1985); see also Raimundo Panikkar, *Interreligious Dialogue* (New York: Paulist Press, 1978), and "The Invisible Harmony: A Universal Theory of Religion or a Cosmic Confidence in Reality?" in Leonard Swidler, ed., *Towards a Universal Theology of Religion* (Maryknoll: Orbis Books, 1987), 118-53.

31. Gavin D'Costa, ed., *Christian Uniqueness Reconsidered: The Myth of a Pluralistic Theology of Religions* (Maryknoll: Orbis Books, 1990), 18.

32. Veli-Matti Kärkkäinen, *An Introduction to the Theology of Religions* (Downers Grove: InterVarsity Press, 2003), 11.

33. Gerald R. McDermott, *Can Evangelicals Learn From World Religions: Jesus, Revelation and Religious Traditions* (Downers Grove: InterVarsity Press, 2000), 38.

34. Denis Okholm and Timothy Phillips have suggested abandoning *exclusivism* in favor of a less offensive label such as *particularism*. See Denis Okholm and Timothy Phillips, eds., *Introduction to Four Views on Salvation in a Pluralistic World* (Grand Rapids: Zondervan, 1996), 171-81.

35. See Neal Punt, *Unconditional Good News: Towards and Understanding of Biblical Universalism* (Grand Rapids: Eerdmans, 1980), and Norman Anderson, *Christians and World Religions: The Challenge of Pluralism* (Downers Grove: Inter Varsity Press, 1984).

36. For a more detailed delineation of the developments of Evangelical perspectives on the theology of religious dialogue, see Kärkkäinen, *Introduction to the Theology of Religions*, chs. 15, 29, and 30.

37. Notto Thelle, "Interreligious Dialogue: Theory and Experience," in Viggo Mortensen, ed., *Theology and the Religions: A Dialogue* (Grand Rapids: William B. Eerdmans Publishing Company), 130-31.

38. Wilfred Cantwell Smith, *The Meaning and the End of Religions* (New York: Harper & Row, 1978), 154-55.

39. Ibid., 43.

40. Ibid.

41. See Donald K. Swear, *Dialogue: The Key to Understanding other Religions* (Philadelphia: Westminster Press, 1977).

42. See Arnulf Camps, "Le dialogue inter-religieux et al situation concretè de l'humanitè," *Bulletin of the Secretariat for Non-Christians* 10 (1975): 315-18; cf. Masatoshi Doi, *Search for Meaning through Interfaith Dialogue* (Tokyo: Kyo Bun kwan, 1976).

43. See Dupuis, *Christianity and the Religions*, 219-20.

44. Ibid., 220.

45. Steven Land, *Pentecostal Spirituality: A Passion for the Kingdom* (Sheffield: Sheffield Academic Press, 1993).

46. *Is Christianity the Only Way* (Cleveland, Tenn.: Pathway Press, 1975).

47. See "Jerusalem Report: Mid-East Superintendent Interviews High Priest of Al Aqsa Mosque," *The Church of God Evangel* (November 17, 1969): 7; see also "Evangelist T. L. Lowery Meet's Jordan's King" and "The King and his Country: A sense of Destiny and Responsibility," both in the May 5, 1969, issue of *The Church of God Evangel.*

48. Yong, *Discerning the Spirit (s)*, 60-61.

49. Clarke Pinnock, *Flame of Love: A Theology of the Holy Spirit* (Downers Grove: InterVarsity Press, 1996), 274.

50. Allan Anderson, *Spreading Fires: The Missionary Nature of Early Pentecostalism* (London: SCM Press, 2007), 77.

51. Ogbu Kalu, *African Pentecostalism: An Introduction* (Oxford and New York: Oxford University Press, 2008).

52. Johannes Nissen, "Seeking God – Sought by God: New Testament Perspectives on the Gospel in a Multifaith Context," in Viggo Mortensen, ed., *Theology and the Religions: A Dialogue* (Grand Rapids: William B. Eerdmans Publishing Company, 2003), 330.

53. Amos Yong, *Beyond the Impasse: Toward a Pneumatological Theology of Religions* (Grand Rapids: Baker Academic, 2003), 22.

54. Harvey Cox describes Yong as the most creative and promising of the young Evangelical/Pentecostal theologians; see Amos Yong, *The Spirit Poured out on All Flesh: Pentecostalism and the Possibility of Global Theology* (Grand Rapids: Baker Academic, 2005), back cover.

55. Yong, *Beyond the Impasse*, 60-61.

56. Yong, *Discerning the Spirit(s)*, ch. 7.

57. Ibid., 99-104.

58. Veli-Matti Kärkkäinen, *Towards a Pneumatological Theology: Pentecostal and Ecumenical Perspectives on Ecclesiology, Soteriology and Theology of Mission*, ed. Amos Yong (Lanham, New York, and Oxford: University Press of America, 2002), 237.

59. Allan Anderson, *An Introduction to Pentecostalism* (Cambridge: Cambridge University Press, 2004), 198.

60. Arnulf Camps notes the collapse of the colonial systems, the failures of Western developmental strategies, and the superiority among Western religious tradition has led to an increase in old traditional religions; see Camps, *Partners in Dialogue*, 6.

61. Anderson, *Introduction to Pentecostalism*, 198.

62. Amos Yong, *Hospitality and the Other: Pentecost, Christian Practices, and the Neighbor* (Maryknoll: Orbis Books, 2008), 2.

63. Ibid., 100.

64. Ibid.

65. See Yong, *Beyond the Impasse*, ch. 4.

66. See R. A. James Merrick "The Spirit of Truth as Agent in False Religions? A Critique of Amos Yong's Pneumatological Theology of Religions with Reference to Current Trends," *Trinity Journal* 29:1 (2008): 107-25. Merrick's critique of Yong's pneumatological theology, though echoing some concerns among some classical Pentecostals, fails to grasp the entirety of Yong's approach particularly as it pertains to Yong's proposals. For an excellent response to Merrick, see Tony Richie, "The Spirit of Truth as Guide into All Truth: A Response to R. A. James Merrick, "The Spirit of Truth as Agent in False Religions? A Critique of Amos Yong's Pneumatological Theology of Religions with Reference to Current Trends," *Cyberjournal for Renewal Research* 19 (2010) [http://www.pctii.org/cyberj/cyberj19/richie2.pdf].

67. Yong, *Beyond the Impasse*, 166.

68. Ibid., 165.

69. Ibid., 175.

70. Ibid.

71. Ibid., 176.

72. Sydney George Williamson, *Akan Religion and the Christian Faith: A Comparative Study of the Impact of Two Religions* (Accra: Ghana Universities Press, 1965), 86.

73. Anderson, *Introduction to Pentecostalism*, 198.

74. Paul K. Moser, "Introduction," in Paul K. Moser, ed., *The Oxford Handbook of Epistemology* (Oxford: Oxford University Press, 2002), 45.

75. David Bosch, *Transforming Mission: Paradigm Shifts in Theology of Mission* (Maryknoll: Orbis Books, 1991), 423.

76. Elleni Tedla, *Sankofa: African Thought and Education* (Frankfurt: Peter Lang, 1996), 11.

77. N. K. Dzobo, "African Symbols and Proverbs as Sources of Knowledge and Truth," in Kwasi Wiredu and Kwame Gyekye, eds., *Person and Community* (Washington: The Council for Research in Values and Philosophy, 1992), 89.

78. Rowan Williams, "Religious Imagery," in Alan Richardson and John Bowder, eds., *The Westminster Dictionary of Christian Theology* (Philadelphia: SCM Press, 1983), 182.

79. A good book which explores the history and significance of Islamic symbols is Tanja Al Harari-Wendel, *Symbols of Islam* (New York: Sterling Publishing Co., 2002).

80. Placide Tempels, *Bantu Philosophy* (Paris: Presence Africaine, 1958), 30.

81. William Placher, *The Domestication of Transcendence: How Modern Thinking about God Went Wrong* (Louisville: Westminster, 1996).

82. Ibid., 182.

83. George A. Theodorson and Achilles G. Theodorson, *Modern Dictionary of Sociology* (New York: J. Y. Crowell, 1969), 285.

84. Vansina, *Oral Tradition* (1961; reprint, London: Routledge & Kegan Paul, 1969), 1.

85. Yong, *Discerning Spirit(s)*, 171.

Chapter 2

The Wide Reach of the Spirit: A Renewal Theology of Mission and Interreligious Encounter in Dialogue with Yves Congar

Tony Richie

How do and should Pentecostal and Charismatic Christians understand religious others? How do and should Pentecostals and Charismatics evangelize and missionize people of other faiths? Are there different theologies and mission strategies required for the various world religious traditions? I will return to these questions later. I am particularly interested in engaging these and similar questions as my own denomination, the Church of God (Cleveland, Tennessee)—one of the oldest, continuing Classical Pentecostal denominations—increasingly confronts intersecting lines of commitment to the Great Commission and of the contemporary reality of world religions.[1] My distinctive contribution to this conversation will be to suggest an inclusive heritage for Pentecostal and Charismatic theology of religions compatible with and conducive to commitment to the Great Commission.[2] Further, I identify and discuss key issues in the context of Charismatic renewal theology with a carefully chosen conversation partner, Yves Congar. Always, I affirm the non-negotiable centrality of Jesus Christ for Christian theology, indisputably distinguishing it from all other religions and their respective centers of reference.[3] Throughout the process of this present work, I propose a gracious and glorious width in the Spirit's revelatory and redemptive reach, arising out of God's incomparable wisdom and righteousness in Christ (Rom. 11:33-36). Simply put, my goal is uncompromisingly Christian, Charismatic, and inclusive.

As for my primary conversation partner, Veli-Matti Kärkkäinen considers Yves Congar as the "most prominent contemporary Catholic theologian on the Spirit."[4] He objects to any suggestion that even the great Karl Rahner could compare to Congar in the field of pneumatology.[5] In fact, both Kärkkäinen and Amos Yong point out that Rahner borrowed from and built on Congar's pneumatological ecclesiology.[6] Specifically, Kirsteen Kim credits Congar with "refounding" Catholic pneumatology and drawing out latent elements of its "true pneumatology."[7] Congar's major treatise on the Spirit is the multivolume, *I Believe in the Holy Spirit*.[8] As Nichols notes, a major interest of this work is the Charismatic Renewal Movement.[9] In fact, Pentecostal theologian Simon Chan even thinks Congar's view of confirmation is close to that of some Pentecostals on Spirit baptism.[10] In a word, Congar's ecumenical reputation, including extraordinary openness to Protestantism, and sympathetic interest in the Charismatic Renewal Movement is remarkably well-established.[11] Therefore, I select Congar as a suitable conversation partner in this project intent on exploring a broadminded pneumatology in relation to ecclesial mission and interreligious encounter.[12]

However, before directly discussing the Great Commission in the context of inclusivism or the implications of Congar's theology, I find it helpful to draw briefly on J. Rodman Williams in laying a foundation for affirmative Charismatic reflection on theology of religions. Williams' *Renewal Theology* is considered "a major study in systematic theology from a charismatic perspective."[13] Furthermore, his role as a major leader and thinker in the Charismatic Renewal Movement is well established.[14] Synan notes that when Williams was baptized in the Spirit, he was "already an experienced and able theologian," and therefore "added a serious theological depth to the charismatic movement as a whole."[15] His influence as an educator was vital to the developing movement.[16] Additionally, although in a somewhat different context, Yong clearly demonstrates the ongoing significance of Williams' inclusive ecclesiology for the ministry of the Church.[17] Williams' insights on our topic should help establish a shared starting point.

Pentecostal/Charismatic Inclusivism and the Great Commission

There is—I hope to show—ample evidence of historical and theological precedence for developing a distinctively Pentecostal-Charismatic approach to Christian theology of religions, including understanding of other religions, the fate of the unevangelized, the nature of interreligious encounter and dialogue, and the performance of Christian mission in a pluralistic world. In particular, I hope to show that this heritage of inclusivism can be and ought to be developed and applied in a manner consistent with a traditional concept of and commitment to the evangelism mandate of the Great Commission. I argue that inclusivism is not only compatible with but actually complementary to evangelism; together, these comprise a coherent and consistent approach for the Church's mission in Christ by the Spirit's power (e.g., Acts 1:8).

Examples of Pentecostal-Charismatic Inclusivist Attitudes

Several important early Pentecostals exhibit what we would call today inclusivist theology of religions. I have written elsewhere of the Pentecostal theology of religions developed by J. H. King, Charles Parham, A. A. Boddy, and, later, George L. Britt.[18] (By the way, the exclusivist-inclusivist-pluralist paradigm is comparatively recent nomenclature. I do not claim that early Pentecostals used these terms or would agree with all they imply; instead, the terms as we now know them identify for us specific characteristics that we have come to name in a certain way.) Yet in spite of great variety, a common denominator under the inclusivist umbrella is their commitment to both the uniqueness and necessity of Jesus Christ and the possibility that some who do not know Christ outwardly may know him in some sense inwardly.[19] However, here I focus on a more contemporary charismatic, Rodman Williams. In the process, an interrelatedness of the Great Commission and evangelism with inclusivism and interreligious dialogue will be indicated.

Frances Adeney rightly warns against developing "a constricted view of Christian mission" that is "limited to a particular and culturally-determined interpretation" of the Great Commission.[20] She suggests that theologies of mission be seen "in their prism-like variety and wholeness" as arising out of "multiple mandates for mission in the New Testament."[21] For her, Christian mission clearly includes such diverse ministries as "medical work, evangelistic preaching, speaking out for human rights of slaves, women, and children, sheltering the poor and caring for widows," as well as "calling for economic justice, planting the church in remote parts of the world, developing agricultural techniques and cottage industries so that no one remains hungry."[22] She finds that theology based on missionary biographies "celebrates diversity in Christian mission."[23] In any case, overstating the colossal significance of the Great Commission (see Matt. 28:18-20 and parallels) for Christ's Church today indeed would be difficult. For example, Renewal theologian Larry Hart insists that the Church's mission today is "to spread the good news of the kingdom around the world," but he admits that all is not "ideal" with that task.[24] Therefore, he warns Charismatic churches not to forget "their Great Commission mandate."[25] For him, theology emerges out of the missionary context of the Great Commission.[26] He acknowledges the discipleship task and ecumenical endeavors, but evangelism is obviously primary.[27]

Williams takes a similar stance but develops it more fully and addresses the humanly unreached. I agree wholeheartedly with him that the Church "stands constantly under the Great Commission of the risen Christ."[28] For Williams, this primarily implies evangelism as a precursor to the stated aim of discipleship.[29] Because all are lost who are without Christ, the Church's chief imperative in regard to the world is to proclaim the gospel.[30] Thus, the "universal proclamation of eternal salvation" is the Church's "high challenge and task."[31] However, Williams reminds that, "True disciples of Christ should be concerned, as was their Master, with the whole human condition."[32] Yet everything else is clearly "secondary" to focusing on the "spiritual plight" of humankind.[33] Of course, discipleship includes water baptism, and the relation with the Triune God it involves, and teaching, in particular on obedience to Christ.[34] Williams also stresses the gift of the Holy Spirit as an important element of full discipleship, but insists that it too is secondary to the "central" task of evangelism.[35]

The following proceeds from a very similar mindset; I would only amplify a bit. First, "secondary" should not be made to mean nonessential. Second, "spiritual" should not be made to mean opposed to physical or social. Third, "central" should not be made to mean everything else is utterly peripheral. I am quite sure Williams would agree with the gist of these statements.[36] Additionally, I would argue that in the contemporary context where religious pluralism is both a global and local reality, interreligious dialogue may be conceived as a legitimate extension of ecclesial mission as couched in the Great Commission so long as the primary task of evangelism is not diminished or undermined. Further, this safeguard requires proposing a precise theology of religions that can sustain Christian mission in the face of the extremes of either radical pluralism or rigid exclusivism. As will be seen, I suggest that robust inclusivism meets the criteria.

I am persuaded that commitment to the above concept of the Great Commission can contribute greatly to the practice of ecclesial mission in contemporary renewal movements. In this regard, Williams' open optimism is encouraging. His highest respect for the evangelistic emphasis of the Great Commission has been shown already. Further, in the context of strong discussion on the last judgment in which he emphasizes God's holy and loving character and the importance of human decision for salvation, he nonetheless posits "the possibility of God's mercy in Christ being extended to some who do not outwardly know him."[37] Williams then advances several supporting arguments in favor of his hypothesis—all common arguments for Christian inclusivism—simultaneously maintaining the nonnegotiable necessity of Christ, the importance of evangelistic proclamation, and the redemptive possibility of a width in God's mercy for the unreached (John 1:9; 3:21; 14:6; Acts 4:12; 1 Ti 2:5).[38] Fully aware of potentially controversial responses, Williams boldly presses on to explain:

I am aware of the possible hazards of such a statement, for it might seem to lessen the urgency of proclaiming Christ Himself as the only hope of salvation. However, on the other hand to state bluntly that the countless numbers of people who have never heard the gospel verbally are all consigned to hell seems to go beyond the New Testament message. I am, of course, not speaking here of anything like universal salvation, but rather of the possibility of God's grace *in Christ* reaching beyond the actual gospel proclamation. That this may be the case should not lessen the urgency of proclaiming the gospel, for not only are many far from the light but some who are doing "what is true" are all the more eager to come to the light of Christ when they hear the gospel.[39]

In the passage above, focus is directed toward the unevangelized without explicit reference to world religions *per se*. Elsewhere, Williams stresses the significance of Judaism, Christianity, and Islam having common commitment to monotheism.[40] Tragically, idolatry appears to be "the prevailing condition" of humankind and "the source of human perversion."[41] True enough, Williams ordinarily stresses need for basic knowledge of the gospel and response of faith for salvation to occur.[42] Yet, Williams appears simply unwilling to press that position to the point of denying the possibility that God might work otherwise on some occasions. He insists that God's will is revealed inwardly to every human being.[43] For Williams, "Paul intimates" (Rom. 2:14-15) on the basis of natural law written inwardly by God on all hearts so that "some may be excused," adding parenthetically that "God surely will honor any genuine witness to truth."[44] Nevertheless, the merely human search for God "never really achieves success" on its own.[45]

Accordingly, with the preceding Pentecostal precedents and Renewal theology in mind, and as shall be further suggested below, Pentecostal-Charismatic inclusivism—with an impulse toward dialogue—and commitment to the Great Commission—with its implied evangelistic impulse—arguably are not only not contradictory but complementary.

Inclusivist Pentecostals and Charismatics and the Great Commission

In the discipline of Christian theology of religions, "exclusivism" posits that a conscious personal response to the preached gospel is not only normative but also necessary for salvation. Typically, it argues that there is no salvation outside the Church or apart from the Church's proclamation of the gospel. On the other end of the spectrum, "pluralism" essentially equates all religions while denying the superiority of any. Typically, it focuses on the more general level of God ("Ultimate Reality") rather than on the particularity of Christ (or Buddha or Mohammed). The more moderating position, "inclusivism," is optimistic in Christ. It affirms that salvation is only of and by Christ even as it allows for the possibility that the unevangelized or adherents of other faiths may mysteriously experience the magnanimous grace and mercy of God. Among these broad categories, each has a fundamentally different view of religious others.[46]

Usually, Pentecostals are assumed to be exclusivists. Indeed, in spite of the above examples, there is a track record to that effect.[47] On one level, Pentecostal exclusivism connects to its understanding of the Great Commission. The call to go into the world and proclaim the gospel to everyone has led them to view religious others only as objects of evangelism. Hence, Pentecostals have asserted that the Spirit's saving work is limited to the Church. It is precisely as members of the Church allow themselves to be used by the Spirit to witness to their non-Christian neighbors—even to those of other religions—that salvation is also made available to the world.[48] In so far as Pentecostals assume that the evangelism mandate and inclusivist openness are incompatible, their ardent evangelistic orientation requires—they often assume—that they must be exclusivists.[49] Some may also assume that interreligious dialogue is an inappropriate rival of evangelism.

However, not all Evangelicals—with whom Pentecostals and Charismatics have been so often associated—agree. For instance, Hesselgrave argues that the question for contemporary Evangelicals is not whether to engage in dialogue but in what kinds of dialogue they ought to engage.[50] Accordingly, interreligious dialogue that answers questions and objections of unbelievers, that proclaims the good news of Christ and invites repentance and faith, and that does not compromise the gospel or countermand the Great Commission is fully acceptable.[51] Practically speaking, Hesselgrave recommends dialogue on the nature of interreligious dialogue. He suggest that healthy religious dialogue promotes freedom of worship and witness, is concerned with meeting human need, is designed to break down barriers of distrust and hatred, and is aimed at mutual comprehension of conflicting truth claims.[52] Hesselgrave concisely challenges ecumenists to consider dangers of compromise in past approaches to dialogue. Further, he encourages Evangelicals to reconsider attitudes of disinterest and nonparticipation.[53]

Many Evangelicals and Charismatics are beginning to realize that the Great Commission cannot—or at least, ought not to—be confined to evangelism. Thus, popular Charismatic leaders such as Peter Wagner and Cindy Jacobs are declaring that the Great Commission is much more than evangelism. Wagner, in his foreword to Jacobs' *The Reformation Manifesto* confesses that many, including him, "have for too long harbored a truncated view of the kingdom of God."[54] He explains further that they "began by over-identifying the church with the kingdom" and proceeded to limit their mission to saving souls without improving society. He specifically names the Great Commission, confessing again that he "used to think making disciples meant getting people saved and multiplying churches," but that he has come to see a broader vision—in agreement with Jacobs—that includes "sustained social transformation." While neither he nor Jacobs focuses on interfaith issues, their expansion of the Great Commission is nevertheless significant for others contexts as well.

Specific Pentecostal grievances against inclusivism include concerns that anything other than traditional, exclusivist approaches to other religions is contrary to Scripture (Acts 4:12 and Jn. 3:18) and replaces the obligation for world evangelism with interreligious dialogue (Matt. 18:28; Mk. 16:15).[55] Further, this view holds that those who fail to fulfill the Great Commission are compromising Christ's Lordship.[56] If true, especially across the board or without qualification, these are devastating charges.[57] Undoubtedly, an appropriate concern would be an inclusive theology replacing obligation for world evangelism with an alternate emphasis on interreligious dialogue (Matt. 18:28 and Mk. 16:15).[58] For exclusivists, inclusivists are deemed to be compromising Christ's Lordship by failing to fulfill the Great Commission.[59] However, is this necessarily the case? It is not. As stated above, Williams' primary reservation about exclusivism is that it goes "beyond the New Testament message." Further, Pentecostal exegete, James Shelton, notes that the grammar—especially the repetitive *pas* in verses 18-20 of Matthew 28:18-20, the basic Great Commission text—pointedly signifies the universality of Christ and of the Church's commission.[60] At a minimum, this prompts a broad ecclesiology and missiology. Thus, there appears no inherent biblical contradiction between evangelism and interreligious dialogue. Obviously, the biblical testimony bears reexamination.

Wolfhart Pannenberg suggests that citing Acts 4:12 in a soteriologically exclusivist sense actually conceals the greater point of its Christological truth and power.[61] New Testament scholar, F. F. Bruce, insists that Acts 4:12 indicates salvation is "inextricably bound up" with the name of Jesus and persistent refusal will "bring destruction." Intriguingly, he adds, "The founders of the great world-religions are not to be disparaged by followers of the Christian way. But of none of them can it be said that there is no saving health in anyone else; to one alone belongs the title: the Savior of the world."[62] Pentecostal scholar, French Arrington, approvingly references Bruce's contention that "salvation" in this text includes both physical and spiritual healing. He adds that it indicates, "Jesus was made indispensable by God," and that "the message of the gospel excludes every other way of salvation and demands trust in Jesus and obedience to him."[63] The majority of Pentecostals would agree with the gist of these statements. The difficulty lies in determining to what extent an exclusive Christology requires an exclusive soteriology, or if and how either is tied to epistemology. Augustine contends that Acts 4:12 indicates there is no other savior than Jesus and no other salvation save through faith in Jesus, but he expands the nature of that faith to include not only pre-Incarnation Israelites but even those before and beyond that nation. Referencing John 3:8, Augustine argues that God's redemptive grace in Christ was applied broadly through the mysterious working of the Holy Spirit.[64] Bede argued from Acts 4:12 that there is no other savior than Jesus and no other salvation save through faith in Jesus, but he insists that "although the sacramental signs differed by reason of the times," "the same faith" and "the same dispensation of Christ…learned from the apostles" is always everywhere present because "there is no redemption of human captivity [from sinfulness] except in the blood of him who gave himself as a redemption for all."[65] Thus, utilizing Acts 4:12 for espousing epistemological exclusivity apparently goes beyond its clear teaching.

Furthermore, Leon Morris suggests that John 3:16-21 conveys the breadth of God's love for the whole world and the centrality of Christ as God's saving gift against a backdrop of eternal life vis-à-vis perishing or judgment.[66] John attributes salvation "ultimately to the Father," but faith in Christ is essential for salvation, and persistent unbelief brings inevitable condemnation.[67] Yet, the divide between faith and unbelief or salvation and condemnation occurs as part of a process of responding either to the light or to darkness.[68] Those who choose darkness, rejecting Christ, are those who already make a practice of persistent wrongdoing. Those who choose light, accepting Christ, are those who already do what is true.[69] J. Ramsey Michaels says, "Coming to Jesus proves God has *already* been at work in one's life," and that faith in Christ expresses that reality.[70] Apparently, the complexity of responsiveness to Christ in faith exhibited in John 3:18-21 leaves ample room for pre-explicit response inclination to faith, which could be referred to as implicit faith.

Appeals to texts such as Acts 4:12 and John 3:18 to support traditional exclusivism or to refute inclusivism appear superficial upon inspection. A similar pattern can be seen in other "proof texts." Concerning John 14:6, Pentecostal commentator Benny Aker rightly contends that though there is no doubt that "Jesus uses this to emphasize the uniqueness of his redeeming work" and that "[o]nly through him can one get to God," central to Jesus' conversation with His disciples is the problem that the disciples still did not really know Jesus; therefore, they could not really know the Father either.[71] Another Pentecostal commentator, Van Johnson, observes regarding Romans 10:9-15 that Paul's fashioning of these verses on Deuteronomy 30:14 qualify their content. Thus, "while confession and belief are both necessary responses to the gospel, we should not understand that they are two steps to salvation or that confession somehow precedes belief."[72] When facing objections about the nature of the Church's "missionary mandate" and its relation to issues of conversion, dialogue, and truth, reexamining superficial assumptions is helpful and enlightening.

Indeed, one may view evangelism and dialogue as two sides of the same inclusivist coin.[73] Evangelism is committed to proclaiming God's good news in Christ to all in hopes that the hearers may respond in faith. Inclusivism is committed to articulating and acting upon the principle that God is not limited to humanity's efforts. However, though the practice of dialogue arises partially out of recognition that God has been at work already and will continue to be so, it does not conclude that God's call to humanity to enter together into that work as co-laborers has been suspended. Pinnock puts it well:

> Isn't it wiser to engage in mission with hope, trusting the God who has been at work beforehand? Hope can be an encouragement rather than an impediment to evangelism. It fosters good relationships and encourages points of contact. God does not send us into mission

knowing the final destiny of every soul. It is not our job to judge the world or identify the elect. Jesus did not do so, and he warned that there would be surprises for those who tried. He said the first would be last and the last first.[74]

Let us briefly recap the discussion so far and then point the way forward. First, I have suggested there is a consistent inclusivist strain represented within the Pentecostal and Charismatic Renewal Movements. Second, I have suggested that Renewal missiology could and should be broad and deep enough to encompass an inclusive theology—and practice of interreligious dialogue— without compromising commitment to the Great Commission's enthusiastic evangelism. However, such an inclusive theology involves several intricately interrelated themes. At times, a tendency to misunderstand or misrepresent important theological categories has led to confusion regarding Christian inclusion.[75] Therefore, I will identify and discuss several key issues in conversation with the broader renewal tradition representing this perspective. In short, the subsequent section suggests that examining the intricate interrelatedness of Christology and pneumatology—with implications for ecclesiology and cosmology—may help to provide a viable framework for a Pentecostal-Charismatic theology of religions such as outlined above.

Developing Renewal Theology of Religions in Discussion with Yves Congar

Herein, my intended objective is to suggest a positive theological construct conducive to Christian mission and contemporary interreligious encounter consistent with the Charismatic Renewal movement, taking seriously first, the relation between Christ and Holy Spirit; and second, the role of the Church and the reality of God's eternal purpose for the cosmos. These areas are of supreme significance in the task of understanding and directing authentic, dynamic Christian belief and practice in today's religiously plural world.[76]

As stated above, I address this topic by drawing on the thought of Yves Congar in delineating a Pentecostal-Charismatic perspective. In addition to his charismatic credentials, as stated above, and admirable diversity, which will be discussed below, a primary reason I chose Congar for this conversation is because of what Nichols calls his "prophetic yet traditional" achievement and agenda.[77] I deeply appreciate and respect his dual ability to retain a sense of the verity and value of the ancient heritage of the faith, while recognizing the continuing need for reform and development.[78] This twofold vision is most helpful for the present task. Only thus can we successfully and safely navigate the dangerous waters between the Scylla of compromising authentic Christianity and the Charybdis of conceding to relativistic religious pluralism.[79] Congar's *The Word and the Spirit,* a small volume summing up many of his main and most mature ideas on the intricate interrelationships between Christology and pneumatology, also involving ecclesiology and cosmology, is especially useful in this regard.[80] My intention is not so much to do an exhaustive critical analysis of Congar, as it is to apply relevant insights gleaned from his already widely recognized work, to a possible Pentecostal-Charismatic Renewal approach to ecclesial mission and interreligious encounter.

Relationship of Christology and Pneumatology

Pentecostal theology of religions appears to be developing in uniquely pneumatological directions. In other words, there is an accent on the agency of the Holy Spirit. The work of Kärkkäinen and Yong is indicative of this trend.[81] Of course, Clark Pinnock has paved the way for much of this approach.[82] However, this trend has come under intense scrutiny and sharp criticism by some from within the evangelical camp.[83] Rather than continuing to cry foul (however correctly) against those who claim discomfort with pneumatology because of alleged desires to safeguard Christology (however misguided), the present approach explores relations between Christology and pneumatology with an eye toward delineating a more precise Christian theology of religions, drawing on pneumatological insights informed by Renewal theology.

Delineating and maintaining a healthy balance, respecting Christ and the Holy Spirit, is absolutely paramount for Pentecostal theology of religions. In the "Preface to the French Edition" of *The Word and the Spirit*, Joseph Doré affirms a sturdy mutuality regarding the person and work of Jesus Christ and the person and work of the Holy Spirit.[84] In other words, he warns against focusing exclusively on Christ to the neglect of the Holy Spirit or vice versa. Referencing Irenaeus' famous phrase regarding Christ and the Spirit, "the two hands of the Father," Doré explains that "[t]he present work aims to show that, and how, these two hands work together."[85] He is not reticent to utilizing terms like "Christomonism," against which he recommends "pneumatological Christology"; or "autonomism," against which he recommends "Christological pneumatology."[86] These remarks seem to agree with Congar's following self-assessment: "If I were to draw but one conclusion from the whole of my work on the Holy Spirit, I would express it in these words: no Christology without pneumatology and no pneumatology without Christology."[87]

Chan says that Congar's balance of Christological pneumatology and pneumatological Christology "means our Christology and pneumatology must find their unity in God the Father."[88] The Catholic Charismatic, Kilian McDonnell, seems to agree with Chan. He argues that, because of common pneumatological and Christological Old Testament roots in Yahweh's identity and activity, Congar's position that a healthy pneumatology is found in its Christology could easily and accurately be reformulated as the health of pneumatology in the Trinity. In other words, "The controls for both christology and pneumatology are in the Trinity."[89] Understanding a dynamic interrelatedness of the Trinity—of theology proper as well as of Christology and pneumatology—with ecclesiology and cosmology and their implications for an inclusive theology of religions and missiology is integral to this project's proposal.

The intriguing "and how" of Doré interests me greatly at this point. Congar explains that he wishes to address "very real problems and needs in the Christian world today, above all those of the so-called charismatic renewal."[90] Specifically, he suggests that it needs "the vigour of a lived out pneumatology" that is "to be found in Christology," adding that "[t]here is only one body which the Spirit builds up and quickens and that is the body of Christ."[91] Thus, Christology, pneumatology, and ecclesiology will be investigated in an interrelated fashion, providing special interest for Pentecostal and Charismatic Christians.

The Bible provides rich resources for understanding the relations of Christ and the Holy Spirit. Congar bases this study on the scriptural anthropomorphism, linking Christ and the Spirit as Word and Breath proceeding out of God the Father as Mouth, arguing thereupon that the entire Bible "bears witness to the intimate connection between the word and the Spirit."[92] Of course, the Spirit and the Word do God's work together.[93] As the Spirit of Truth, the Holy Spirit is relative to Christ, "the way, the truth, and the life" (John 14:6),[94] who is the fullness of the Word of God. Although truth is ultimately eschatological, it is experienced presently by the Spirit. God's truth is not merely conceptual but moral and personal, being addressed not only to the head but also to the heart, communicating the content of God's plan of grace.[95]

The relations of the person and work of Christ and of the person and work of the Holy Spirit and therefore of the derivative theological categories of Christology and pneumatology are exceedingly complex; however, they are not at all convoluted. One is inclined to agree with Elizabeth Teresa Groppe's assertion that Congar should be "remembered as a theologian of the Holy Spirit, a man who gave new life to a neglected tradition in which pneumatology, theological anthropology, and ecclesiology had been seamlessly united," including that "[w]e can learn much from Congar's approach, and his legacy can bear fruit in the contemporary renewal of pneumatology and in the life of the church at large."[96] Therefore, Congar's contribution to our understanding of the intricate interrelatedness of Christology, pneumatology, ecclesiology, and cosmology can be of immense importance in their implications for an inclusive Renewal theology of mission.

Significantly, Congar questions any so-called "autonomy of the Spirit."[97] Even in the Spirit's distribution of spiritual gifts, or charismata, the Church is still not construed as "the Body of the Spirit, but that of Christ."[98] Yes, the Spirit's "freedom really exists, but it is the freedom of the living and glorified Lord Jesus together with his Spirit."[99] However, Congar avoids Christomonism as well. Not only does he insist that "[t]he Spirit is the Spirit of the Word, of the Lord, of the Son, of Christ," he states that "Jesus Christ is also of the Spirit."[100] Nevertheless, it is "primarily in Christ" that the two hands of the Father are united as Word and Breath.[101] And yet, Congar is not at all reticent in articulating the ever present activity of the Holy Spirit in and with Christ—that is, of a prominent role of pneumatology in Christology.[102] However, the Holy Spirit is the Spirit of Christ and the Spirit of God even if "first and foremost" of God, still working in Jesus Christ for human salvation.[103]

Finally, Congar helpfully offers a clear "Christological criterion" for "the authenticity of a pneumatology," nevertheless defining this firmly but flexibly "to look for the way in which the actions and fruits that are attributed to the Holy Spirit are of a piece with or at least in accordance with the work of the incarnate Word, Jesus Christ the Lord."[104] In a discussion of "exuberant manifestations of the Spirit," Congar says, "Christ is the 'all' of Christianity. All the activity of the Spirit goes back to this 'all', which is the criterion of the active presence of that Spirit."[105] Within contexts of specifically Christian worship, the standard for authentic expressions of the Spirit is fidelity to the confession of Jesus' lordship.

One may observe that, overall, Congar's integration of biblical, historical, and theological reflection indicates that Christ and the Holy Spirit—and therefore, Christology and pneumatology—ought always to be related yet considered distinct. To be sure, relation should not be interpreted in terms of assimilation, nor should distinction be considered in terms of separation. Arguably, Charismatic inclusivism can simultaneously affirm the Spirit's expansive activity in the world and among the unevangelized and religious others while ardently insisting on the absolute essentiality of Christ in and for all the Spirit does anywhere or anytime—even beyond the borders of the Church.

The Roles of Ecclesiology and of Cosmology

The appropriate place of the Church in relation to God's vision for and work in the world are of fundamental importance. Some even go so far as to insist that salvation is inextricably tied to visible, formal membership in the Church.[106] Congar does not agree.[107] Congar argues against the "heresy" of "ecclesiolatry," that is, making the Church central rather than Christ or God. However, he ardently espouses "an immense, deep and warm love of the Church" that he finds "very favorable to a life of prayer and praise."[108] Together with ecumenism, ecclesiology was "the great passion" of Congar's life.[109] Charismatics will be interested that, without neglecting Christological nuances of ecclesiology, Congar increasingly "gave greater weight to the mission of the Holy Spirit, by whose agency the gifts of the Christ to the church are concretely realized in the lives of believers."[110] In fact, Congar came to think of the Church's life "as a prolonged *epiclēsis,* or prayer for the Spirit's advent."[111] Perhaps this explains, in part, why Yong suggests Pentecostals might have more in common with Congar's dynamic and charismatic ecclesiology than ordinarily might be suspected due to its Roman Catholic background.[112] For Congar, the people of God are those who through the aid of the Holy Spirit hear the Word, believe, and obey.[113] The Church's genesis in this initial relation to the Word is also its ongoing reality.[114] Accordingly, there is a clear "unity of function" of witness coming from the Father, concerning Jesus, given by the Spirit, and continuing in the Church.[115] There is an inner, individual and outer, ecclesial testimony of the Spirit. Thus, the dangers of individualism are overcome through looking for the Spirit's bearing witness "not only in the believing individual, but also in the believing community of the Church."[116] In any case, it is essential to recognize the necessity of the Spirit's giving life to everything: to all the tradition and liturgy, including it's "highly Christological structure."[117] It is an error to fail to make explicit this profoundly necessary pneumatology. In short, as Congar summarizes, the Spirit and the Word do God's work together, an observation manifestly evident in the Church.[118]

Regarding the Renewal, Congar declares that "[t]here could be no doubt that God is active in it," and he avidly affirms its positive contribution to the Church.[119] However, he also questions some of its terminology, warning, in the interests of ecumenism, "that those who belong to the Renewal should recognize that they have no monopoly on the Spirit and its activities do not form a Church for them."[120] Congar's interest in pneumatology increased and progressed, being fueled in part by the Charismatic Renewal Movement, moving forward from the Spirit's ecclesial role as "animator" to "co-institutor."[121] Congar freely confesses that Acts presents speaking in tongues as a sign of the Spirit's intervention.[122] However, Congar is often critical of Charismatics who limit charisms to extraordinary gifts such as speaking in tongues.[123] For him, full appreciation of the charisms of the Spirit "requires a proper understanding of the inseparability of Jesus Christ and the Holy Spirit," not only allowing but also inviting inclusion of a broad range of ecclesial ministries just as the Spirit was involved in all of Christ's life.[124] For precisely this reason, I suggest that Congar can contribute much to Pentecostal and Charismatic Renewal theology of mission in regards to interreligious encounter.

As with Christology and pneumatology, ecclesiology calls for careful balance. Congar always seems to be aiming for "an equilibrium" regarding Christ and the Spirit and the Church.[125] Nichols notes that the Church is, for Congar, "at once the people of God and the Body of Christ, the temple of the Holy Spirit and a communion, a society and an extended sacrament," explaining that "[t]his linguistic generosity" derives from "a desire to keep in equilibrium the institutional aspect of the church, linked chiefly with the mission of the Son, and its charismatic side, connected mainly to that of the Spirit"; in Congar, "There can no more be ultimate incompatibility between these two dimensions than there can be dissonance between the two divine missions. The humanity of the Word Incarnate is Spirit-filled, just as the Spirit himself is always the Spirit of the Son."[126] However, Congar admits that knowing "how to separate the work of the Word who reveals the Father from that of the Spirit" is problematic; after all, "[t]hey co-institute the Church."[127] Importantly, Congar argues that "[t]he Spirit is not autonomous in the substantial aspect of the work to which the Word of God, the incarnate Son, has to give form." Intriguingly, he adds that "it is possible to cite a number of ways of attributing initiatives to the Spirit without reference or at least with insufficient references to the Word."[128] For him, the

Church finally comes from both "the Word in his incarnation and from the Spirit."[129] "Everything" depends on recognizing that "the Church is constituted and lives, in continuity from its origins, from the gifts distributed by the Lord and the Spirit for the building up of the body of Christ" (1 Cor. 12:4-30).[130] And yet, Congar agrees that the Church's dialogue with the world and its cultures, including dialogue with other religions, benefits both and presupposes the Spirit's presence in both.[131]

Therefore, the Holy Spirit is bonded to Christ and his Church, but the Spirit is not bound. Congar carefully distinguishes between "two lines of action in God's work" which he calls, "the way of mediation and the way of immediacy."[132] While he never allows for their complete divorce, discovering subtle correspondences, mediation occurs more through institutionalized means. In other words, mediation occurs through the Church and immediacy through personal initiative and individual experiences of the Holy Spirit.[133] He warns against allowing codified norms that become "a sort of ready-made straightjacket," preferring to think of the Church as "a spiritual communion with a social structure."[134] Thus, "past forms are preserved," but "criticism and creativity" are also possible.[135] Although convinced that the public testimony—the apostolic witness of revelation—is complete, he denies that the Church now "knows the whole content of the Word of God," leaving ample room for "private revelations."[136] It is a small wonder that Kärkkäinen stresses Congar's ceaseless bent toward balance and stern concern over unhealthy tension between charism and institution.[137]

The overflowing activity of the Spirit of Christ into God's created order ought to be acknowledged. Congar argues that the Spirit's wind blows mysteriously and unpredictably (John 3:8); therefore, genuine prophetism may occur without explicit reference to Christ beyond the borders of the institutional Church.[138] Congar asks, "Does the charism of prophecy still exist today? Has it continued in the Church? Is it to be found outside its visible boundaries?" He replies, "My answer is certainly 'yes.'"[139] However, he explains that there are several different forms of prophetism, including that which is unique to the Church and its ministry, that which is distinctively charismatic, and that which may even be non-religious.[140] Afterwards, he warns that the Word should never be considered an obstacle to the Breath: "We do not, after all, know where the Breath comes from or where it is going!"[141] Nonetheless, when "the Spirit displays something that is new, in the novelty of history or variety of cultures," says Congar, "it is a new thing that comes from the fullness that has been given once for all by God in Christ."[142] This is the case even though there remains that which is to be "totally revealed or totally fulfilled in Christ according to the flesh."[143] Thus, Congar says that the Spirit "is constantly an inspiration from Jesus and an aspiration for Jesus as the Lord."[144]

Functioning properly, Christ's Church and God's world need not necessarily be at odds. Congar advocates a strong ecclesiology but with a remarkable lack of rigidity. This is a position he came to hold, in contrast to much of the Western Church's tendency to neglect the person and work of the

Holy Spirit, in a gradual process of increasing appreciation and utilization of pneumatology as ecclesiology's "own deepest basis."[145] Williams also laments a historical and theological "tendency to subordinate the work of the Holy Spirit to the work of Christ," resulting in *"ontological* equality" but *"functional* subordination."[146] Interestingly, Williams argues that God's omnipresence not only means God is present throughout creation, but also that through the Holy Spirit, "God is immediately present to every human being" (Psa. 139:7-12).[147] At the same time, God is uniquely present with those indwelled by the Spirit through faith.[148] One may discern a consistent tendency in each to apply pneumatology to both ecclesiology and to cosmology.

Accordingly, a clear pneumatological trait is discernable in Congar's reflections on cosmology. He regrets the lack of theological reflection on the cosmic role of the Holy Spirit (Gen. 1:3; Rom. 8:17-21).[149] In this regard, he bases "pneumatological anthropology" and "pneumatological cosmism" on "pneumatological Christology" or "Christological pneumatology."[150] He argues for "a close and intimate connection between the part played by the Spirit in our hearts and his cosmic role."[151] For him, "history is inseparably Christological and pneumatological."[152] The incarnate Christ "draws the world to him" so that "his redemption is cosmic."[153] Therefore, Christology, pneumatology, ecclesiology, and cosmology appear intertwined.

However, Congar's pneumatological cosmology clearly means more than that the material creation will someday participate in salvation's restoration. "The Spirit is in labor" in the world now, and "the active presence of the Holy spirit is recognized in the world and in its constant seeking."[154] Of course, evil is real, and there is therefore much in human history and the world that does not come from the Holy Spirit.[155] Yet, there is also much that is positive. While the Spirit is working specifically to build up the Body of Christ—a work that certainly is central—there are also "unknown dimensions" of the Spirit's working. While the Church "has a visible form that can be named," there is more to it as well.[156] Tellingly, he thinks that "it may be possible to say where the Church is, but not possible to say where it is not."[157] Thus, divine redemption and its expressions are multilayered, according to God's own gracious manner.

The Spirit of liberty cannot be limited. For Congar, "We simply do not know the frontiers of the Spirit's work in this world, nor the ways in which he acts" although "[w]e can be sure that they are related to Christ."[158] In fact, he is convinced that though the Christians know and call Christ and the Spirit "by name" and we have the Scriptures, the sacraments, and the ministries, "The Spirit is active beyond the visible frontiers of the Church, and for the world, the Church is the sacrament of Christ and his Spirit."[159] Thus, we pray for the world, and give God glory for it, trusting that "the Spirit is the one who in secret gathers up and binds together everyone who is trying to stammer the words 'Our Father.'" Further, "The Spirit is, after all, the one through whom we cry or who cries for us: 'Abba, Father!'(Rom. 8:15; Gal 4:6)."[160]

And yet, no one should ever lose sight of the Spirit's association with Christ. After all, "the Holy Spirit is active in the cosmos and is the *Spiritus Creator* only because he is one with the Word and with 'God.'"[161] Though he admits he has not given it sufficient attention in the present writing—regrettably for us because it is a focus of this volume—Congar affirms the work of the Spirit in evangelism.[162] Elsewhere, Congar contends that, "The time of the Church is essentially a time of mission, bearing witness and kerygma."[163] Nevertheless, the eschatological element in the Spirit's work in bringing to fulfillment and consummation God's promise in Christ still "points emphatically to the tendency towards the kingdom of God which secretly inspires the history of mankind."[164]

Congar's reflective work on ecclesiology and cosmology helpfully suggests—similarly to that on Christ and the Spirit, Christology and pneumatology—that they ought always to be kept related but distinct.[165] Again, relation is neither reducible to assimilation nor distinction expandable to separation. In an ecclesial context, Congar insists, "The essential thing is to respect the two missions, of the Word and of the Spirit, on the pattern of the succession which derives from the procession within the Trinity."[166] However, "Christ and the Spirit both carry out the same work of salvation."[167] Thus, the "relationships between the Paraclete and Christ are also extremely close in the economy of salvation."[168] Congar agrees that one might say, "Jesus is the way (*hē hodos*) and the Spirit is the guide (*ho hodēgos*) who enables man to go forward on that way."[169] Accordingly, there is always a distinction in relation and relation in distinction. Significantly for an inclusive renewal theology of religions, the uniqueness of the Church and its mission cannot be diminished. Equally as important, God's plan and purpose for all of God's creation ought never to be minimized (Psa. 145:9). A healthy balance will bring together in proper tandem both theological verities and their attendant realities.

At this point, I will highlight three broad implications of Congar's work in the context of the present discussion. First, an inclusive theology of religions with a strong pneumatological accent does not sacrifice classical Christian orthodoxy. The burden of proof rests with those who would argue otherwise. Christ is no less the utterly unique Lord and Savior because his Spirit reaches wide into the world to invite participation in the redemption that he alone can provide. The Church is no less Christ's agent and servant because God's kingdom cannot be contained within institutional boundaries, or because God's eternal purpose graciously touches all creation and every creature. Second, the inherent complexity of Christology, pneumatology, ecclesiology, and cosmology resists facile oversimplification. Pitting Christ and Spirit or Church and creation against each other is a horrible and an inexcusable error precisely because it is guilty of ignoring the copious subtlety of the beauty and symmetry of Christian truth. Third, the breadth and depth of Christian theology invites an amazing fertility in the developing area of theology of religions. It is a rich and reliable resource. Renewal Christians are perhaps uniquely poised to plumb the vast reservoirs of a Pentecostal-Charismatic theology of religions due to their divinely ordained place in contemporary global society. In my judgment, it would be a shame to miss or dismiss such an excellent opportunity for ministry.

Conclusion

Before closing, I will address concerns and questions regarding an inclusive theology of Christian mission.[170] These can be divided into two categories: those which are really *fair* and those which are merely *fearful*. In this writing, I have tried to address fair and reasonable concerns regarding the legitimate implications of inclusivism for Pentecostal and Charismatic sense of mission and ministry. These include how inclusivism affects our theology and praxis regarding evangelism and dialogue as well as whether it is genuinely sound in its overall theological implications and interrelations. Obviously, my assessment is positive. Concerns which arise out of unfounded phobias or overblown biases are more difficult to address. For instance, there is simply no evidence that inclusivism undermines evangelistic urgency. Amazingly, great evangelists and apologists such as John Wesley and C. S. Lewis were avidly inclusivist.[171] As another example, inclusivism and universalism are poles apart; the former does not lead to the latter and the latter is, in fact, countered by the former. Yet, we continue to hear claims that inclusivism replaces evangelism with dialogue, and that it amounts to insipient universalism. Admittedly, part of the problem is the not almost but outright promiscuous misuse of terminology that fuses and confuses inherently incompatible concepts. Many Pentecostals and Charismatics will perhaps be familiar with Carlton Pearson's "gospel of inclusion." Pearson variously defines his so-called "gospel of inclusion" as "universal reconciliation," "universal redemption," or "universal salvation."[172] This is *not* at all classical Christian inclusivism. It *is* universalism and it *is* unacceptable. Of course, Pearson's explication of it as "inclusion" is also confusing.

For me, the solution is to simply keep telling the facts until the falsehood finally fades away, trusting that the overcoming power of truth will "win the day." Here, the practice of authentic Christian mission requires our perseverance. Important to bear in mind is that salvation is God's work (Eph. 2:8-9). It is not dependent upon human righteousness or wisdom. In short, we are not saved by what we know or do. Conversion and salvation are graciously accomplished by what God knows and by what God does. The biblical doctrine of the atonement is based on that abiding truth (Lev. 4:1-5:13; Rom. 5:12-21).

In summary, the discussion above developed first by supplying historical examples or precedents of Pentecostal inclusivism and biblical and theological arguments for its complementarity with uncompromising commitment to the evangelism mission of the Church as couched in the Great Commission. Second, the discussion developed by surveying issues at stake in pneumatological theologies of religions, namely the intricate interrelations of Christology, pneumatology, ecclesiology, and cosmology through the thought of a leading theologian, Yves Congar. Congar is particularly noted for his contributions to ecumenical and charismatic theology. Our original questions resurface: How do and should Pentecostal and Charismatic Christians understand religious others? How do and should Pentecostals and Charismatics evangelize and missionize people of other faiths? Are there different theologies and mission strategies required for the various world religious traditions? Perhaps now, a few brief suggestions may be inoffensively offered.

According to the norm of biblical revelation, Pentecostal and Charismatic Christians should aspire to attain to a nuanced understanding of religious others in order to account for the diversity and variety of humanity's experience of God. Renewal Christian mission should, of course, continue to emphasize evangelism and proclamation, seeking to understand and implement mutual dialogue and cooperation as inherent within Christ's calling and command to his disciples throughout the world in all its cultures. As obedient disciples, Christ's command to "go into all the world" presupposes our connecting and engaging with its cultures, including its religions. In this process, different theologies and mission strategies required for intelligent and articulate interaction with various world religious traditions will undoubtedly arise providing unique opportunities for Christian ministry for today's Church in the world. In any case, witness in word and deed should always characterize Christian mission. Gauging everything by the norm of God's revelation in Christ through the Holy Scriptures, Pentecostals and Charismatics should be able to embrace enthusiastically fresh, visionary venues as the Spirit graciously guides. I am sure that Spirit-filled believers have much to offer along this avenue. Therefore, I suggest, in unapologetic continuity with historic Pentecostal-Charismatic commitments, the movements should face the future with bold creativity.[173]

In closing, I note that Paul's prayer in Ephesians 3:16-18 presents itself to me as remarkably expressive of the preceding comments and conclusions.

> I pray that out of his [the Father's] glorious riches he may strengthen you with power through his Spirit in your inner being, so that Christ may dwell in your hearts through faith. And I pray that you, being rooted and established in love, may have power, together with all the saints, to grasp how wide and long and high and deep is the love of Christ (NIV).

In Jesus' name, Amen![174]

Notes

1. Church of God Presiding Bishop Raymond Culpepper urges new ways of obeying Christ's Great Commission in a postmodern, pluralistic, politically correct, and pragmatic world; see discussion in James Cossey, "I Still Feel a Heartbeat!" *Church of God Evangel* (*COGE*) 99:12 (December 2009): 6-7 and 27. Readers should also consult the articles by Robert D. Crick, "A Global Pentecostal Perspective" (November 17, 2009),

http://www.faithnews.cc/2009/11/17/a-pentecostal-global-perspective/, and Bill George, "Symposium Calls Church to Great Commission Obedience" (September 29, 2009), http://www.faithnews.cc/2009/09/29/symposiums-call-church-to-great-commission-obedience/. During personal attendance at said symposium, I found that the subject of other religions and their adherents forcefully surfaced.

2. Broadly speaking, "inclusivism" describes a possibility of some openness (in Christ) regarding the unevangelized or adherents of other religions; "exclusivism" refers to a more closed or restrictive attitude; and "pluralism" essentially equates all religions. See Dennis L. Okholm, and Timothy R. Phillips, eds., *Four Views on Salvation in a Pluralistic World* (Grand Rapids: Zondervan, 1996).

3. See Larry D. Hart, *Truth Aflame: Theology for the Church in Renewal*, 2nd ed. (Grand Rapids: Zondervan, 2005), 19-20.

4. Veli-Matti Kärkkäinen, *Pneumatology: The Holy Spirit in Ecumenical, International, and Contextual Perspective* (Grand Rapids: Baker Academic, 2002), 15.

5. Kärkkäinen, *Pneumatology*, 111n28. Nevertheless, Kilian McDonnell, *The Other Hand of God: The Holy Spirit as Universal Touch and Goal* (Collegeville: Liturgical Press, 2003), 102, points out that Congar, though basically agreeing with Rahner, rightly wished to "limit the absolute character of his dictum" in the sense that the historical revelation of the Trinity can never exhaust the eternal reality.

6. Kärkkäinen, *Pneumatology*, 116, and Yong, *Discerning the Spirit(s): A Pentecostal Charismatic Contribution to Christian Theology of Religions* (Sheffield: Sheffield Academic Press, 2000), 43; cp. Karl Rahner, "Anonymous Christians," in *Theological Investigations*, trans. K. H. Kruger and B. Kruger (Baltimore: Helicon, 1969), 6.394.

7. Kirsteen Kim, *The Holy Spirit in the World: A Global Conversation* (Maryknoll: Orbis Books, 2007), 38, 145.

8. Yves Congar, *I Believe in the Holy Spirit*, 3 vols., trans. David Smith (New York: Seabury, 1983).

9. Aidan Nichols OP, "Yves Congar," in David F. Ford, ed., *The Modern Theologians: An Introduction to Christian Theology in the Twentieth Century*, 2 vols. (Cambridge: Blackwell, 1990), 1.226.

10. Simon Chan, *Pentecostal Theology and the Christian Tradition* (Sheffield: Sheffield Academic Press, 2000, 2003), 90; also Congar, *Holy Spirit*, 1.106.

11. See Chan, *Pentecostal Theology*, 98, and Kärkkäinen, *Pneumatology*, 39-40, 74, and 95. See also Veli-Matti Kärkkäinen, "Pneumatology," in William A. Dryness and Veli-Matti Kärkkäinen, gen. eds., *Global Dictionary of Theology: A Resource for the Worldwide Church* (Downer's Grove: InterVarsity Press, 2008), 659-69, esp. 662 and 665, and P. D. Hocken, "Charismatic Movement," in Stanley M. Burgess and Eduardo van der Maas, eds., *New International Dictionary of Pentecostal and Charismatic Movements* [hereafter referred to as *NIDPCM*] (Grand Rapids: Zondervan, 1992), 477-519, esp. 494, and "Church, Theology of the," 544-52, esp. 549.

12. As Hart, *Truth Aflame*, 552-53 (also 27-29 and 9), accurately observes, the Pentecostal/Charismatic Revival at its best can be a potent force for Christian unity.

13. C. M. Robeck, Jr., "Williams, J. Rodman," *NIDPCM*, 1198. See J. Rodman Williams, *Renewal Theology: Systematic Theology from a Charismatic Perspective*, 3 vols. in one (Grand Rapids: Zondervan, 1996).

14. Hocken, "Charismatic Movement," *NIDPCM*, 481, 493, and 497; Hocken, "Church, Theology of," 550; G. B. McGee, "Initial Evidence," *NIDPCM*, 784-91, esp. 79; H. D. Hunter, "International Pentecostal-Charismatic Scholarly Associations,"

NIDPCM, 795-97, esp. 796; and V. H. Synan, "Presbyterian and Reformed Charismatics," *NIDPCM*, 995-97, esp. 997.

15. Synan, "Presbyterian and Reformed Charismatics," 997.

16. See C. M. Robeck, Jr., "Seminaries and Graduate Schools," *NIDPCM*, 1045-50, esp. 1047, and R. P. Spittler, "Society for Pentecostal Studies," *NIDPCM*, 1079-80, esp. 1079. In honor of his legacy in renewal theology, Regent University School of Divinity established the J. Rodman Williams Chair of Theology (now held by Amos Yong). See http://www.regent.edu/news_events/?article_id=544&view=full_article.

17. Amos Yong, "Disability and the Gifts of the Spirit: Pentecost and the Renewal of the Church," *Journal of Pentecostal Theology* 19 (2010): 75-92.

18. See Tony Richie, "'Constitutionally Christian': A Classical Pentecostal Appraisal of Founders and Figures of World Faiths with Attentiveness to Inclusivist Implications," *Testamentum Imperium* 2 (2009) [http://www.preciousheart.net/ti/2009/28-049_Richie_Constitutionally_Christian.pdf]; "Eschatological Inclusivism: Exploring Early Pentecostal Theology of Religions in Charles Fox Parham," *Journal of the European Theological Association* 27:2 (2007): 137-52; "Azusa-era Optimism: Bishop J. H. King's Pentecostal Theology of Religions as a Possible Paradigm for Today," in Veli-Matti Kärkkäinen, ed., *The Spirit in the World: Emerging Pentecostal Theologies in Global Contexts* (Grand Rapids: William B. Eerdmans Publishing Company, 2009), 227-44; and "Continuing the Conversation on King: My Really Final Response to Tony Moon?" *Journal of Pentecostal Theology* 19 (2010): 169-78.

19. E.g., the Psalmist described those outside Zion who knew the Lord (87:4). Craig C. Broyles, *New International Biblical Commentary: Psalms* (Peabody: Hendrickson, 1999), 350-51, calls Psalm 87 "the most explicit, positive statement about the nations" that "catches us by surprise" until duly noting parallels in Isaiah. Inclusivists argue along similar lines: the Christ, not the Church, is the Savior.

20. Frances S. Adeney, "Why Biography? Contributions of Narrative Studies to Mission Theology and Mission Theory," *Mission Studies: Journal of the International Association for Mission Studies* 26:2 (2009): 153-72, quote from 158. Adeney is a professor of evangelism and mission at Louisville Presbyterian Seminary in Louisville, Kentucky.

21. Ibid., 160.

22. Ibid., 160-61.

23. Ibid., 161.

24. Hart, *Truth Aflame*, 23.

25. Ibid., 26.

26. Ibid., 30, and (for the quote) 491; cp. 375 and 495.

27. Ibid., 555-56; cp. 552-53 and 557-58.

28. Williams, *Renewal Theology*, 3.133.

29. Ibid., 3.135.

30. Ibid.

31. Ibid., 3.136.

32. Ibid., 3.135; e.g., see ministries to the poor, hungry, sick, outcast, and demon-possessed.

33. Ibid.

34. Ibid., 3.135-41.

35. Ibid., 3.138. The Church of God (Cleveland, Tennessee) Presiding Bishop, Raymond F. Culpepper, *The Great Commission: The Solution...* (Cleveland, Tenn.:

Pathway Press, 2009), certainly makes evangelism central as well. However, he also insists (35-36, 49-50, and 161-65) on connecting and identifying with peoples and their cultures, and includes dialogue as a part of that approach. For him, this is all part of "the Spirit's stretching ministry" and helps "prevent dull and stolid thinking" (169). Nevertheless, although he admits church ministry is "multifaceted" and that Jesus' ministry was "multilayered," he warns against "a serious error" in confusing even good ministries with the Great Commission, meaning winning souls and making disciples (182-83).

36. After all, Williams highlights wise relations with the world, regarding "not only what one says but also in how one says it" (*Renewal Theology*, 3.154).

37. Ibid., 3.474-76, quotation from 476.

38. Ibid.

39. Williams, *Renewal Theology*, 3.476n126; italics original.

40. Ibid., 1.84.

41. Ibid., 1.246 and 1.253. Therefore, the great need of humankind is to hear the gospel (Culpepper, *The Great Commission*, 190-91).

42. Williams, *Renewal Theology*, 2.29. Hart, *Truth Aflame*, 420, sums up faith as combining knowledge of the truth, intellectual assent to it, and personal trust in God.

43. Williams, *Renewal Theology*, 3.459; however, he certainly limits natural knowledge (3.186).

44. Ibid., 1.239-40.

45. Ibid., 1.266; see also Hart, *Truth Aflame*, 43-45.

46. For a classic presentation of these categories, see Alan Race, *Christians and Religious Pluralism: Patterns in the Theology of Religions* (Maryknoll: Orbis Books, 1983).

47. Yong, *Discerning the Spirit(s)*, 185.

48. See Veli-Matti Kärkkäinen, *An Introduction to Theology of Religions: Biblical, Historical, and Contemporary Perspectives* (Downers Grove: InterVarsity Press, 2003), 140-42.

49. Yong, *Discerning the Spirit(s)*, 184, 186. Of course, Pentecostals are certainly not pluralists (e.g., Culpepper, *The Great Commission*, 189-90).

50. David J. Hesselgrave, "Evangelicals and Interreligious Dialogue," in Donald A. Pittman, Ruben L. F. Habito, and Terry Muck, eds., *Ministry and Theology in Global Perspective: Contemporary Challenges for the Church* (Grand Rapids: William B. Eerdmans Publishing Company, 1996), 425-28, esp. 425.

51. Ibid., 425-26.

52. Ibid., 426-27.

53. Ibid., 427.

54. C. Peter Wagner, in his "Foreword" to Jacobs, *The Reformation Manifesto: Your Part in God's Plan to Change the Nations Today* (Bloomington, Minn.: Bethany House, 2008), 10. The rest of the Wagner quotations in this paragraph come from this page.

55. Although Matthew 18:28-35 actually focuses on appropriate interpersonal responses to divine forgiveness, Robert H. Mounce, *New International Biblical Commentary: Matthew* (Peabody: Hendrickson, 1991), 178. The emphasis on miraculous signs in the longer ending of Mark 16:9-20—e.g., Larry W. Hurtado, *New International Biblical Commentary: Mark* (Peabody: Hendrickson, 1989), 287—may make it more attractive to some Pentecostals, but it supplies no reason to assume that evangelism and dialogue are incompatible. E.g., William J. Brown, review of Pradip N. Thomas, *Strong Religion, Zealous Media: Christian Fundamentalism and Communication in India* (Sage,

2008) in *PNEUMA: The Journal of the Society for Pentecostal Studies* 31:2 (2009): 291-92, welcomes "a covenantal approach to reconciliation among differing religious groups" and suggests "Pentecostals and evangelical Christians should strongly promote mutual respect and understanding with those of other faiths" (292), even as he ardently defends enthusiastic Christian evangelism.

56. Yong, *Discerning the Spirit(s)*, 184.

57. Also note that in actual practice those who advocate interreligious dialogue often argue for the import of retaining dialogue and social action alongside evangelism for a full orbed missiological engagement with the religions—e.g., Amos Yong, *Hospitality and the Other: Pentecost, Christian Practices, and the Neighbor* (Maryknoll: Orbis Books, 2008), ch. 5.

58. See Mounce, *Matthew*, 178, and Hurtado, *Mark*, 287. However, as indicated by Reginald H. Fuller, "Matthew," in James L. Mays, gen. ed., *Harper's Bible Commentary* (San Francisco: Harper & Row, 1988), 951-82, esp. 981, the classic "Great Commission" text, Matthew 28:16-20, probably comparable to Moses' farewell speech (Deut. 33), emphasizes discipleship, teaching, and Christ's abiding presence rather than explicit evangelism (although certainly implicit). Mounce, *Matthew*, 268, notes that "the teaching is here set forth as ethical rather than doctrinal."

59. Yong, *Discerning the Spirit(s)*, 184. Many Pentecostals see themselves as existing expressly for the purpose of fulfilling the "Great Commission." See James Cossey, "The Holy Spirit and the Great Commission," *Church of God Evangel* 99:9 (September 2009): 3, and Charles Fischer, "The Theology of the Great Commission," *Church of God Evangel* 99:9 (September 2009): 8-9. However, this evangelistic emphasis is usually considered compatible with social ministries, as in George Moxley, "Commissioned to Care," *Church of God Evangel* 99:9 (September 2009): 12-13.

60. James Shelton, "Matthew," in French L. Arrington and Roger Stronstad, eds., *Full life Bible Commentary to the New Testament: An International Commentary for Spirit-Filled Christians* (Grand Rapids: Zondervan, 1999), 119-253, at 252.

61. See Wolfhart Pannenberg, *An Introduction to Systematic Theology* (Grand Rapids: William B. Eerdmans Publishing Company, 1991), 53-55.

62. F. F. Bruce, *The Book of Acts*, rev. ed. (Grand Rapids: William B. Eerdmans Publishing Company, 1988), 94.

63. French L. Arrington, *The Acts of the Apostles: Introduction, Translation, and Commentary* (Peabody: Hendrickson, 1988), 47.

64. See Francis Martin, ed., *Ancient Christian Commentary on the Scriptures, New Testament V: Acts* (Downers Grove: InterVarsity Press, 2006), 49.

65. Bede, in Martin, ed., *Ancient Christian Commentary*, 49.

66. Leon Morris, *The Gospel According to John* (1971; reprint, Grand Rapids: William B. Eerdmans Publishing Company, 1987), 229-31.

67. Ibid., 232.

68. Ibid., 233.

69. Ibid., 234-35.

70. J. Ramsey Michaels, *New International Biblical Commentary: John* (Peabody: Hendrickson, 1989), 59; italics original. For OT evangelism in inclusive context, see John N. Oswalt, *The Book of Isaiah: Chapters 40-66* (Grand Rapids: William B. Eerdmans Publishing Company, 1998), 283 and 487. For missionary implications of the prophetic message, see Oswalt, "The Mission of Israel to the Nations," in William V. Crockett and James G. Sigountos, eds., *Through No Fault of Their Own: The Fate of Those Who Have Never Heard* (Grand Rapids: Baker, 1991), 85-95. See also Oswalt, *Isaiah*, 284n88.

71. Benny C. Aker, "John," in French L. Arrington and R. Stronstad, eds., *Full Life Bible Commentary on the New Testament: An International Commentary for Spirit-Filled Christians* (Grand Rapids: Zondervan, 1999), 84. Alternatively, cf. Ramesh P. Richard, *The Population of Heaven: A Biblical Response to the Inclusivist Position on Who will be Saved* (Chicago: Moody, 1994), 66-67. Note that Richard essentially ignores the context to which Aker is pointing.

72. Van Johnson, "Romans," in French L. Arrington and R. Stronstad, eds., *Full Life Bible Commentary on the New Testament: An International Commentary for Spirit-Filled Christians* (Grand Rapids: Zondervan, 1999), 693-797, quotation from 762. Again, note that, e.g., Richard, *Population*, 67, in arguing against inclusivism, ignores this context and its possible implications. Interestingly, John Wesley argued that the Pauline principle that, "What the law speaketh, it speaketh to them that are under the law" implies that those who do not have the Scriptures are exempt from its epistemological demands. See Tony Richie, "John Wesley and Mohammed: A Contemporary Inquiry Concerning Islam," *Asbury Theological Journal* 58:2 (2003): 79-99, quote from 84; see also *The Complete Works of John Wesley* (Rio, Wis.: The Wesleyan Heritage Collection; Ages Software, Inc, 2002), 7:58.

73. An approach embracing evangelism and inclusivism appears compatible with the biblical text of the Great Commission itself; see Fuller, "Matthew," 981; Mounce, *Matthew*, 268; and Shelton, "Matthew," 252.

74. Clark H. Pinnock, *Flame of Love: A Theology of the Holy Spirit* (Downers Grove: InterVarsity Press, 1996), 213.

75. E.g., James R. A. Merrick, "The Spirit of Truth as Agent in False Religions? A Critique of Amos Yong's Pneumatological Theology of Religions with Reference to Current Trends," *Trinity Journal* 29:1 (2008): 107-25. For my response to Merrick, see below.

76. I am aware that I am taking on major aspects of Congar's contributions, and I acknowledge that I cannot adequately discuss all aspects in depth or resolve the major interpretive issues; however, I have these specific goals in mind that I outline here. In other words, this is not an interpretation of Congar for Congar specialists but one that seeks to draw from Congar's work in a very general sense to provide further theological scaffolding for my inclusive Renewal theology of mission.

77. See Nichols, "Congar," 233.

78. Additionally, I can hardly help but appreciate Congar's pastoral sensitivity in doing theology, as Nichols mentions ("Congar," 233-34).

79. I am not denying the obvious reality of multiple faiths co-existing in close quarters in today's global society. Rather, I am contesting any ideology, philosophy, or theology asserting that all major world religions are of comparatively equal value. See Ninian Smart, "Pluralism," in Donald W. Musser and Joseph L. Price, eds., *A New Handbook of Christian Theology* (Nashville: Abingdon, 1992), 360-64, and John Hick, "A Pluralist View," in Dennis L. Okholm, and Timothy R. Phillips, eds., *Four Views on Salvation in a Pluralistic World* (Grand Rapids: Zondervan, 1996), 27-59.

80. Yves Congar, *The Word and the Spirit*, trans. David Smith (San Francisco: Harper & Row, 1986).

81. E.g., Veli-Matti Kärkkäinen, *Trinity and Religious Pluralism: The Doctrine of the Trinity in Christian Theology of Religions* (Aldershot and Burlington: Ashgate, 2004), 2; see also Kärkkäinen's *Toward a Pneumatological Theology: Pentecostal and Ecumenical Perspectives on Ecclesiology, Soteriology, and Theology of Mission*, ed. Amos Yong (Lanham: University Press of America, 2002), ch. 14. On Yong, see

Discerning the Spirit(s) and *Beyond the Impasse: Toward a Pneumatological Theology of Religions* (Grand Rapids: Baker Academic, 2003). Although Yong emphasizes pneumatology more directly and explicitly than Kärkkäinen in his trinitarian theology of religions, Kärkkäinen's energetic pneumatological accent ought not to be missed—e.g., see his "Toward a Pneumatological Theology of Religions: A Pentecostal-Charismatic Inquiry," *International Review of Mission* 91:361 (2002): 187-98, and "How to Speak of the Spirit among Religions: Trinitarian 'Rules' for a Pneumatological Theology of Religions," *International Bulletin of Missionary Research* 30:3 (2006): 121-27.

82. See Clark H. Pinnock, "Toward an Evangelical Theology of Religions," *Journal of Evangelical Theological Society* 33:3 (1990); 359-68; *A Wideness in God's Mercy: The Finality of Jesus Christ in a World of Religions* (Grand Rapids: Zondervan, 1992); and *Flame of Love*, esp. ch. 6.

83. I discuss this aspect of the debate in my "The Spirit of Truth as Guide into All Truth: A Response to James R.A. Merrick, 'The Spirit of Truth as Agent in False Religions? A Critique of Amos Yong's Pneumatological Theology of Religions with Reference to Current Trends,'" *Cyberjournal for Pentecostal Charismatic Research* 19 (2010) [http://www.pctii.org/cyberj/cyberj19/richie.html].

84. Joseph Doré, "Preface to the French Edition," in Congar, *Word and Spirit*, ix-x.

85. Ibid., ix. Nichols, "Congar," 230, says Irenaeus' "two hands" terminology and theology is "beloved of Congar" and behind much of his balancing of Christology and pneumatology.

86. Doré, "Preface to the French Edition," ix.

87. Congar, *Word and Spirit*, 1. Simon Chan, *Spiritual Theology: A Systematic Study of the Christian Life* (Downers Grove: InterVarsity Press, 1998), 49, says Congar's balance of Christological pneumatology and pneumatological Christology "means our Christology and pneumatology must find their unity in God the Father"; see also Congar, *Holy Spirit*, 3.165-71. McDonnell, *Other Hand of God*, 193, seems to agree with Chan, arguing that because of common pneumatological and Christological OT roots in Yahweh's identity and activity, Congar's position that a healthy pneumatology is in its Christology could easily and accurately be reformulated as the health of pneumatology in the Trinity. In other words, "The controls for both christology and pneumatology are in the Trinity."

88. Chan, *Spiritual Theology*, 49; also Congar, *Holy Spirit*, 3.165-71.

89. McDonnell, *Other Hand of God*, 193.

90. Congar, *Word and Spirit*, 6. For Congar, Charismatic Renewal includes what is today termed "Classical Pentecostalism" (50-51).

91. Ibid., 6.

92. Ibid., 15 and 19; cp. Kärkkäinen, *Pneumatology*, 26.

93. Congar, *Word and Spirit*, 21-35. Thus, in Yong's words, building in part on Congar, "the Word and the Spirit are related and yet distinct" (*Discerning the Spirit(s)*, 116).

94. Throughout this work, Congar cites enormous amounts of biblical texts, but for purposes of brevity, I only list a very few representative examples.

95. Congar, *Word and Spirit*, 42-46.

96. Elizabeth Teresa Groppe, *Yves Congar's Theology of the Holy Spirit* (Oxford and New York: Oxford University Press, 2004), 12.

97. Congar, *Word and Spirit*, 48-77.

98. Ibid., 60.

99. Ibid., 61.

100. Ibid., 62.

101. Ibid. According to Congar three volume *The Holy Spirit*, the Spirit and the Christ "condition each other" (2.211), even as the Church and the Spirit "condition each other" (1.68).Yet, Congar could also speak of the Spirit as the "go-between-God," i.e., "the God who acts as a kind of broker and who penetrates subtly everywhere in order to create true relationships" (2.220). Similarly, he spoke of kind of "a 'kenosis' of the Spirit" or the Spirit "who acts without revealing himself except in the acts he secretly inspires" (2.222; cp. General Introduction, vii). Thus, so much of what the Spirit does may be inexpressible (referencing Lk. 17:21) or implicit (referencing Matt. 25:35ff.) and have a hidden aspect (2.23; cp. 1.58).

102. Congar, *Word and Spirit*, 87-92.

103. Ibid., 101-02.

104. Congar, *Holy Spirit*, 2.210; cp. 2.211.

105. Ibid., 1.34.

106. Kärkkäinen, *Theology of Religions*, 318-52, discusses this approach and some proponents under the heading of "Ecclesiocentrism."

107. E.g., Congar, *Holy Spirit*, 2.219-24.

108. Ibid., 2.209-10.

109. Nichols, "Congar," 221; Nichols also says, "[T]he heart of Congar's theology" was his doctrine of the Church (226). Hans Schwarz, *Theology in a Global Context: The Last Two Hundred Years* (Grand Rapids: William B. Eerdmans Publishing Company, 2005), 429, calls Congar, "the most prominent ecumenical scholar of his church in the twentieth century."

110. Nichols, "Congar," 225. See also Yves Congar, *Tradition and Traditions: An Historical and a Theological Essay*, trans. Michael Naseby and Thomas Rainborough (London and New York: Macmillan, 1966).

111. Nichols, "Congar," 226. Amos Yong, *The Spirit Poured Out on All Flesh: Pentecostalism and the Possibility of Global Theology* (Grand Rapids: Baker, 2005), 133-34 and 139, observes that Congar argues that the Holy Spirit and the Church are always linked in creedal history; see also Kärkkäinen, *Pneumatology*, 39-40. Like many Pentecostals and Charismatics, Congar emphasized "living pneumatology," but he also pressed for its theological reflection and development (Groppe, *Yves Congar's Theology of the Holy Spirit*, 3).

112. Yong, *Spirit Poured Out on All Flesh*, 147-48 and 150.

113. Congar, *Word and Spirit*, 21-23.

114. Ibid., 27.

115. Ibid., 30.

116. Ibid., 32. Groppe suggests that Congar's "distinctive contribution" to pneumatology was his integration of the Holy Spirit's indwelling individuals with reflection on the Spirit's work in the Church (4), i.e., he "reunited spiritual anthropology and ecclesiology" through his "elaboration of both a pneumatological anthropology and pneumatological ecclesiology" (*Yves Congar's Theology of the Holy Spirit*, 137; cf. 107).

117. Congar, *Word and Spirit*, 35.

118. Ibid., 21-35.

119. Congar, *Holy Spirit*, 2.145; also 2.149-60.

120. Ibid., 2.209, and also 2.161-72.

121. See Groppe, *Yves Congar's Theology of the Holy Spirit*, 34-35, 49.

122. Congar, *Holy Spirit*, 1.45.

123. Groppe, *Yves Congar's Theology of the Holy Spirit*, 105.

124. Ibid., 133.

125. Congar, *Word and Spirit*, 79.

126. Nichols, "Congar," 230.

127. Congar, *Word and Spirit*, 79.

128. Ibid. Congar's qualifying clauses are important to notice in this regard. For example, in *The Holy Spirit*, he says, "The Pneuma, *as given to us*, relates entirely to Christ," and "*As regards the content of a work of the Spirit as opposed to a work of Christ*, it is neither autonomous nor different" (1.37, italics added). Of course, Congar agrees that within the life of the Trinity the Spirit "must be an autonomous, free person" (1.40).

129. Congar, *Word and Spirit*, 83.

130. Ibid., 115. Congar admits that in the early OT documents, "there are parallels and similarities in other religions" (e.g., shamanism) regarding the "external effects" of the Spirit, but he notes that the OT distinctively attributes to God what others ascribe to the forces of nature (*Holy Spirit*, 1.5).

131. Congar, *Holy Spirit*, 2.219.

132. Congar, *Word and Spirit*, 52.

133. Ibid., 53.

134. Ibid., 55.

135. Ibid. Congar's discussion of ecclesiology is framed by a Catholic conversation with the Protestant Reformers and their heirs in an ecumenically amicable and open fashion. Congar even admitted Roman Catholicism has tended to "forget" the Holy Spirit and to find "substitutes" for the Holy Spirit in the Eucharist, the pope, and Mary; see Congar, *Holy Spirit*, 1.159-66, and Kärkkäinen, *Pneumatology*, 74.

136. Congar, *Word and Spirit*, 57. The discussion is in the context of questioning whether revelation is closed. In a sense, the answer may be both "yes" and "no." God's decisive revelation in Christ to and through the Church is a settled matter, but fresh revelatory insight and understanding in the Church and in individuals may continue in carefully qualified senses through the Spirit's ongoing work (see Nichols, "Congar," 227-28).

137. See Kärkkäinen, *Pneumatology*, 15 (on balance) and 95 (on tension); cp. Congar, *Holy Spirit*, 2.152-53 and 2.165-69, and Groppe, *Yves Congar's Theology of the Holy Spirit*, 213n184.

138. Congar, *Word and Spirit*, 66n54 and 75-76.

139. Ibid., 66-67.

140. Ibid., 67-71.

141. Ibid., 71.

142. Ibid. Thus, fresh appreciation for the fullness of Christ actually may encourage Christians to recognize and encounter different religions in new and welcoming ways (Groppe, *Yves Congar's Theology of the Holy Spirit*, 110).

143. Congar, *Word and Spirit*, 71.

144. Congar, *Holy Spirit*, 1.58.

145. Nichols, "Congar," 231.

146. Williams, *Renewal Theology*, 2.206-07n103.

147. Ibid., 1.78.

148. Ibid., 1.77-79 and 2.204. See also Congar, *Holy Spirit*, 2.219-24.

149. Congar, *Word and Spirit*, 122; see also Tony Richie, "Revelation, Redemption, and World Religions: A Pentecostal Perspective on the Inclusive Embrace of Divine Providence," *Journal of Beliefs and Values* 30:3 (2009): 313-22.

150. Congar, *Word and Spirit*, 122.

151. Ibid., 123.

152. Ibid., 123.

153. Ibid., 124. Timothy I. MacDonald criticized Congar's earlier work, in part, for failing to maintain adequately enough "the unity-in-difference" dialectic of the Church and world relationship, a tendency that Congar later corrected through a more philosophically informed underpinning of the supernatural character of the Church; see Timothy I. MacDonald, *The Ecclesiology of Yves Congar* (Lanham: University Press of America, 1984), and Nichols, "Congar," 231-32.

154. Congar, *Word and Spirit*, 125.

155. Ibid., 125-26. Charles MacDonald, *Church and World in the Plan of God: Aspects of History and Eschatology in the Thought of Père Yves Congar, OP* (Frankfurt-am-Main: Peter Lang, 1982), who criticized Congar's ecclesiological and cosmological eschatology for being, in Nichols' ("Congar," 232) words, "too redolent of an ideology of progress," may not have given due consideration to Congar's caveat concerning the reality of evil.

156. Congar, *Word and Spirit*, 126.

157. Ibid. Groppe, *Yves Congar's Theology of the Holy Spirit*, 133, points out that Congar drew on the temple imagery of Israel and other ancient religions to incorporate a cosmic character into his pneumatological ecclesiology.

158. Congar, *Word and Spirit*, 126.

159. Ibid., 127.

160. Ibid.

161. Ibid., 131. Chan, *Pentecostal Theology*, 114, wisely cautions against possible pitfalls in a too casual approach to the *Creator Spiritus* concept, not arguing against it altogether but advising that "its usage must be carefully circumscribed." Congar's emphasis on the conjoined identity and activity of Christ and the Spirit appears to avoid the admittedly real dangers.

162. Congar, *Word and Spirit*, 131.

163. Congar, *Holy Spirit*, 1.58.

164. Congar, *Word and Spirit*, 132. Interestingly, Culpepper, *The Great Commission*, 37-38, boldly argues that the Kingdom of God is "the overarching reality" of which the Church is "an expression," adding that "[t]hose who observe with spiritual eyes know that God is at work outside the church as well as within and through it."

165. Pentecostals and Charismatics such as Rodman Williams are already accustomed to maintaining such complex and subtle relations in their understanding of regeneration and Spirit baptism; see also F. D. Macchia, "Theology, Pentecostal," *NIDPCM*, 1120-41, at 1130. Furthermore, Pentecostal ecclesiology suggests regarding the Church and the Kingdom that "the two are related, but they are not precisely the same" (Culpepper, *The Great Commission*, 37). Obviously, careful distinctions regarding related realities are not foreign to Pentecostal theology.

166. Congar, *Holy Spirit*, 1.25

167. Ibid., 1.50.

168. Ibid., 1.56.

169. Ibid., 1:57.

170. The following flows out of response and discussion at the "Symposium on World Religions and the Great Commission," which occurred at Regent University School of Divinity, Virginia Beach, Virginia, 27 February 2010, and at which an earlier

draft of this chapter was presented. Special thanks to Antipas Harris for the formal response.

171. See Tony Richie, "Wesley and Mohammed," 90-91, and "Hints from Heaven: Can C. S. Lewis Help Evangelicals Hear God in Other Religions?" *Evangelical Review of Theology* 32:1 (2008): 38-55.

172. Carlton Pearson, *The Gospel of Inclusion: Beyond Religious Fundamentalism to True Love of God and Self* (New York: Atria, 2009), 9-10, 158, 164, 217, 247, and 251.

173. Adeney, "Why Biography?" 169, suggests theologies of mission adjust to changing societies and human needs, bringing "different aspects of the good news of Jesus Christ to the fore." Catherine M. Mooney, "Ignatian Spirituality, A Spirituality for Mission," *Mission Studies: Journal of the International Association for Mission Studies* 26:2 (2009): 192-213, proposes that a discerning approach to mission should consider what particular ministries may be most helpful at a particular time and place and shape its mission practice accordingly (209).

174. Special thanks to Raymond Hodge for constructive comments on an earlier version of this chapter.

Chapter 3

Christian Mission and the Religions as Participation in the Spirit of Pentecost

Steven M. Studebaker

Pentecostal mission has usually proceeded on the assumption that, outside of explicit faith in Jesus Christ, there is no salvation—or, at least, very little. Pentecostal mission, therefore, assumes a negative theology of religions, which is to say that non-Christian religions are not only misguided efforts but also, most likely, serious impediments to salvation.[1] However, this traditional posture toward missions and theology of religions is out-of-step with the biblical narrative of the Spirit of Pentecost. From creation to Pentecost, the mission of the Spirit of God is not only to breathe life into all human beings but also to draw them into the fellowship of the trinitarian God, and that mission is universal and perennial.

This chapter suggests that 1) the Spirit of Pentecost, from creation to the eschatological event of Pentecost, is a liminal and constitutional agent within the history of biblical redemption, and 2) the work of the Spirit of Pentecost can fund a Pentecostal theology of religions and missions. In order to develop the liminal and constituting nature of the Spirit's work and its utility for a Pentecostal theology of religions and missions, the first part of the following illustrates the Spirit's work in creation-redemption, the Incarnation, and Pentecost; the second part brings these findings into the service of a Pentecostal theology of missions and religions.

Spirit of Creation as Spirit of Redemption

Although it is common to think of creation and redemption as distinct movements in the drama of biblical redemption, Scripture coordinates the Spirit's work in these two areas.[2] In short, the Spirit of creation is also the Spirit of redemption. Creation and redemption should not be understood as unrelated activities. In order to demonstrate the continuity between the Spirit of creation and redemption, the following looks at the Spirit's role in creation and the significance of that work for the Hebrew prophets' vision of redemption.

The Spirit and Creation as Redemption

First, the Spirit's creative work in Genesis 1:2 is also a redemptive work. The structure of Genesis 1:2 looks like this:

Now the earth was formless and empty . . .
Darkness was over the surface of the deep . . .
and the Spirit of God was hovering over the waters.

With regard to Genesis 1:2, a key interpretive question is whether the third nominal clause, "*and* the Spirit of God was hovering over the waters," continues to modify the "formless and empty" space and the watery abyss of the first part of the verse, or if it contrasts with them and transitions to the creative movement of God, which complements 1:3: "And God said, 'Let there be light.'" According to Wilf Hildebrandt, the *waw*, or "and," introducing the third clause is adversative; that is, it separates the third clause from the preceding two in a contrasting way.[3] Understood in this way, the Spirit of God hovering over the waters contrasts with the disorder of "formless and empty" and "darkness . . . over the surface of the deep." Thomas L. Brodie suggests that the "striking picture—God's spirit amid the darkness—is like an intimation, a nucleus, of the vast drama that is about to unfold."[4] The hovering Spirit of God sets the stage for and initiates the creation process. Genesis 1:2b is a pneumatological transition from cosmic chaos to God's creation. The hovering Spirit of God is the pneumatological threshold across which primordial chaos gives way to a fecund creation.[5]

The work of the Spirit of God in Genesis 1:2 establishes the fundamental nature of the Spirit's work throughout Scripture with regard to both creation and redemption. Moreover, the Spirit's work in creation suggests that the Spirit of God is a liminal and constituting agent—liminal, because through the activity of the Spirit, creation crosses over from darkness and chaos to light and ordered life. The Spirit's work is constitutive because the Spirit's work achieves God's design for the world. In this light, Karl Barth's pneumatology of creation is unsatisfactory. Barth maintains that the "'Spirit of God' who . . . hovers or broods over [the nothingness of Genesis 1:2a]—a divine power which is not that of the creative Word—cannot make good this lack but can only reveal it more sharply . . . 'the Spirit of *Elohim*' who is not known in his reality therefore hovers and broods over it impotently because wordlessly."[6] Even if we grant the necessity of the Spirit and the Word working in tandem to bring forth creation, we also need to recognize that if the Spirit is impotent without the Word, then so is the Word without the Spirit. In the narrative structure of creation, the Spirit hovering over the waters is the liminal stage between lifeless cosmic chaos and the days of creation that bring forth a creation bursting with life. Thus, the Spirit is the Spirit of creation because the Spirit is the initial divine agent of creation. The Spirit leads the primordial elements from chaos to creation.

Also important for pneumatology is the portrayal of creation as a redemptive act of God. The ancient Near Eastern myths of cosmic origins often portrayed the pre-creation state of things as churning waters welling up from an unfathomable abyss.[7] The creative process that begins with the Spirit of God hovering over the waters and proceeds through the six days of creation should be understood as a redemptive act of God and not purely as an act of "creation." This is because God delivers the primeval elements from their chaotic abyss and produces an earth that is harmonious and fruitful. Psalm 74 expresses the redemptive nature of the Hebrew theology of creation. The psalm highlights, "But you O God . . . bring salvation upon the earth. It was you who split open the sea by your power; you broke the head of the monster in the waters. . . . It was you who opened up springs and streams; you dried up the ever flowing rivers . . . you established the sun and moon. It was you who set all the boundaries of the earth" (Psa. 74:12–17). In Genesis 1, the Spirit of God is the primordial presence of God who initiates creation and frees the elements from primal pandemonium.[8] Creation, therefore, is the Spirit's first act of divine deliverance and redemption.

The Spirit and Redemption as Creation

Second, the Hebrew prophets drew a connection between the Spirit's work of creation and redemption.[9] Coming to shape in the exilic and post-exilic period, the Genesis 1 creation narrative likely served a religious and liturgical function for the people of Israel during their Babylonian captivity and repatriation.[10] Exile in Babylon was a national and religious crisis because the seeming invincible Babylonian military forces appeared to be supported by equally insuperable gods. The destruction of Jerusalem and the temple suggested to the people of Israel that Yahweh was impotent before the might of the Babylonian pantheon.[11] In contrast to the chaos of their circumstances, Genesis 1 portrays the God of Israel as the one who effortlessly brings forth creation and is its supreme master without need or even the presence of other gods.[12] Contrary to other ancient Near Eastern creation stories, Yahweh does not struggle with other gods in the beginning but is there alone as the one true God.[13] Isaiah shows the significance of creation theology for redemption when he promises, "[H]e who created the heavens and stretched them out, who spread out the earth and all that comes out of it . . . I, the Lord, have called you in righteousness; I will take hold of your hand . . . to free the captives from prison and release from the dungeon those who sit in darkness" (Isa. 42:5–7). The theological argument is that because Yahweh created the heavens and the earth and the people of Israel, Yahweh can redeem them from their exile.[14] Additionally, Isaiah 32:15 supports the connection of the Spirit of God with creative activity. In this text, the Spirit poured out from on high transforms the "desert" into a "fertile field" and also empowers the people to live in justice and righteousness. The Spirit's restoration of the people and the land are inseparable, which suggests the synthesis of the Spirit's creative and redemptive work.

Ezekiel's description of the Spirit's work in redeeming Israel from exile coheres with the liminal and constituting nature of the Spirit's work in creation. Ezekiel promises that Yahweh will put the Spirit of God in them and that the Spirit will restore the people of Israel to their homeland. Ezekiel uses the vivid imagery of the Spirit of God revivifying a valley of dry bones (Ezek. 36–37). Ezekiel's use of pneumatological images to describe Yahweh's fulfillment of the promise to restore the people of Israel to their homeland coheres with that of Genesis 1:2. The Spirit of God, who Ezekiel sees as the divine power that sets the people of Israel free from the despair of their captivity and returns them to Jerusalem as the faithful covenant people of God, is the same Spirit who set the primordial chaos free and ushers in the creative process that concludes with a planet teeming with life.[15] Just as the Spirit moved over the cosmic chaos of Genesis 1:2 and brings forth a lush creation, so the Spirit of God will breathe new life into the dead bones of exiled Israel in Ezekiel 37:1–14. The imagery of dry bones infused with new life by the Spirit of God also is reminiscent of Genesis 2:7 in which God breathes life into the lifeless dirt and through the breath of God, the dirt becomes a living human being.[16]

Thus, the creation narrative of Genesis 1 and the promises delivered by Isaiah and Ezekiel concerning the restoration of the people of Israel and revitalization of the land of Israel portray the Spirit as the presence of God that brings life and freedom from despair and disrepair. The purpose of the Genesis 1 creation narrative is not to supply the ancients and moderns with a scientific account of creation but rather to buttress faith in God's power to save those called to relationship with this God. In other words, the creation story supports soteriology.[17]

To summarize to this point, first, in both the creation of the world and the redemption of the people of Israel from exile and re-establishment in the land of Israel, the Spirit is the liminal agent who facilitates the transition from chaos to the realization of God's purposes—from cosmic chaos to creation and from exile to restoration. The Spirit inhabits the liminal space between chaos and exile and between creation and redemption. The Spirit is the divine person who enables creation and the people of Israel to cross the threshold from chaos and exile to creation and restoration. Second, continuity characterizes the work of the Spirit in creation and redemption. Creation itself is a form of redemption, and the Spirit's work of redemption parallels the creative work of the Spirit. Having established the continuity between the Spirit's work of creation and redemption, the next step in the argument is to show that this continuity informs the identity and work of the Spirit as Spirit of Christ and Spirit of Pentecost.

That is, the Spirit's work as Spirit of creation has the Spirit's work as Spirit of Christ and Pentecost as its *telos*.

The Spirit of Christ

The work of the Holy Spirit in Christ shares continuity with the Spirit's creative-redemptive work in the Old Testament. Specifically, the Holy Spirit plays a liminal and constituting role in the Incarnation of Jesus Christ. Furthermore, this work informs the nature of the Spirit's work as "the Spirit of Christ."[18] The traditional way of referring to the Holy Spirit as "the Spirit 'of' Christ" can give the impression that the Spirit's work is derived from and relative to Christ's. However, the "of" in Spirit of Christ has two meanings. "Of" can mean from, but it also carries the connotation of specifying "the source or starting point of action" and "indicating the creator of a work" (*Oxford English Dictionary*). For example, the description of the Spirit as the Spirit of creation means that the Spirit is the source and creator of creation. In Christology, both senses of "of" apply to the Spirit as the Spirit of Christ. Though the second sense of the Spirit of Christ is less familiar in the history of pneumatology and Trinitarian theology, it nonetheless expresses the fundamental nature of the Spirit's work in Christ and carries forward the nature of the Spirit's liminal and constituting work noted in the Old Testament creation-redemption themes. In order to detail the second and less familiar way of thinking about the Spirit of Christ, I first outline the traditional and more recognized one.

The most familiar usage is to refer to the Spirit as Spirit of Christ in the sense that the risen Christ pours out and sends the Holy Spirit on the Day of Pentecost and, thus, the Spirit is *of* Christ because the Spirit is *from* Christ. Acts 2:33 supports this imagery when it portrays the risen Christ receiving the "promise of the Father" (see Luke 11:13 and 24:49 and Acts 1:4) and giving the Spirit at Pentecost. This way of thinking about the Spirit as "the Spirit of Christ" also reflects the influence of the Gospel of John and Logos Christology. John portrays the Father sending the Son while the Father and the Son send the Holy Spirit. Read back into the immanent Trinity, traditional theology infers that the Holy Spirit originates or proceeds from the Father and the Son. These relations led to the familiar Western doctrine of the *filioque*, according to which the Son is begotten from the Father and the Holy Spirit proceeds from the Father *and* from the Son. The Orthodox tradition is similar except that it rejects the *filioque*, but in respect to processions establishing divine personal identity, it is in agreement with the West because the Holy Spirit is from the Father and, in some expressions, through the Son. Furthermore, the influence of the Gospel of John and the traditional tendency to derive the identities of the divine persons from the processions has meant that Trinitarian theology has relied on Christological data. The relations between the Father and the Son have provided the primary content for Trinitarian theology in general and the identity of the Spirit in particular.

The Spirit is also the Spirit of Christ in the second sense of "of." In this respect, the Spirit is the source of the Incarnation of Jesus Christ. Of course, the Spirit does not create the eternal Son of God, but the Spirit does facilitate the Incarnation of the Son. The Spirit of Christ, in this sense, means that the Spirit is the divine person who unites the humanity of Jesus Christ with the eternal Son of God (Luke 1:35 and Matt. 1:18–21). The technical term for this understanding of the Incarnation is Spirit Christology. The theological insight of Spirit Christology is that the Spirit plays a constitutional role in the Incarnation. The phenomenon that theology calls the Incarnation—the union of the humanity of Jesus with the eternal Son of God—was as much an event of the Holy Spirit as of the Son. The Son becomes incarnate, but the Spirit is the agent of the hypostatic union.[19]

The Spirit's work in the Incarnation as "the Spirit of Christ" shares continuity with the Spirit's creative-redemptive work in the Old Testament. First, the work of the Spirit in the creation-redemption episodes discussed in the Old Testament is paradigmatic for the Spirit's work in the Incarnation. Put more forcefully, the Spirit's work that begins in Genesis 1:2 with the redemption of creation from chaos, that is carried on further in the breathing of life into the dirt in Genesis 2:7, and revivifies the valley of dry bones in Ezekiel 37:1–14, finds its historical zenith in Christ. In other words, the union of creation with Creator attains its highest possible concrete manifestation in Jesus Christ. Although Christ is the definitive historical instance of the Spirit's work to bring creation into union with its Creator—i.e., he is the incarnation of the eternal Son of God—the preceding creative-redemptive work of the Spirit is in continuity with the work of the Spirit in Christ (i.e., as "the Spirit of Christ").

Second, the Spirit is the liminal and constituting agent of the Incarnation. The Spirit who precedes and initiates the redemption of the primordial chaos in the creation account of Genesis 1:2 is the same Spirit who precedes and instantiates the union of the humanity of Jesus and the Son in the Incarnation. Genesis 2:7 describes God breathing the breath of life into the dirt and thereby creating living, human persons. The creation story then portrays the purpose of the creative act. The text describes Adam and Eve living in sublime harmony with each other—i.e., the significance of their 'nakedness"—creation, and their God, who comes walking to them in the garden during the cool of the day. God's Spirit breathes life into the dirt so that human beings can live in loving relation with their creator and with each other.

In Matthew 1:20, the angel of the Lord assures Joseph, "[D]o not to be afraid to take Mary home as your wife, because what is conceived in her is from the Holy Spirit." In Luke 1:35, the angel Gabriel comforts Mary: "The Holy Spirit will come upon you, and the power of the Most High will overshadow you. So the holy one to be born will be called the Son of God." The Spirit's work is the threshold of the union of the eternal Son of God with the humanity of Jesus. The Holy Spirit facilitates the Incarnation of the Son of God to fulfill the Spirit's original animation of the dirt (i.e., the creation of the human beings in Gen. 2:7). Furthermore, Matthew and Luke present the Spirit as the liminal and constituting agent of the Incarnation. The Spirit is the liminal agent of the

Incarnation because just as the Spirit of God led the primordial elements across the threshold from chaos to creation—the dirt across the threshold to living creature—so the Spirit is the divine agent that precedes and facilitates the Incarnation. The Spirit is the constituting agent of the Incarnation because the Spirit is the primordial agent that brings the humanity of Jesus into union with the eternal Son of God.

The work of the Spirit in Jesus, moreover, is an abiding presence. The Spirit remains as an active agent in his life. At his baptism, the Spirit comes upon Jesus and thus inaugurates his messianic ministry (Matt. 3:3–17; Mark 1:9–11; Luke 3:21–22; and John 1:29–34). The descent of the Spirit at his baptism should not be understood as a new reception of the Spirit in the sense that the Spirit was not previously present with Jesus. Rather, the descent of the Spirit is a public manifestation of his identity as the Messiah. The event was public in two senses: first, for Jesus, it undoubtedly confirmed his sense of a unique relation to and mission from God; thus, as a public event, it helped Jesus to embrace his identity and calling. Second, it was a public announcement to all who witnessed the event and later would testify about him, especially John the Baptist (John 1:35–36). The Spirit also leads Jesus into the wilderness and empowers him to forswear Satan's temptations (Matt. 4:1–11; Mark 1:12–13; and Luke 4:1–14). Finally, the Spirit's work in Jesus Christ reaches its fullness when the Spirit raises Jesus from the dead (Rom. 8:11 and 1 Pet. 3:18).[20] The work of the Spirit in the life of Jesus continues to reflect continuity with the previous work of the Spirit. The Spirit's work is the threshold from Jesus' public life to public ministry, from untested capacity for faithfulness to the Father to renouncing Satan, and from death to resurrected life.

The Spirit of Pentecost

The outpouring of the Holy Spirit on the Day of Pentecost is an eschatological work of the Spirit. The work of the Spirit that is the foundation of the creation of the cosmos, breathes life into all living creatures, and brings forth the Incarnation of the Son of God attains its fullness in the outpouring of the Spirit of Pentecost. As an eschatological event, the outpouring of the Spirit of Pentecost is a critical threshold in the history of redemption. As such, it comprehends the liminal and constitutive work of the Spirit and the two senses of the Spirit as the Spirit of Christ—i.e., Christ *sends* the Spirit and the Spirit is the divine person who *establishes* the community of believers, the body of Christ. The following discussion illustrates that the Spirit of Pentecost fulfills the liminal and constitutive nature of the Spirit's creative-redemptive work.

The Liminal work of the Spirit of Pentecost

The outpouring of the Spirit on the day of Pentecost is a liminal and eschatological work of the Spirit.[21] The outpouring of the Spirit as the Spirit of Christ draws the disciples into union with the risen Christ. However, Pentecost is not primarily about the disciples' charismatic experience in the Upper Room but a climactic point in redemptive history; thus, Pentecost is an eschatological event. Calling Pentecost an eschatological event does not mean that salvation history comes to an abrupt end in Acts 2.[22] It means that at Pentecost, salvation history crosses a critical threshold no less than at the moment of the Incarnation, the cross, and the resurrection of Jesus Christ. The work of the Spirit in creation and in the incarnate Christ achieves its fullest historical expression as the Spirit of Pentecost. The redemptive event that occurs through the particular and historical mediation of the person of Christ becomes universally available through the Spirit of Pentecost as the Spirit of Christ. The Spirit of Pentecost, therefore, fulfills the work of redemption even though the historical actualization of that redemption remains penultimate until the everlasting kingdom.[23]

The eschatological nature of Pentecost is similar to that of the crucifixion. Jesus' cry, "it is finished," is eschatological because it expresses the fact that on the cross, he fulfilled humanity's devotion to the Father even though that devotion is penultimate in historical terms because the everlasting kingdom and the concrete realization of Jesus' redemption in the lives of individual believers remain in the future. Graham Ward uses the term, "eschatological remainder," to describe the eschatological nature of Christian discipleship. The eschatological remainder means that the Christian participates in the future kingdom of God because that kingdom is operative in the present.[24] Although Ward primarily draws on Christology to develop the details of the eschatological remainder, the notion has utility for understanding the eschatological nature of the Spirit of Pentecost. The outpouring of the Spirit of Pentecost is eschatological because, on the one hand, it culminates the previous creative-redemptive work of the Spirit, but, on the other hand, it has not ended because the Spirit is still being poured out on all people—hence, the eschatological, and I suggest, the *pneumatological* remainder. Thus, although the Day of Pentecost fulfilled certain eschatological expectations, it also remains a fulfillment with a surplus of fulfillment.

The Constitutional Work of the Spirit of Pentecost

The Spirit of Pentecost is also a constitutional agent because the Spirit establishes or creates the community of believers both on individual and corporate levels. In respect to the individual, the Spirit "creates" and actualizes redemption in the believer (John 3:1–8 and 7:37–39). Spirit baptism is a central biblical metaphor for describing the experience of participation in the Spirit of Pentecost that enables the human person to cross the threshold from being dead in sin to experiencing new life in Christ. Spirit baptism can be understood as a comprehensive metaphor for participating in the Spirit of Pentecost.

The biblical justification for seeing Spirit baptism as a comprehensive metaphor is its canonical position. Scripture frames Jesus' redemption in terms of the metaphor of Spirit baptism: John the Baptist promises, "[H]e will baptize in the Holy Spirit" (Matt. 3:11; Mark 1:8; Luke 3:16; and John 1:33). Jesus promises the fulfillment of that promise on the Day of Pentecost: "'do not leave Jerusalem, but wait for the gift my Father promised. . . . For John baptized with water, but in a few days you will be baptized with the Holy Spirit'" (Acts 1:4–5). On the Day of Pentecost, the Spirit also creates the body of Christ. As the Spirit was the divine presence that preceded and brought the humanity of Jesus into union with the divine Son, so the Spirit of Pentecost goes before and instantiates what Scripture refers to as the body of Christ. The body of Christ, in the ecclesiological sense, is not the physical human body of Jesus of Nazareth, but the extended "body" of all those united to the risen Christ by the Spirit of Pentecost.

The Consummative Work of the Spirit of Pentecost

The Spirit of Pentecost consummates the Spirit's creative-redemptive work in the drama of biblical redemption. The Spirit of Pentecost is consummative because it stands in continuity with and brings to full expression the liminal and constitutional nature of the Spirit's creative-redemptive work in two ways. First, the Spirit's work as Spirit of Pentecost is in continuity with the preceding work of the Spirit in creation-redemption, and this is the case not only in respect to the larger history of redemption but also in the individual human person. In the macro-plot of biblical redemption, the Spirit is the divine agent who empowers and fosters the transition from one existential plane to another: a transition from darkness to light, from a cosmic morass to a garden bursting with life, and—as the Spirit of Pentecost—the formation of the Church of Jesus Christ. The Spirit's work in the individual reflects the same continuity. The eschatological goal—both cosmic and individual—of Genesis 1:2 and 2:7 is Acts 2:1–4, which ultimately leads to the new heaven and new earth (Rev. 21:1). The Spirit who initiates creation and breathes life into all human persons is the Spirit who liberates creation from its bondage to decay (Rom. 8:21) and brings new life to all those drawn into fellowship with the Trinitarian God. Thus, the Spirit of Pentecost is the eschatological culmination of the Spirit's creative-redemptive work.

Second, a similarity marks the various ways in which the Spirit is the pneumatological threshold and liminal point for the emergence of creation-redemption: the emergence of life and of the living creatures in Genesis 1 and 2, the promise of the restoration of Israel in Isaiah and Ezekiel, the Incarnation of the Son of God, and the formation of the Church of Jesus Christ through the union of all those who participate in the Spirit of Pentecost. In each of these creative-redemptive events, the movement of the Spirit precedes and then empowers the transition of creation into a pneumatological horizon of redemption. In the ultimate liminal and constitutional work of the Spirit, the Spirit will redeem creation by liberating it from its bondage to decay (Rom. 8) and by raising to new life all those drawn into fellowship with Christ and the Father in the everlasting kingdom (Rom. 8:11). Thus, the Spirit of Pentecost fully manifests the personal work of the Holy Spirit in the biblical drama of creation-redemption. The eschatological kingdom is but the final realization of these redemptive works.

The Mission of the Spirit of Pentecost

The mission of the Spirit is the Spirit's work within creation to bring creation to its proper way of participating in redemption.[25] When we think of mission and evangelism, we may think in terms of the scope of the Spirit's redemptive work and conceptualize the scope of the Spirit's mission in compartmental terms: the Spirit is at work here in Christian religious and mission contexts but not there in non-Christian religious and mission contexts. However, the mission of the Spirit of Pentecost is universal and perennial. This section presents the case for the universal work of the Spirit of Pentecost, and that the mission of the Spirit of Pentecost brings to full expression the creative-redemptive work of the Spirit charted in the Old Testament and Incarnation.

On the Day of Pentecost, Peter identifies the outpouring of the Holy Spirit as the inauguration of the promise of Joel 2:28: "I will pour out my Spirit on all people." The key qualifier for the scope of the Spirit's mission is the "all" of the promise, "I will pour out my Spirit on all people" (Joel 2:28 and Acts 2:17). "All" means all. The Spirit of Pentecost has been poured out on all people.[26] Perhaps to reinforce the inclusive nature of the promise, Luke concludes Peter's Pentecost quote of Joel 2:32 with "everyone who calls on the name of the Lord will be saved," and he drops the ending of the verse that spotlights "for on Mount Zion and in Jerusalem there be deliverance."

The outpouring of the Spirit on all people draws attention to the fact that people within a faith community often intuitively believe that people outside their faith community are either bereft of the presence of God or, at the very least, do not have the same favors and benefits of God as they possess—e.g., God's redemptive work and forgiveness. The inclusive delineation of "all" in Joel 2:28–32 and quoted by Peter in Acts 2 presupposes this tendency to elevate one's own faith community to privileged status before God. That is why the Joel passage instructs the reader that "all" really means all. Whether Joel specifically envisioned an outpouring of the Spirit that transcended Israel or meant more minimally that all the people of Israel would receive the Spirit is an important issue. The historical context suggests that he had the people of Israel, specifically the people of Jerusalem, most directly in mind. However, Douglas Stuart points out that the outpouring of the Spirit in Joel is a promise "for a covenant people" and not only the people of Jerusalem or Israel.[27]

Reinforcing its inclusive nature, the outpouring of the Spirit transcends typical patterns of social segregation—e.g., gender, age, and class. The book of Acts narrates not only the historical instances of the outpouring of the Spirit on all people but also the early-Christians' difficulty in embracing that truth. Indeed, although Peter declared the fulfillment of Joel's promise of an outpouring of the Spirit, he probably thought of the Jews as its primary recipients and did not grasp its comprehensiveness.[28] Even though his address, "fellow Jews and all of you who are in Jerusalem," could be read in an inclusive way, his later difficulties with inclusion suggest otherwise. When the Samaritans receive the Gospel, the suspicious Jerusalem church dispatches Peter and John to confirm and ratify it (Acts 8:4–17). Later, when the Gentile household of Cornelius receives the Holy Spirit, it requires a council of the church to verify its veracity (Acts 10–11 and 15:1–35). However, I also want to press the point further. The outpouring of the Spirit is not only available to all—e.g., Jew and Gentile—but has been received by all. Of course, that immediately raises the issue of universalism in respect to salvation. I am sympathetic with the desire to expand redemption to all people—e.g., the Christian and Pentecostal universalism of pastor Carlton Pearson—but I do not believe that the universal outpouring of the Spirit and access to grace means that all people will yield their lives to and thus participate in God's redemptive work. Later, I make a distinction between the universal outpouring of the Spirit and the particular participation in the Spirit of Pentecost. I now want to consider this question: "What is this Spirit doing who has been poured out on all people?"

The preceding question brings the discussion to the mission of the Spirit of Pentecost. The mission of the Holy Spirit is for all people to participate in the Spirit as the Spirit of Pentecost. The work of the Spirit in Christ—the Spirit of Christ—illuminates the nature of the universal work of the Spirit of Pentecost. As the Spirit established the union of Jesus' humanity with the eternal Son of God, so the Spirit unites the believer with Christ and draws them into the ambit of the Trinitarian fellowship. The work of the Spirit that finds its fullest expression in the Incarnation of the Son of God is a universal work that spans all of history and touches every human person. The Spirit of Pentecost is present with all persons, drawing them toward union with the God revealed in Jesus Christ. The outpouring of the Spirit of Pentecost is but the full revelation of the Spirit, who breathes life into all human beings—thus, Genesis 2:7 and Acts 2 are coordinate events.

Although all people have *received* the Spirit of Pentecost, not all people have *yielded* and *participated* in the Spirit of Pentecost. When people yield to the Spirit's work, participating in the Spirit of Pentecost, they cross a Pentecostal and pneumatological threshold that draws them into union with the Trinitarian God, which makes them children of God (John 1:12). The Spirit's mission as Spirit of Pentecost is, therefore, consistent with the liminal and constitutional creation-redemptive work of the Spirit charted in the Old Testament and the Incarnation. Because the Spirit has been poured out on all people, the threshold of participation in the Spirit of Pentecost is a universal one and is not limited by the formal boundaries of the church and Christian ministry. Furthermore, because the Spirit enables the person to cross over into the horizon of the Spirit of Pentecost and the fellowship of the Trinitarian God, the potential for that participation also is not sequestered to the traditional lines of demarcation between the church and the non-church world.

The Spirit of Pentecost and a
Pentecostal Theology of Missions and Religions

The previous segments of this essay set forth the trajectory of the creative-redemptive work of the Holy Spirit in the drama of biblical redemption. This section outlines some of the implications of the mission of the Spirit of Pentecost for a Pentecostal theology of religions and mission. Specifically, what does the universal mission and work of the Spirit of Pentecost mean for a Pentecostal theology of mission and religions?

The Work of the Spirit of Pentecost Transcends Religious Boundaries

The Spirit of Pentecost is at work in every person, regardless of his or her posture toward a particular religion. The Spirit of Pentecost is present with and active in the atheist, the Muslim, the Christian, and all human beings. Sure, not everyone responds and yields to the work of the Spirit. But where sin abounds, grace does much more (Rom. 5:20), which in this context, implies that resistance to the Spirit does not lead to the abdication of the Spirit. The universal work of the Spirit of Pentecost opens the possibility for universal access to grace and redemption.[29] It does not necessarily imply universalism—the actualization of universal salvation—but it does mean that the opportunity to participate in grace and redemption is universal. A consequence of the universal scope of the Spirit's work is that the mission of the Spirit of Pentecost always precedes Christian mission. We need to remember that when we do missions work, we do not bring the Spirit of Pentecost to a place where the Spirit otherwise was not present.

I recognize that this point is contrary to what Kirsteen Kim describes as the traditional tendency to locate and largely limit the Spirit's work to the institutional and sacramental functions of the church and/or individual spirituality—e.g., Spirit reveals truth and sanctifies the inner dimensions of the person.[30] It also stands in tension with the traditional role of the Holy Spirit and the experience of Spirit baptism within Pentecostalism. Pentecostals normally see the Spirit empowering Pentecostal missions, rather than enabling people to participate in salvation outside the scope of Christian mission initiatives.[31] Notwithstanding these traditional tendencies, the Spirit of Pentecost, *working as* the Spirit of Pentecost in the lives of people, always precedes the Christian mission task and is unbounded by explicit Christian mission activities.

The Work of the Spirit of Pentecost in Religions

The universal work of the Spirit of Pentecost in all people opens up some possibilities for a Pentecostal theology of religions. The first possibility is that some people have responded and thereby received grace and redemption. This prospect suggests an inclusive soteriology.[32] Inclusivism can affirm that people are saved who respond to the work of the Spirit as Spirit of Pentecost and can do so in a way that is authentic to the Spirit of Pentecost—though not necessarily "authentic" to "our" way of responding. Just as Abraham expressed faith in God in a way that was sensible to him and authentic to the work of the Spirit in his life, so people today in non-Christian religions can do so too. Essential for a theology of religions are two interrelated notions: that if the Spirit of Pentecost is at work in all people then people can respond to the Spirit's work; and that some of the concrete ways people respond to the Spirit of Pentecost can be manifestations of grace.

The first possibility regarding individual responses to the Spirit implies the second, namely, that some non-Christian religious thought and activity is a product of the Spirit of Pentecost. This point suggests a positive theology of religions. Traditionally though, Pentecostals have held a negative theology of religions.[33] Even if they were open to the idea that those who had never heard the Gospel might receive grace and be judged on the light available to them— agnostic inclusivism—Pentecostals tend to reject the religions as avenues and expressions of grace.[34] One reason for defaulting to a negative theology of religion is that Pentecostals, following the logic of evangelical exclusivism, assume that inclusivism conflicts with their commitment to missions.[35] However, as Amos Yong insists, pragmatism and consequentialism should not be the exclusive drivers of Pentecostal theology.[36] Moreover, as indicated above, the universal work of the Spirit of Pentecost lays a foundation for a positive theology of religion. Although not traditional within the Pentecostal movement, Pentecostal theology should follow its pneumatological instincts and not remain tethered to its inherited evangelical viewpoint. A positive theology of religion means that the religions in certain ways may be 1) legitimate ways people respond to the Spirit of Pentecost and 2) sacramental means for the work and experience of the Spirit. These two points raise a controversial question: Is there a biblical basis for seeing non-Christian religions as possible conduits, points of contact, and expressions of the Spirit and means of experiencing the Spirit? For two reasons, I suggest the answer to that question is "yes."[37]

First, the question has an erroneous assumption built into it. It assumes that the "Christian" religion, or at least, biblical revelation, is reified and a-cultural, but this is not the case. For example, in Acts, the Holy Spirit is manifest in terms of wind and "tongues of fire." However, "wind" and "fire" have no intrinsic ontological connection to the Holy Spirit; the Spirit is not inherently "wind" and "fire." The visible manifestation of the Spirit takes the form of wind and fire probably because it has clear precedent in the religious tradition of Israel—e.g., creation narratives, flood, exodus, burning bush, pillar of fire, and fire on the altar in the tabernacle—which, in turn, resonated with religious ideas common in the ancient Near East. The association of divine presence with wind and fire was common in the Near Eastern religions.[38] For instance, as Greeks attributed the storm (wind) that floundered the Persian fleet at Chalkis (480 BCE) to divine activity, so the Hebrews escaped annihilation from Pharaoh's army by a wind from God that divides the sea. The point is not that the Old Testament borrows or co-opts popular religious thought in a cut-and-paste manner with merely a change in the names of the deities and circumstances, but rather that it describes the revelation and work of God in ways that were sensible to people living in the ancient Near East. They lived in a world that associated divine activity and presence with the wind and the storm. Thus, the Old Testament association of God and God's Spirit with wind and fire is the provision of redemption and revelation through religious forms that were common in the ancient Near East, including the Hebrew religious tradition.

In respect to a Pentecostal theology of mission, if we begin with the assumption that the Gospel that we preach in missions is the pure and culturally transcendent Gospel, we have already in a sense distorted biblical revelation. The Bible and the epoch of divine deliverance contained in it are not a-cultural, "biblical" categories. The categories through which the God of the Bible spoke and acted were contextual revelations and redemptive activities. Of course, the biblical traditions transform and, at times, even demythologize the ancient Near Eastern religious categories; however, the point is that they use them too—e.g., the creation narratives draw on a plethora of ancient Near Eastern cosmic myths, but also demythologize those myths.

Second, the assumption of an a-cultural Gospel also carries with it an "us" to "them" mission's posture: "we" bring the truth of the Gospel to "them, who are otherwise bereft of saving knowledge and experience of God. The "us" to "them" stance is unsustainable for at least two reasons. Initially, it assumes that our—or, the Western view of the Gospel—is a-cultural, timeless, and non-contextualized; thus, "our" version of the Gospel is *the* form of the Gospel for all people. The "us" to "them" posture also presupposes that all authentic articulations and expressions of the Gospel will mirror ours. This attitude is perhaps the Pentecostal religious parallel of other Western and modernist "universalisms."

For example, I remember a colleague involved with missions in Africa who asked me if I had any standard evangelical theology texts that I could donate for the library of the Bible institute he worked with in Africa. I asked him why he did not use theologies produced by African theologians. His response was that evangelical formulations were basically right and better than the indigenous theologies produced by African Pentecostals. He followed up with the judgment that many African theologies are too influenced by their African cultural and religious assumptions. In other words, they are syncretistic.[39] Yet, not without irony, the text my colleague planned to use in Africa was a North American evangelical text that clearly carried on the "rational" approach of Charles Hodge's doctrine and the Princeton theology. In turn, this theology reflects the scientific method (Baconian) and Scottish Common Sense philosophies of the early modern period. In the postmodern context, a compelling objection would be that, not only are theological approaches indigenous to the Enlightenment not helpful in non-Western settings, they are no longer even appropriate to the postmodern Western context. During the ascendancy and height of modernism, such an approach to evangelical theology may have made sense because it addressed theological issues in the culture's intellectual idiom. Nevertheless, post-conservative Evangelicals, for example, maintain that we need to replace the modernist styles of theology with ones more appropriate to our current culture's postmodern climate.[40] Moreover, to think that traditional Pentecostal and evangelical theologies are somehow not as imbued with cultural assumptions, philosophical commitments, and worldviews indigenous to the West perhaps misses the forest for the trees.

Additionally, as the biblical narrative of the Spirit illustrates, the revelation and manifestation of the Holy Spirit for salvation happens in terms of indigenous cultural and religious expectations. The manifestation of the Spirit on the Day of Pentecost, being in terms of wind and fire, was not timeless and "biblical." Instead, it was situated in a cultural and religious context which made them sensible. It is my guess that most of us have not experienced the Spirit in terms of "fire" and "wind," but we have nonetheless had authentic experiences of the Spirit. The point is that the Spirit of God encounters and speaks to human beings in terms that are sensible to them. The Spirit's redemptive work bears continuity, but it can occur in diverse religious and cultural contexts.

Two biblical examples illustrate that access to grace is not contingent upon holding certain religious beliefs and observing specific religious rites. Amos 9:7 rhetorically declares, "are not you Israelites the same to me as the Cushites? . . . Did I not bring Israel up from Egypt, the Philistines from Capthor, and the Arameans from Kir?" These are staggering statements. Israel is God's special covenant people, and the deliverance from Egypt is the key historical event in which God establishes Israel as a nation and provides them with the covenant. However, Amos suggests that exodus-type acts of deliverance are not exclusive to the people of Israel, nor is Israel an exclusive recipient of God's compassionate affection: "are not you Israelites the same to me as the Cushites?" To think that the Cushites, Philistines, and the Arameans all adopted the religious thought and practices of Israel as either the precondition or consequence of God's redemptive work among them strains the pale of credulity.

The Ninevite's repentance at hearing the warning of Jonah is another example of people experiencing God's redemptive activity or at least the withholding of judgment without adopting Israel's approved set of religious beliefs and activities. The Ninevites expressed their repentance by "declaring a fast," covering themselves with sackcloth, and "giving up their evil ways and violence" (Jonah 3:5–8). Their religious expressions were not unique to Israel but common to the ancient Near East. The text gives no indication that they gave proper, covenant sanctioned sacrifices to Yahweh, abandoned polytheism, or destroyed their idols. In fact, Douglas Stuart notes that the text does not even make it clear that they directed their repentance to Yahweh or to one of the deities in the Assyrian pantheon.[41] Although Yahweh's requirement for the people of Israel was far more specific, perhaps the specificity related to the fact that they had received fuller revelation rather than to delineating exclusive channels of grace. The repentance of the Ninevites shows that God is not miserly with grace, nor does God narrowly restrict authentic religious response among people in order to receive that grace.

The Amos and Jonah texts suggest that we can expect God to work within and through religious and cultural expectations of people whom we seek to evangelize, and this is true whether we are engaged in domestic or foreign missions. We should expect the Spirit to speak and act in ways that people will understand. We also should expect the Spirit to contradict and transform those elements of peoples' religious expectation that are inconsistent with the revelation and activity of the Spirit which we find in the biblical traditions. Recognizing the contextual nature of divine activity and the Spirit's manifestation in the Bible does not relativize the Spirit; instead, it calls into question a facile rejection of culture and non-Christian religions as graceless and inappropriate for divine activity and expression. Furthermore, recognizing the cultural-contextual nature of biblical revelation opens up the space to consider the religions of the world as possible ways the work of the Spirit of Pentecost achieves concrete manifestation in the lives of people.

Progressive and Partial Participation in the Spirit of Pentecost

The canonical narrative of the Spirit of Pentecost begins with creation, moves to Incarnation, and then to thematic climax on the Day of Pentecost. Just as the experience of the Spirit of Pentecost is incremental and progressive in the biblical accounts, so the experience of the Spirit by people, regardless of their religious tradition, can be incremental and progressive. Tony Richie intimates that the early Pentecostal leader J. H. King's progressive doctrine of salvation could be applied to theology of religions when he states, "King does not directly relate his pneumatology and soteriology at this point to theology of religions, but it seems a small step to apply his dynamic and progressive Pentecostal pneumatology and soteriology beyond the pale of conventional Christianity."[42] I want to go ahead and make that step. Consider that Abraham's experience of God as a flaming pot bears little or no correspondence to the religious experience of most North American Pentecostals, but that in no way impugns its legitimacy. So, perhaps people in other religious traditions can concretely experience God in a way that is 1) sensible to their cultural and religious context and 2) authentic to the Spirit of Pentecost.[43]

The test of authentic manifestation and experience of the Spirit is whether the experience and the practice it sponsors are consistent with the nature of the Spirit as revealed in Scripture—e.g., does it lead people to act justly, act with mercy, etc (cf. Matt. 25:31–46). This applies not only to non-Christian religions but also to Christianity and Christians. Pentecostals typically do not believe that religion saves anyone. Christianity, per se, does not save a person.[44] People are saved when they receive the Spirit as the Spirit of Pentecost, the Spirit of Christ. Moreover, just as other religions may detract and obscure the manifestation of the Spirit of Pentecost, so too may certain forms of Christian thought and practice prevent a full manifestation of the Spirit of Pentecost as demonstrated by the story of the Jerusalem council in Acts 15, Paul's struggle against the "Judaizers" (Gal. 5:1–12), and John's critique of gnostic permutations of the Gospel (2 John 7). Furthermore, the Christian doctrine of sanctification assumes an incremental experience of the Spirit of Pentecost—hence, the on-going need to "be filled with the Spirit" (Eph. 5:18).

Religion is both the work of the Spirit of Pentecost and the human attempt to bring the Spirit of Pentecost to an authentic expression and, as such, religion is a "mixed bag"—again, this is true for Christianity too.[45] Religion is a work of the Spirit because the Spirit is ever seeking to initiate people into and develop in them a fuller experience of the Spirit of Pentecost. Religion is also the effort—never perfect and sometimes defunct—of human beings to respond in authentic ways to the Spirit of Pentecost. A caveat is in order. Discerning the Spirit of Pentecost is important. I think we need to recognize that some religious traditions and practices simply are not and perhaps cannot be authentic manifestations of and responses to the Spirit of Pentecost. Human sin and evil is real, and sometimes in human systems, it obviates the redemptive work of the Spirit. However, in most cases, just as in Christianity, human religious thought and practices are a mixture of authentic and aberrant responses to the Spirit.

Conclusion

The work of the Spirit of God begins with creation and reaches its thematic-canonical culmination as the Spirit of Pentecost. Although often understood as distinct works, the Spirit's work within creation and redemption is unified. The nature of the Spirit's creative and redemptive work is liminal and constitutional. In creation, Incarnation, and redemption, the Spirit enables creation to achieve its divine purposes, which is to participate in the fellowship of the Trinitarian God. The scope of the creative-redemptive work of the Spirit of Pentecost is also universal. The Spirit ever seeks to initiate people into and develop in them a fuller experience of the Spirit of Pentecost. The universal outpouring of the Spirit of Pentecost provides a theological basis to develop a Pentecostal theology of religions and mission as participation in the Spirit of Pentecost. Specifically, it recommends first that religion can be both the work of the Spirit of Pentecost and the human attempt to bring the Spirit of Pentecost to authentic and concrete expression. Second, it suggests that Christian mission is a way that Christians participate in the mission of the Spirit of Pentecost. The mission of the Spirit is to bring all people to participate in the outpouring of the Spirit as the Spirit of Pentecost. When Christians engage in missions, they join with the mission of the Spirit to help a person or group of people to begin their participation in and/or progressively experience the Spirit of Pentecost.

Notes

1. Amos Yong indicates that Pentecostals tend to contrast their *faith* with other *religions* along the following lines: Pentecostal faith is a divinely given means of salvation that provides for genuine relationship with God whereas other religions are human rituals contrived to attain salvation at best and demonic distractions to authentic

faith at worst. See Yong, "From Azusa Street to the Bo Tree and Back: Strange Babblings and Interreligious Interpretations in the Pentecostal Encounter with Buddhism," in Veli-Matti Kärkkäinen, ed., *The Spirit in the World: Emerging Pentecostal Theologies in Global Contexts* (Grand Rapids: William B. Eerdmans Publishing Company, 2009), 215–16. However, Tony Richie shows in respect to the early Pentecostal leader, J. H. King, that Pentecostals have resources for a more optimistic theology of religions within their tradition. See Tony Richie, Richie, "Azusa-Era Optimism: Bishop J. H. King's Pentecostal Theology of Religions as a Possible Paradigm for Today," in Veli-Matti Kärkkäinen, ed., *The Spirit in the World: Emerging Pentecostal Theologies in Global Contexts* (Grand Rapids: William B. Eerdmans Publishing Company, 2009), 240–41.

2. Creation and redemption are distinct in the sense that God redeems creation, but they are not distinct as to their economic program and end. The economic order is one: the redemption of creation. Thus, in Scripture, creation and redemption are not two separate orders, spheres, or modalities of divine activity. Rather, they are one program in that God's acts of redemption *redeem* creation. The unity of creation and redemption does not deny a conceptual distinction between creation and redemption, but it does set aside a dichotomy, which implies that creation and redemption are completely separate economic orders. For example, at the moment that God creates a new human life, God does so for no other purpose than to nurture in that person loving patterns of life and relationship with creation, other human persons, and the triune Godhead. Moreover, whatever that person does in and through his/her life, more or less, either contributes to or detracts from the actualization of God's creative purpose for his/her life. Thus, conceptually, a distinction can be drawn between God's act of creating a human person and the purpose for that creation, but the distinction is more logical and abstract than illuminative of separate divine programs. From Studebaker, "The Spirit in Creation: A Unified Theory of Grace and Creation Care," *Zygon: Journal of Religion and Science* 43:4 (2008): 947. Roger Haight proposes a similar relation between nature and grace in "Holy Spirit and the Religions," in David H. Jensen, ed., *The Lord Giver of Life: Perspectives on Constructive Pneumatology* (Louisville: Westminster John Knox, 2008), 65–68.

3. Wilf Hildebrandt, *An Old Testament Theology of the Spirit of God* (Peabody: Hendrickson, 1995), 32–35. Tuvia Freedman and John H. Sailhamer draw the same exegetical conclusion and recommend the translation of *ruach elohim* as "Spirit of God" rather than as a "mighty wind." Sailhamer also sees a thematic link between the image of God's Spirit hovering over and superintending the creation process at the beginning of the Pentateuch in Genesis 1:2 with the presence of Yahweh hovering over the people of Israel at its close in Deuteronomy 32:11. He also sees narrative symmetry between the Spirit as the source of divine power in creation and the source of Bezalel's ability to construct the tabernacle in Exodus 31:5: "in both accounts the work of God . . . is to be accomplished by the 'Spirit of God.'" See Tuvia Freedman [trans. Aviva Wolfers-Barazani], "רוח אלהים—and a Wind from God, Genesis 1:2," *Jewish Bible Quarterly* 24 (1996): 13, and Sailhamer, *The Pentateuch as Narrative: A Biblical-Theological Commentary* (Grand Rapids: Zondervan, 1992), 32 and 87.

4. Thomas L. Brodie, *Genesis as Dialogue: A Literary, Historical, and Theological Commentary* (New York: Oxford University Press, 2001), 133.

5. For an interpretation of Genesis 1:2 as the Spirit's superintending Big-bang cosmology, planetary formation, and biological evolution, see Paul Elbert, "Genesis 1 and the Spirit: A Narrative-Rhetorical Ancient Near Eastern Reading in Light of Modern Science," *Journal of Pentecostal Theology* 15:1 (2006): 23–72. Amos Yong interprets

Genesis 1 in terms of a canonical-pneumatological approach and brings the Spirit's role in the creation narrative into dialogue with Philip Clayton's theory of emergence; see Yong, "*Ruach*, the Primordial Chaos, and the Breath of Life: Emergence Theory and the Creation Narratives in Pneumatological Perspective," Michael Welker, ed., in *The Work of the Spirit: Pneumatology and Pentecostalism* (Grand Rapids: William B. Eerdmans Publishing Company, 2006), 183–204.

6. Karl Barth, *Church Dogmatics*, vol. 3, *The Doctrine of Creation*, ed. G. W. Bromiley and T. F. Torrance (Edinburgh: T & T Clark, 1958), III/1.2 (p. 108). Biblical scholars are just as prone to prefer Word/Christological categories over the complementary pneumatological ones in the text; see for example, Bruce Waltke, who describes the Genesis one creation account in terms of "Creation by Word"; Waltke, *Genesis: A Commentary* (Grand Rapids: Zondervan, 2001), 69.

7. Henry J. Flanders, Robert W. Crapps, and David A. Smith, *People of the Covenant: An Introduction to the Hebrew Bible*, 4th ed. (New York: Oxford University Press, 1996), 107–10 and David Toshio Tsumura, *The Earth and the Waters in Genesis 1 and 2: A Linguistic Investigation*, Journal for the Study of the Old Testament Supplement Series, 83 (Sheffield: Sheffield Academic Press, 1989).

8. James E. Huchingson refers to the primal elements as the "pandemonium tremendum" and employs contemporary communication and systems theory to understand divine agency in the process of creation; Huchingson, *Pandemonium Tremendum: Chaos and Mystery in the Life of God* (Cleveland, Oh.: Pilgrim, 2001).

9. Bernhard W. Anderson remarks that "Yahweh's power as Creator is the basis of the proclamation that he is Redeemer"; *Understanding the Old Testament*, 3rd ed. (Englewood Cliffs: Prentice-Hall, 1975), 451. Elke Toenges similarly points out that Scripture has an inner coherence between creation and redemption. The final vision of salvation in Revelation 21 indicates that "the eschatological theology of creation . . . is intended to demonstrate the inner connection between creation and salvation, redemption as perfection of the creation"; "'See, I am making all Things New': New Creation in the Book of Revelation," in Henning Graf Reventlow and Yair Hoffman, eds., *Creation in Jewish and Christian Tradition*, Journal for the Study of the Old Testament Supplement Series 319 (London: Sheffield Academic Press, 2002), 139.

10. Walter Brueggemann, *Theology of the Old Testament: Testimony, Dispute, Advocacy* (Minneapolis: Fortress, 1997), 153–54, and Winfried Thiel, "God as the Creator and Lord of Nature in the Deuteronomistic Literature," in Henning Graf Reventlow and Yair Hoffman, eds., *Creation in Jewish and Christian Tradition*, Journal for the Study of the Old Testament Supplement Series 319 (New York: Sheffield Academic Press, 2002), 54–55.

11. Brueggemann, *Theology of the Old Testament*, 149–51.

12. John Goldingay, *Old Testament* Theology, vol. 1, *Israel's Gospel* (Downers Grove: InterVarsity Press, 2003), 44.

13. Interestingly, Job 24:12–13 incorporates pneumatological imagery and elements of ancient Near Eastern cosmological beginnings when it describes creation in the following terms: "[God] marks out the horizon on the face of the waters for a boundary between lights and darkness. . . . By his power he churned up the sea; by his wisdom he cut Rahab to pieces. By his breath the skies became fair; his hand pierced the gliding serpent." The use of *ruach*/breath here correlates with the *ruach's* activity at creation and the receding waters of the flood—*ruach* brings order to chaos.

14. The development of biblical pneumatology in the context of exile has a possible point of correspondence with the experience of many early Pentecostals in North America and of many around the world today. The early Pentecostals and many

contemporary ones are "exiled" people; they do not operate in the centers of cultural and ecclesiastical power but on the political, social, economic, and religious margins.

15. Bruce Vawter and Leslie J. Hoppe, *A New Heart: A Commentary on the Book of Ezekiel*, International Theological Commentary (Grand Rapids: William B. Eerdmans Publishing Company, 1991), 166–67.

16. R. Jerome Boone, "The Role of the Holy Spirit in the Construction of the Second Temple," in Terry L. Cross and Emerson B. Powery, eds., *The Spirit and the Mind: Essays in Informed Pentecostalism* (Lanham: University Press of America, 2000), 52–53, and Joyce, *Ezekiel*, 209.

17. Gerhard von Rad, *Genesis: A Commentary* (Philadelphia: Westminster, 1972), 45–46.

18. The case for a united understanding of the Spirit's work in creation, Incarnation, and redemption endeavors to resolve the commonplace "disconnection between the Spirit and Christ and/or the Spirit and the Creator" in pneumatological theologies of religions is made by Veli-Matti Kärkkäinen; see his "'How to Speak of the Spirit among Religions': Trinitarian Prolegomena for a Pneumatological Theology of Religions," in Michael Welker, ed., *The Work of the Spirit: Pneumatology and* Pentecostalism (Grand Rapids: William B. Eerdmans Publishing Company, 2006), 48.

19. See Steven M. Studebaker, "Integrating Pneumatology and Christology: A Trinitarian Modification of Clark H. Pinnock's Spirit Christology," *PNEUMA: The Journal of the Society for Pentecostal Studies* 28 (2006): 5–20.

20. The interpretation of 1 Peter 3:18, "He was put to death in the body but made alive by the Spirit," is difficult. The basic point of the text is the affirmation of the early Christian faith that Christ was crucified and raised from the dead. More specifically, the statement can mean that Christ died on the cross ("put to death in the body") and was resurrected by God's Spirit and subsequently through the same Spirit "preached to the spirits in prison who disobeyed long ago when God waited patiently in the days of Noah while the Ark was being built" (1 Pet. 3:19–20). Also, this way of reading 1 Peter 3:18 is consistent with Romans 8:11, which declares that "the Spirit . . . raised Jesus from the dead." For support of the above interpretation and other readings of 1 Peter 3:18, see Paul J. Achtemeier, *A Commentary on First Peter*, Hermeneia: A Critical and Historical Commentary (Minneapolis: Fortress, 1996), 246–53; Karen H. Jones, *1 Peter* (Grand Rapids: Baker Academic, 2005), 237–42; and J. N. D. Kelly, *A Commentary on the Epistles of Peter and Jude* (1969; reprint, Grand Rapids: Baker, 1977), 150–53.

21. On the basis of Pauline literature and Jürgen Moltmann's theology, T. David Beck develops a pneumatological eschatology around six ideas: inauguration, eschatological tension, universality, historical character, advent, and *novum*; see Beck's *The Holy Spirit and the Renewal of All Things: Pneumatology in Paul and Jürgen Moltmann*, Princeton Theological Monograph Series 67 (Eugene: Pickwick Publications, 2007), 234.

22. My description of Pentecost as an eschatological event is also distinct from the common characterization of the Pentecostal movement in terms of an eschatological harbinger of the Second Coming of Christ within a broader pre-millennial eschatological framework. For example, D. William Faupel, *The Everlasting Gospel: The Significance of Eschatology in the Development of Pentecostal Thought*, Journal of Pentecostal Theology Supplement Series 10 (Sheffield: Sheffield Academic Press, 1996), presents a case for Pentecostalism as primarily an eschatological or end-time mission movement with Spirit baptism and charismatic manifestations serving as its principal signs. More recently Allan Anderson and Wonsuk Ma emphasize Pentecostal eschatological identity as a key motivating factor of Pentecostal missions; see Anderson, *Spreading Fires: The*

Missionary Nature of Early Pentecostalism (Maryknoll: Orbis Books, 2007), 219–23 and Ma, "'When the Poor are Fired Up': The Role of Pneumatology in Pentecostal/Charismatic Mission," in Veli-Matti Kärkkäinen, eds., *The Spirit in the World: Emerging Pentecostal Theologies in Global Contexts* (Grand Rapids: William B. Eerdmans Publishing Company, 2009), 43–44.

23. Frank D. Macchia, *Baptized in the Spirit: A Global Pentecostal Theology* (Grand Rapids: Zondervan, 2006), 42–49 and 85–88, argues that Spirit baptism is eschatological in the sense that it proleptically provides the believer with an experience of the future kingdom of God. I agree with Macchia that Spirit baptism is a proleptic experience of the everlasting kingdom, but I also affirm that it is eschatological in the sense that it consummates God's work of redemption.

24. Graham Ward, *The Politics of Discipleship: Becoming Postmaterial Citizens* (Grand Rapids: Baker Academic, 2009), 167–80.

25. I prefer the terminology of "mission of the Spirit" to that of "Spirit of mission" because the latter portrays mission as an instrumental function of the Spirit rather than as something intrinsic to the Spirit. For example, David J. Bosch's discussion of the Holy Spirit as the one who initiates, guides, and empowers mission reflects the conceptuality of the Spirit of mission because mission is not so much the Spirit's work per se, as a work the Spirit helps the disciples fulfill; see Bosch, *Transforming Mission: Paradigm Shifts in Theology of Mission* (1991; reprint, Maryknoll: Orbis Books, 1995), 113–15. Moreover, mission of the Spirit highlights that mission is fundamentally theological and pneumatological—not ecclesiastical. The Spirit is not merely the power supply for the Church to fulfill *its* mission. In this respect, Bosch's work has been very helpful in charting the rise of a shift from ecclesiological to theological notions of missions—e.g., *missio Dei* (Bosch, *Transforming Mission*, 368–93). Exhibiting this perspective, Jürgen Moltmann underlines that, "It is not the church that has a mission of salvation to fulfill to the world; it is the mission of the Son and the Spirit through the Father that includes the church, creating a church as it goes on its way"; Moltmann, *The Church in the Power of the Spirit: A Contribution to Messianic Ecclesiology*, trans., Margaret Kohl (1977; reprint, New York: HarperCollins, 1991), 64.

26. F. F. Bruce, *The Book of Acts*, rev. ed. (1988; reprint, Grand Rapids: William B. Eerdmans Publishing Company, 1989), 61.

27. Douglas Stuart, *Hosea-Jonah*, Word Biblical Commentary 31 (Waco: Word, 1987), 261–62.

28. Darrell L. Bock, *Acts* (Grand Rapids: Baker Academic, 2007), 118–19; Bruce, *Acts*, 61; and Ajith Fernando, *Acts* (Grand Rapids: Zondervan, 1998), 101.

29. Indeed, as Kirsteen Kim, *The Holy Spirit in the World: A Global Conversation* (Maryknoll: Orbis Books, 2007), 140, points out, if the Spirit were not operative outside the visible boundaries of the Church, mission itself would be impossible.

30. Ibid., 4–7.

31. See Anderson, *Spreading Fires*, 212–15, and Veli-Matti Kärkkäinen, "Pentecostal Pneumatology of Religions: The Contribution of Pentecostalism to Our Understanding of the Work of God's Spirit in the World," in Veli-Matti Kärkkäinen, ed., *The Spirit in the World: Emerging Pentecostal Theologies in Global Contexts* (Grand Rapids: William B. Eerdmans Publishing Company, 2009), 163–66.

32. For a discussion of an early-Pentecostal theology of religions and possible inclusivism, see the dialogue on J. H. King between Tony G. Moon and Tony Lee Richie (listed in order of the dialogue): Richie, "Azusa Era Optimism: Bishop J. H. King's Theology of Religions as a possible Paradigm for Today," *Journal of Pentecostal Theology* 14 (2006): 247–60; Moon, "J. H. King's Theology of Religions: 'Magnanimous

Optimism'?" *Journal of Pentecostal Theology* 16 (2007): 112–32; Richie, "A Moderate Move or Missing the Point? A Response to Tony Moon's J. H. King's Theology of Religions: 'Magnanimous Optimism'?" *Journal of Pentecostal Theology* 16 (2008): 118–25; Moon, "Richie Misses the Point: A Reply to Tony Richie's 'A Moderate Move or Missing the Point?'" *Journal of Pentecostal Theology* 171 (2008): 110–32; Richie, "Getting Back to the Heart of the Matter: The Way Forward and a Final Response to Tony Moon," *Journal of Pentecostal Theology* 18 (2009): 141–49; and Moon, "'Getting back to the Heart of the Matter': A Brief Rejoinder to Tony Richie," *Journal of Pentecostal Theology* 18 (2009): 312–18.

33. Anderson, *Spreading Fires*, 221; Veli-Matti Kärkkäinen, *Toward a Pneumatological Theology: Pentecostal and Ecumenical Perspectives on Ecclesiology, Soteriology, and Theology of Mission*, ed., Amos Yong (Lanham: University Press of America, 2002), 229–30 and 231–34; and Amos Yong, *Discerning the Spirit(s): A Pentecostal-Charismatic Contribution to Christian Theology of Religions*, Journal of Pentecostal Theology Supplement Series 20 (Sheffield: Sheffield Academic Press, 2000), 185–87 and 189.

34. For example, in the final report of the Roman Catholic-Pentecostal Dialogue, the Pentecostals expressed reticence at considering redemptive elements in the religions and preferred to limit the Spirit's work therein to preparing people for hearing the gospel. See "Evangelization, Proselytism, and Common Witness: The Report from the Fourth Phase of the International Dialogue (1990–1997) between the Roman Catholic Church and Some Classical Pentecostal Churches and Leaders," *PNEUMA: The Journal of the Society for Pentecostal Studies* 21 (1999) 16.

35. Amos Yong references the intrinsic connection between exclusivism and evangelism in evangelical theology in *Hospitality and the Other: Pentecost, Christian Practices, and the Neighbor* (Maryknoll: Orbis Books, 2008), 72. Kärkkäinen also notes Pentecostalism's historical connection with conservative Evangelicalism as a primary source for its negative theology of religions and penchant for soteriological exclusivism ("Pentecostal Pneumatology of Religions," 170–71).

36. For Yong's critique of the "pragmatic" rationale, see *Beyond the Impasse: Toward a Pneumatological Theology of Religions* (Grand Rapids: Baker Academic, 2003), 26.

37. I realize this is a controversial point. For example, Veli-Matti Kärkkäinen affirms that the religions play an important role in helping the church arrive at a deeper understanding of God, but he nonetheless denies that that they are "salvific as such"; Kärkkäinen, *Trinity and Religious Pluralism: The Doctrine of the Trinity in Christian Theology of Religions* (Burlington: Ashgate, 2004), 179. However, if the Spirit of God is active in the religions of the world and this activity reveals divine mysteries, then why are they not salvific in the sense of providing acceptable means to experience the Spirit's redemptive work? In proposing that the religions may be conduits for redemptive experience of the Spirit, I am not entirely alone among Pentecostals; Amos Yong suggests that "the potentiality of the Spirit's presence and activity in the religions and their adherents means both that the religious traditions of humankind are redeemable for the glory of God and that the gospel can be communicated . . . even found manifest in new ways, in the other faiths"; see Yong, *The Spirit Poured Out on All Flesh: Pentecostalism and the Possibility of Global Theology* (Grand Rapids: Baker Academic, 2005), 247.

38. For example, in ancient Egypt, the four winds were perennially identified as gods. See Susanne Woodhouse, "The Sun God, His Four Bas and the Four Winds in the Sacred District at Saïs: The Fragment of an Obelisk (BM EA 1512)," in Stephen Quirke,

ed., *The Temple in Ancient Egypt: New Discoveries and Recent Research* (London: British Museum Press, 1997), 136–37. Furthermore, the Egyptian high god Shu, who was associated with the air, was considered the ultimate source of the winds, and reigned with his sister-goddess Tefnut, ultimately controlled the four winds and was a chief actor in ancient Egyptian cosmology; see G. J. Botterweck and Helmer Ringgren, ed., *Theologisches Wörterbuch zum Alten Testament*, 10 vols. (Stuttgart: W. Kohlhammer, 1973–2000), vol. 7, s.v., "רוח rûah." The Assyrian King, Adad-Nerari II appropriated to himself the status of the Sun god and associated his power with the "onslaught of the wind" and "the gale." See Albert Kirk Grayson, *Assyrian Royal Inscriptions: From Tiglath-pileser I to Ashur-nasir-apli II*, 2 vols. (Wiesbaden: Otto Harrassowitz, 1976), 2:85–86. Also see, K. van der Toorn, Bob Becking, and Pieter Willem van der Horst, *Dictionary of Deities and Demons in the Bible*, 2nd rev. ed. (Leiden: Brill, and Grand Rapids: William B. Eerdmans Publishing Company, 1999), s.v., "wind-gods," and Leland Ryken, James C. Wilhoit, and Tremper Longman, III, eds., *Dictionary of Biblical Imagery* (Downers Grove: InterVarsity, 1998), s.v. "whirlwind."

39. Others too have noted this penchant; see Kärkkäinen, "Pentecostal Pneumatology of Religions," 161–62.

40. E.g., John R. Franke, *The Character of Theology: An Introduction to Its Nature, Task, and Purpose* (Grand Rapids: Baker Academic, 2005).

41. Stuart, *Hosea-Jonah*, 494. The hard restrictivist or exclusivist position seems to be the contemporary version of Jonah's fear: "O LORD, . . . you are a gracious and compassionate God, slow to anger and abounding in love, a God who relents from sending calamity" (Jonah 4:2).

42. Richie, "Azusa-Era Optimism," 234.

43. Adam Sparks, *One of a Kind: The Relationship between Old and New Covenants as the Hermeneutical Key for Christian Theology of Religions* (Eugene: Pickwick Books, 2010), critiques the inclusivist "Israel analogy" that draws a parallel between the reception of salvation by the people of Israel and the adherents of other religions; that is, non-Christian religions are similar in their relation to Christianity as was the religion of Israel. He argues that the revelation of salvation through the history of Israel, which culminates in Christ, was *sui generis*; therefore, the reception of salvation by the people of Israel without explicit faith in Christ cannot serve as a paradigm for an inclusivist soteriology. However, one can grant the *sui generis* nature of the revelation of salvation through Israel and still find support for an inclusive view of the way people in non-Christian religions access the grace of Christ, a point that Sparks recognizes. First, the necessity for the historical mediation of faith necessitates a particular history of redemption—i.e., the revelation through the people of Israel culminating in the Incarnation of Christ and the outpouring of the Holy Spirit. Second, a parallel between non-Christian religions and the religion of Israel is not necessary and perhaps not that common among inclusivists; for example, few inclusivists see the teachings of Buddha as equivalent to the Law of Moses, which is what they must do for Spark's critique to have traction. Indeed, the prevalent view among inclusivists is that adherents of non-Christian religions can participate in the grace of Christ in spite of and not by virtue of their religion. Furthermore, inclusivists tend to make the more modest claim that figures in the Old Testament, both within and without the people of Israel, received grace and did so without explicit faith in Christ rather than seeing the religion of Israel as a paradigm for understanding the function of non-Christian religions. Thus, though the "Israel analogy" may not support inclusivism, it is not necessary for inclusivists, nor does it seem to be the primary theological point that inclusivists draw from the experience of salvation in the Old Testament. Finally, in respect to the notion that other religions find fulfillment in

Christ—as did Judaism—in so far as they are authentic responses to God's redemptive work, all religious expressions find their fulfillment in Christ and the Spirit of Pentecost, regardless of the person's religious tradition. The key question in respect to the "Israel analogy" is, "Does the Old Covenant have a unique (*sui generis*) role in preparing the way for Christ?" The answer is both "yes" and "no." Yes, because the particular religious history of Israel yields the Incarnation, the cross, the resurrection, and the outpouring of the Spirit. No, because God's redemptive work is not limited to the particular religious history of Israel. If we grant that point, because all redemption is ultimately in continuity with Christ and the Spirit of Pentecost, the Old Covenant is not *sui generis* in respect to being an exclusive place of God's redemptive work. Moreover, it means that Christ and the Spirit are the fulfillment of God's redemptive work in all people, regardless of their particular religion.

44. Tony Richie argues that the early Pentecostal, J. H. King "ascribed saving efficacy to 'the religion of Christ,' not to the Christian religious system per se," and that this opens the door to a more positive Pentecostal theology of religions; see Richie, "Azusa-Era Optimism," 236.

45. Ibid., 239. Or, as Anthea Butler suggests, Pentecostalism includes practices that can be characterized as the good, the bad, and the ugly: see Butler, "Pentecostal Traditions We should pass on: The Good, the Bad, and the Ugly," *PNEUMA: The Journal of the Society for Pentecostal Studies* 27 (2005): 343–53.

Part II

Renewal Missiology &

the Interfaith Encounter

Chapter 4

Dukkha and *Passio*:
A Christian Theology of Suffering in the
(*Theravada*) Buddhist Context

Veli-Matti Kärkkäinen

First Words: Approach and Goal

This essay argues that a key common concern between Buddhist and Christian religions is the issue of suffering.[1] This is because of the prominence of the issue of suffering in both the Buddhist and Christian vision of liberation and "salvation." Consequently, my contention is that a successful missionary encounter in any Buddhist environment requires a lot of careful attention to the meaning of suffering and the means of release from under its power.

I will significantly limit the scope of my investigation. From the Buddhist side, I will concentrate not only on the *Theravada* branch but also on its manifestation in one of the main locations of *Theravada* in the contemporary world, Thailand.[2] From the Christian side, I will focus on the resources of the Renewal Theology and Missiology through the lens of Pentecostal tradition. While I know well that the Renewal tradition is larger than that of Pentecostalism, I am also convinced that Pentecostal theology and missiology may serve as *a* representative.

During the course of discussion I will further explain the rationale for other limitations, including the omission of the traditional theodicy question and of socio-political suffering/liberation. The essay consists of two parts: in the first I attempt to discern the understanding of suffering in each religious tradition. In the second part, I compare and contrast the Buddhist and Christian visions of liberation with a view to proposing theological guidelines for a missionary encounter. I will finish with some tasks and themes for further reflection.

Two Perspectives on Suffering: *Dukkha* and *Passio*

The Buddhist Insight into Suffering

> The Noble Truth of *dukkha,* monks, is this: Birth is *dukkha*, aging is *dukkha*, sickness is *dukkha*, death is *dukkha*, association with the unpleasant is *dukkha*, dissociation from the pleasant is *dukkha*, not to receive what one desires is *dukkha*—in brief the five aggregates subject to grasping are *dukkha*.[3]

In his first sermon after the Enlightenment, "Setting the Wheel of Dhamma in Motion," Gautama Buddha set forth *dukkha* as the basic principle of Buddhist teaching and worldview (the first "Noble Truth"). With all their differences, all Buddhist schools consider *dukkha* ("suffering") to be the main challenge and, consequently, extinction of *dukkha* to be the main goal. Suffering is inescapable as long as one is in the circle of life and death, *samsara*. To be more precise, it is the craving (the second "Noble Truth") which is the real root and cause.[4] Behind the (misplaced) craving, according to the Buddha, is ignorance.[5] The logic of the emergence and continuation of suffering rooted in craving due to ignorance is indebted to the law of *kamma*.[6]

Buddhist scholars consider *dukkha* and the rest of the "Noble Truths" (the origin and way of extinction) as the *summa* of everything in Buddhism and its Scriptures.[7] While most of the Buddhists in Thailand are fairly ill-versed in the doctrinal heritage of their religion—which is understandable in light of a deep and pervasive "animistic"[8] orientation of everyday religiosity and spirituality with its focus on spirits—one can hardly find a Thai who couldn't recite the essence of Buddha's first sermon at the Deer Park. "Consequently, the Buddhist concept of suffering certainly governs the understanding of Thai Buddhists, and, at the same time, it inevitably influences the responses of Thai Christians to the reality of human suffering."[9]

The term *dukkha* is notoriously difficult to translate, as even a quick look at different English renderings of the Pali original reveals: terms such as "suffering," "pain," "stress," and "unsatisfactoriness" are used. None of them, however, can capture the ambiguity of the original term—and most of them, taken in isolation from the Buddhist worldview, can easily lead us astray. The world-renowned Buddhist teacher Walpola Rahula chooses not to even attempt a translation of *dukkha* to avoid obvious misunderstanding.[10]

The common suspicion that according to Buddha life is nothing but suffering and pain, while containing a seed of truth, is also in many ways misleading.[11] Firstly, the term *dukkha* means much more than—and in many ways something much different from—"suffering": along with suffering, pain, and sorrow, the term denotes imperfection, impermanence, emptiness, and insubstantiality.[12] Second, the focus on *dukkha* does not imply that for Buddhism life is pessimistic (any more than optimistic for that matter). The Buddhist vision of life is rather realistic. As is well-known, Gautama gave a long litany of things in life that are enjoyable and should be enjoyed, from economic security and wealth to happiness on account of living a good life.[13]

Gautama's observation according to which "the five groups of existence connected with clinging are *dukkha*" reminds us of the five aggregates that make up a human being, namely, the physical (or material), feeling, perception, mental formations, and consciousness. Besides and beyond these five aggregates there is no permanent "self" or "individual" in the Western sense of the word. Even these aggregates, of course, are nothing permanent! This is the essence of the Buddhist notion of *anattatā*, no-self. Coupled with the idea of no-self and *dukkha*, is the third "characteristic of existence," namely impermanence.[14] Of course, human beings cannot fathom this reality, and thus craving emerges, which helps explain *dukkha*! Sentient beings are instead fooled by the idea of continuity, movement, and wholeness.[15] A most ironic thing about the Buddhist worldview is that while the "self" is impermanent—in other words, a fleeting reality—*dukkha* is something "essential," "permanent." *Dukkha* simply describes how life is! The same can be said of *kamma*; in the world characterized by non-being and impermanence, those two "laws" seem to be in place whatever happens.

In the Buddhist vision, suffering is both a built-in and inevitable reality; on top of that, sentient beings also encounter various types of sufferings such as those outlined above.[16] For the Buddha, *dukkha* has three interrelated meanings:[17] First, *Dukkha-dukkhatā*: the state of suffering in terms of feeling and sensation; this meaning comes closest to the English "suffering." Second, *Viparināma- dukkhatā*: the state of suffering inherent "in the change or the state of suffering which [is] concealed within the infidelity of happiness." This is the "post-enjoyment" realization of the ending of the pleasure. Third, *Sankhāra dukkhatā*: the state of suffering due to formations, related to the "three characteristics of existence" teaching.[18]

Satanun Boonyakiat summarizes succinctly the Buddhist notion of *dukkha* in its various dimensions and forms:

In summary, the term "suffering" in the Buddhism has a complex meaning. On the one hand, it simply means physical and emotional pain. On the other hand, it refers to the state of suffering that is inherent in the change and conflictual state result[ing] from impermanence. The Buddha points out that human beings must encounter various kinds of suffering. Physical and emotional suffering associated with birth, old age, and death is unavoidable because it is the true basis of human nature. The feeling of suffering is the result of craving or clinging to someone or something. Moreover, the Buddha teaches that suffering is the stressful and conflictual nature of all things caused by their impermanence. Therefore, nothing can provide complete fulfillment to those who attach to it. The Buddha proclaims this truth not to add a burden to human misery, but to help people recognize it and to start the process of suffering solving.[19]

The Christian Theology of Suffering

In light of the prevalence in the Thai mind of the idea of suffering, Satanun Boonyakiat laments the fact that Christian "theological approaches to suffering, driven by the agenda of the people in the west, often focus on the problem of evil and theodicy rather than addressing the reality of human suffering per se." As a result, he surmises, those responses make little sense to the Thais.[20] Key questions for Christian missionary responses then are—rather than the classical theodicy question as to how to reconcile the idea of a good, loving God with the problem of evil—the following ones: Do Christians and Buddhists refer to the same reality when speaking of "suffering"?[21] Is craving behind the Buddhist explanation of the root of suffering similar to the Christian notion of sin? What is the way of liberation? In other words, in this dialogical investigation, rather than focusing on the question of *Why* suffering? (which, of course, is a crucial *theological* dilemma), I will place the emphasis on *How* to deal with suffering? and *What* is suffering in light of the gospel?

This orientation helps us limit this part of the investigation to prepare us for a comparison and contrast with a view to implications for mission. Rather than attempting any kind of traditional inquiry into the "whence evil" theodicy question, I will just offer a brief statement about the issue of suffering in Christian tradition and then attempt to highlight the Pentecostal approach.

While Christian theology does not speak about suffering in one voice, all Christian traditions agree that suffering—however it is related to the Fall and sin—only came into existence in the second movement following God's good creation.[22] In that sense, Christian tradition considers suffering and evil in some sense parasitic to goodness.[23] In the main, Christian tradition has denied the idea of an ontological primacy of evil and thus of suffering, even when suffering is related via the Fall and sin to Satan, God's chief opponent. Furthermore, while there is a strong theological tradition in Classical Theism resisting the idea of linking suffering too closely with God, contemporary theology, having rediscovered the biblical teaching[24] and formative contributions of Martin Luther's "theology of the cross,"[25] speaks robustly of suffering in God, in other words, divine suffering.[26] In the words of Jürgen Moltmann, Christian theology has no choice but to replace the *apathy axiom* (idea of an impassible) God for the notion of *theopathy*.[27] The main reason is the biblical idea that God is love.[28] Love that is not engaged and committed to sharing pain is not worth its salt. God's passion can be called "active passion," since it is voluntary identification with the suffering of the world and is based on love.[29]

There is yet another formative Christian idea about suffering: the redemptive suffering of Christ. While, again, Christian tradition does not speak in one voice about *how* redemption happened (and will happen) in the event of

Jesus Christ,[30] there is a shared conviction that without the suffering of the Son of Man salvation would not be available.[31] Finally, to sum up in few strokes of pen the vast area of the theology of suffering with regards to its many forms and motifs, Christian tradition also agrees that there are experiences and forms of suffering that just belong to human life in general, even as some aspects of suffering are peculiar to the Christian experience in particular. In a cautious way, Christian tradition is even saying that suffering in that sense may be conducive to one's growth in faith. This is not to say that suffering is necessarily a "good" thing, but it is to say—differently from Buddhism—that suffering may also play some role in the hands of the loving and caring Father who allows his creatures to undergo moments of suffering.[32]

Now, enter Pentecostals (as representatives of Renewal Theology and Missiology); what is Pentecostalism's take on the topic of suffering? In many ways, Pentecostal-Charismatic spirituality has tended to be on the other side of the question: "Pentecostal/charismatic Christianity has (re)introduced to Christian spirituality an ideal of victorious Christian living, an intensive faith expectation, and emphasis on spiritual power to overcome problems in one's life. The attitude of 'overcoming' is characteristic to Pentecostal and charismatic preaching. Often there is a heightened expectation of divine intervention, even in situations that seem impossible."[33] Indeed, rather than suffering and pain, Pentecostals have highlighted themes such as victory and healing. As a general observation, one has to admit that there is precious little talk about suffering in much of Pentecostal literature.[34] One may thus wonder, to cite the title of my earlier writing, if "Theology of the Cross [is] a Stumbling Block to Pentecostal/Charismatic Spirituality"?[35] This is all the more astonishing when one takes into consideration the fact that even in the midst of victories and deliverances,

> The first Pentecostal churches suffered at the hands of mainline Christian denominations. Their people comprised the poor, the uneducated, those from the margins of society, and the oppressed—in contrast to the rich, the influential and the powerful who occupied the pews of main line churches. The hostility these Pentecostal churches faced from established Christendom and the outside world made them look up with even greater earnestness; thereby enhancing their own spirituality, their spiritual equipment for service, their zeal to suffer for God and their hope in an imminent future with God.[36]

This pointed remark by the Indian Pentecostal theologian Gabriel Reuben Louis, in his response to a presentation, "Toward an Asian Pentecostal Theology," by Korean Pentecostal missiologist-theologian Wonsuk Ma, is a healthy reminder of the important *lacuna* in Pentecostal spirituality. Louis further laments that while today's Pentecostalism has embraced the early vision of the "Latter Rain," it is looking for its benefits mainly for the sake of this-worldly goods and enjoyment. While the theme of suffering, he continues, "may not be that relevant for a Pentecostal theology in a rich and prosperous West . . .

[it is] in a poor and miserable Asia. . . ." Rather than assigning all or even most suffering to the spirit world, Louis contends, contemporary Pentecostalism should rediscover the important lesson from their forebears: "It is human to suffer; it is human to experience pain; it is human to be despised, forsaken and oppressed. This was what our own fore-fathers in the Pentecostal faith went through, and this is what most of the people of Asia go through even today." [37] The omission or downplaying of the theme of suffering among Pentecostals is of course not limited to the Asian or Western contexts; similar kinds of charges have been leveled for example against African Pentecostalism.[38]

On the other hand, there are significant efforts underway by Pentecostal theologians and missiologists to address more intentionally the theme of suffering in human life and Christian experience. While acknowledging and strongly endorsing the Pentecostal mentality of overcoming, The Pentecostal biblical scholar and missiologist William W. Menzies, with wide experience from the Asian context, admits that healings are mysteries and "Good people are not always healed." As a consequence, he suggests a biblical theology of suffering for Pentecostals.[39] This task has been taken up by another Assemblies of God biblical scholar, Martin William Mittelstadt, who has written on *The Spirit and Suffering in Luke-Acts*,[40] focusing his study on the topic seldom discussed by Pentecostals who otherwise have launched major investigations on this most treasured part of the New Testament. The Pentecostal theologian-missionary of Puerto Rico, Samuel Solivan, has contributed a significant theological treatise titled *The Spirit, Pathos and Liberation* in which he attempts an outline of Hispanic Pentecostal theology through the lens of suffering and liberation,[41] and the Sudanese Pentecostal Isaiah Majok Dau has reflected on *Suffering and God* in the context of the tragic civil war in his homeland.[42] What is noteworthy about these two theological treatises is that while Pentecostal in orientation, they engage widely Christian tradition and diverse theological views. I will take up these contributions in my constructive part of the essay.

Two Visions of Liberation: *Ortho-doxy* and *Ortho-pathos*

Liberation through Right Knowledge: The Way of *Ortho-doxy*

While inevitable, "The Buddha believes that suffering is resolvable. He pointed out that overcoming suffering is not accomplish by avoiding problems or neglecting suffering, but by confronting the reality of suffering and learning how to respond to it correctly. Therefore, the essence of the first truth is rightly accepting the reality of suffering as it is, and perceiving life and the world as they are." [43] How, then, would the Buddhist and Christian notions of suffering compare with each other? While both religions agree on the reality and multifaceted nature of suffering, the main differences have to do with three underlying issues. These differences of orientation should be kept in mind and reflected upon when constructing a missionary approach.

For Buddhism, suffering is in some respects an unavoidable structure of reality,[44] whereas for Christian faith, suffering is in some sense parasitic on goodness. In other words, Christian tradition, in light of creation, does not consider suffering as ontologically primary or necessary.[45]

When it comes to the "cause" or "reason" behind the suffering, Buddhist and Christian visions differ sharply. As mentioned above, for Buddhism the cause behind suffering is craving because of ignorance in the framework of *kamma*. In other words, the "something" behind the human dilemma is impersonal. When it comes to the Christian explanation of the cause of suffering, ultimately it is to be found in the personal God rather than in a formal principle of reality. To sharpen and clarify the Christian view, I follow the helpful typology suggested by Boonyakiat who speaks of three ways of looking for the causes behind suffering; these are all interrelated and, as said, finally to be referred to the Almighty and Loving God.[46] First, according to the message of "retribution theology," suffering is the result of sin. This explanation comes closest to the Buddhist notion of retribution in the framework of *kamma* but is also different because the Buddhist explanation is based on an alleged "natural law of action and effect" rather than the actions of a personal God. It is highly significant that the Christian idea of "reaping and sowing" is placed in a theological framework: "Do not be deceived: God cannot be mocked. A man reaps what he sows" (Gal. 6:7 NIV). Another major difference has to do with the Buddhist notion of attributing the consequences to the next life rather than to this life.[47] Retribution theology appeals to Thai Christians since in contrast to the Buddhist *kamma*, sin can be dealt with in terms of repentance and faith.[48] Second, according to the message of liberation theology, part of suffering in the Christian vision is the result of oppression, which of course is not unrelated to the Fall and sinfulness of humanity. This is to say that unlike the Buddhist analysis which assigns one's suffering to one's own acts and dispositions, in the Christian view much suffering comes to the innocent because of the wrongdoings of others, including structural sin. Beginning from the Exodus, there is the biblical promise of God acting on behalf of and empowering those who suffer under oppression, injustice, neglect, and other similar situations. The existence of massive injustice, poverty, oppression (particularly of minorities such as the Mountain Peoples), and corruption both confuse and burden Thais when they realize that so much of that suffering cannot be attributed to the innocent sufferers. In the final analysis, in Christian theology even this suffering must be referred to God in one way or another (depending on one's theodicy) rather than to a nonpersonal, formal principle governing reality. Third, there is also the biblical and theological tradition that simply makes suffering the function of mystery. There is suffering in the world and in Christian experience that simply evades explanation. Just consult the Book of Job—or many Psalms. In comparison with the Buddhist vision, it is highly significant that both Job and Psalms are part of the Wisdom literature. They are meant to heal our ignorance by telling us there is also suffering without any immediate cause or reason—

other than the mystery of God, the Personal God. Again, it is comforting for Thai Christians to receive the message that there simply are sufferings which cannot be attributed to any cause conceived by humans, not even sin in the individual life or in the structures, but that even that kind of suffering is taken up by the Loving and Just God.

Yet another radical difference between the Buddhist and Christian vision is that "Savior has no place in the Buddhist worldview. An individual must control and be responsible for his or her own destiny."[49] One is one's own refuge, and no one else, not even Buddha,[50] can save one from the law of *kamma*. In other words, Buddhism, particularly in its original "orthodox" version is "an atheistic and humanistic system that locates human beings at the center of their existence and believes that humankind can overcome the problem of human suffering by their own endeavors. It also implies the denial of . . . Savior who delivers humankind from suffering."[51]

So, what then is the Buddhist vision of liberation? It is the removal of ignorance, in other words, right understanding and right thought—to name the first two aspects of the "Noble Eightfold Path."[52] I therefore have named it *ortho-doxy*, following the Christian vocabulary.[53] Of course, the Middle Way or the Noble Path also includes other things such as right action and right effort, but still it is true that everything focuses on the right insight, right knowledge, right understanding. Behind suffering is the wrong understanding; healing therefore comes in the form of the removal of ignorance with the coming of enlightened knowledge.[54] And as said, it is each human person's own responsibility to reach the goal. Over against the *Theravada* Buddhist human-centered idea of *ortho-doxy*, I will suggest a Christian idea of *ortho-pathos*.

Liberation through Right Suffering: The Way of *Ortho-pathos*

If the Buddhist strategy of seeking for release from suffering is knowledge-based, for Christians, the problem of suffering demands not only—or even primarily—a rational explanation or even right knowledge but rather, faith-based proper response, patience, trust, and hope. This is the way of *ortho-pathos*, "right suffering" to use constructively the terminology of Solivan.[55] Whereas for him the term is a shorthand for a Pentecostal Hispanic liberation theology, helping complement the weaknesses of mere *orthodoxy* with little focus on concrete action and *orthopraxis* with its distant and disengaged relation to a particular sufferer's life-situation, I make the term *orthopathos* a function of embracing in faith, hope, and love the biblical idea of suffering, both divine and human. Focusing now on a constructive missiological response from a Renewal Perspective through the lens of Pentecostalism, I will suggest four interrelated tasks for such an endeavor. I argue that for Pentecostals to facilitate a proper missionary interfaith encounter, these four interrelated aspects of a "suffering theology" of *orthopathos* should play a role:

- "Divine Suffering": embracing of the biblical God of love who shares in the *passio* and *pathos* of the world and makes it his own;

- "Redemptive Suffering": clinging to the "theology of the cross" that facilitates not only forgiveness of sins but also a concrete hope based on Christ;
- "Integrative Suffering": accepting suffering and pain as part of a victorious Spirit-filled life and ministry;
- "Healing Suffering": engaging in mature faith and hope the ministry of healing and compassion to help those who suffer.[56]

Divine Suffering

In order for Pentecostals to embrace the biblical idea of divine suffering, the implications of the belief in "an apathetic God" need to be exposed and corrected. This is what Solivan is doing in a most helpful way in a critical dialogue with the whole of Christian tradition. As he constructs a liberating theology of *orthopathos*, he sees it necessary to revisit the whole Christian tradition beginning from the Fathers with their engagement with the Greek Hellenistic notion of a passionless deity all the way to Luther's theology of the cross and contemporary revival of the theme of the *Crucified God*.[57] Old Testament study would be a good place for Pentecostals to rediscover the idea of a passionate, engaged, loving God who is in pains for his people and the peoples.[58] The New Testament speaks of the suffering of the Son in submitting his life onto the hands of the Father and of the suffering of the Father in handing over his Son to death, as well as the passionate Spirit sharing—as the bond of love, as tradition says—in this divine suffering.

Consequently, Pentecostals have a need to rediscover the biblical teaching about the relationship between the Spirit and suffering, not only the Spirit and empowerment. Having scrutinized a number of Pentecostal biblical investigations into the Lucan pneumatology, the most precious section in the Pentecostal "canon within the canon," Mittelstadt concludes that there is "a failure to integrate the intersecting of the Spirit with suffering."[59]

With all their emphasis on the power of God in healings, exorcisms, and other kinds of "power encounters" as well as the vibrant expectations of God's desire to intervene miraculously, Pentecostal theology faces poorly the need to embrace the view of the loving, *passio*nate and *com*passionate God who weeps and anguishes over the suffering of his children and whose fatherly heart is broken because of the brokenness of life. As foreign as that view of God is for both the Hellenistic philosophical tradition and the "atheistic" Buddhist religious tradition, it is compelling as well. And even when it is perceived as scandalous, it cannot be abandoned for the sake of "relevance." Embracing the idea of a passionate God makes Pentecostal ministers and missionaries compassionate toward their neighbors and the religious Other.

Redemptive Suffering

While the generic idea of redemptive or "vicarious" suffering on behalf of others is not unknown in Buddhism—think of, for example, the commonly known story of the sixteenth-century Queen Srisuriyothai's self-sacrifice to save her people under the threat from the King of Burma or the annual ritual of *loikrathong*, which seeks to embody the sending away of the sins of the past year exploiting candles and miniature rafts—any notion of somebody suffering (death) to atone for sins or even taking up the other person's suffering onto himself is utterly foreign to the *Theravada* tradition.[60] A resort to such a vicarious act done by another person, even a divinity, would mean shirking one's own responsibility to deal with one's *kamma*.

I leave out of my discussion here the complicated and complex question as to how to deal with the problem of atonement vis-à-vis Thai culture[61] and focus rather on the more general idea of the Christian "theology of the cross" and the redemptive suffering of Christ and the call to Christians to follow the suffering Christ on the way to Golgotha. As mentioned above, a foundational difference between Buddhist and Christian views of salvation/liberation is the emphasis in the former on human initiative and capacity and in the latter on the benefits of the Savior. I just leave it here and move on to the corollary part.

In the Christian vision those who follow the suffering Christ are called to identify with and share in his sufferings. Pentecostals would do well in listening to the call of the late Pope John Paul II who began his encyclical "On the Meaning of Christian Suffering" with the quote from St. Paul: "Declaring the power of salvific suffering, the Apostle Paul says: 'In my flesh I complete what is lacking in Christ's afflictions for the sake of his body, that is, the Church.'"[62] The Holy Father reminded Christians of the fact that while redemption was accomplished by Christ's suffering on the cross, every Christian is called to suffer for the sake of the church and other people.[63] He quotes several times the familiar biblical verse from Romans 5:5 which speaks of the pouring out in our hearts of God's love through the Holy Spirit as the power for a hopeful suffering, suffering which sees meaning beyond suffering.[64]

This is what the Sudanese Pentecostal theologian Isaiah Majok Dau calls "suffering as a direct result of being followers of Christ"[65] Living in that war-stricken land, he rejoices over the fact that in the contemporary situation the Pentecostal church has become "a community capable of absorbing suffering"[66] and thus embodying the sufferings of Christ for the benefit of others.

Integrative Suffering

As a result of having missed the integral relationship in the biblical materials between the Spirit and suffering, "While Pentecostal leadership continues the call for the same empowering of the Holy Spirit and commissioning to gospel proclamation, often lacking is Luke's emphasis on the persistent tension between persecution and Spirit-inspired mission." An important theological and spiritual lesson for Pentecostals thus is to learn that "upon reception of the Spirit, recipients are not all powerful." Indeed, "Luke offers a vivid reminder of the limitations of Spirit-enablement." This all means that Pentecostals need to learn and embrace as an integral part of Christian experience the moments of failure, weakness, despair, sickness, and other forms of suffering.[67] Not only contemporary Pentecostalism but also the first audience of the Lucan message had to tackle this same challenge. Having experienced the empowering, healing, and delivering power of the Holy Spirit in their midst, the first Christians had to come to grips with opposition, harassment, betrayals, and other kinds of struggles. According to Mittelstadt, nothing less is at stake here than the principle that "Opposition is rooted within the plan of God."[68] With a life story filled with tragedies such as epidemic disease in childhood, having one of his eyes permanently impaired, long-time civil war, and his wife's life-threatening diseases, Dau calls suffering "a test of faith and faithfulness."[69]

The Thai theologian Satanun Boonyakiat rightly argues that the term "integrative suffering" "enables Christians to see that some sort of suffering can belong to the human nature from the beginning. It also reveals that suffering is not always wrong because it can serve life and enrich our relationship with God."[70] He continues, saying that the idea that certain kinds of suffering "can belong to and have a positive role in God's good creation also makes Christian faith flourish" as well as relieves Christians from a naïve, unrealistic view of life—so much mocked by the realistic Buddhist vision.[71]

The presence—and hope-filled and patient embrace—of suffering in the Christian life and ministry is wonderfully embodied in Paul Yonggi Cho's experience. A Korean pastor, he comes from and reflects Buddhist (and Confucian) themes. In a collection of sermons titled *When I Am Weak, Then I Am Strong*, the lead sermon reflects on the presence of sufferings—in the form of the "thorn in the flesh" (2 Cor. 12:7-10)—in the life of St. Paul, who also claimed divine revelations, abundance of mercy, and extraordinary victories. Pastor Cho urges "that we should be motivated in our lives of faith in God to let all the thorns of difficulties and trials become opportunities through which we can receive His blessings."[72] Knowing that these sufferings in the life of the Christian minister may turn out to be God's blessings, Cho advises us not to resist them with our own strength.[73] "Pastor Cho's Pentecostal theology of hope is an interesting mixture of bold faith-expectation, the kind of 'stubborn' faith of the woman in the Gospel of Luke (18:1-8) approved by Jesus, and obedient submission to endure suffering and pain as coming from the hand of a good God."[74]

Healing Suffering

In Christian faith the follower of Jesus Christ is called to alleviate the suffering of other men and women. While not denying the role of personal responsibility over the consequences of one's choices, there is the calling for all Christians to follow in the footsteps of their Master who devoted his life to healing, exorcism, hospitality, and reconciliation—at times even at the expense of one's own well-being and safety. Let me highlight here the importance of healing for its obvious importance to Pentecostal spirituality and mission. In the mainline, Buddhism, particularly the *Theravada* tradition, teaches that one should not be too active in intervening in another person's suffering in order to avoid interrupting the *kamma* and *samsara*-nature of reality.[75] Let me offer a personal testimony here to illustrate my point. When I lived with my family in Bangkok, my then young daughters often challenged and questioned my neglect of beggars on the street corners. Every visitor to the capital of Thailand or any other city knows that there is a huge number of beggars, many of them handicapped or otherwise health-impaired, including mothers with small children on their laps. While my own reason for not responding to the needs of many of these desperate people had more to do with—in addition to the obvious incapacity of being able to help the huge number of people because of the financial limitations of a missionary— the justified suspicion of being exploited for the benefit of the greedy "mafia," my Thai Buddhist interlocutors argued that an act of benevolence might be an exercise in intervening with another person's *kamma*.[76]

While I am a bit concerned about the concept of exploiting a "power encounter" as a means of persuading the followers of other religions—because it may easily turn into a "battle" between religions in terms of who represents the most "powerful" form of religion, hardly consonant with the Christian teaching focused on the suffering and crucified Messiah—I also affirm wholeheartedly the biblical idea of healings as a way to affirm God's compassion, love, and care. In the highly "animistic" Buddhist environments, the presence of healings has the potential of alleviating men's and women's suffering in a way that may also open them to the gospel.

When engaging in the ministry of healing, whether in miraculous or more "natural" ways, Christian ministers also have to negotiate the dynamic wisely described in W. M. Menzies' Pentecostal "Reflections on Suffering":

> Prudence requires that we neither capitulate prematurely to the problem of human suffering, nor are we to demand of God that he intervene, as if he were a 'cosmic bellhop' governed solely by urgent calls from his children. A better option seems to be to engage in Apostolic ministry, to reach out to God on behalf of the suffering, and to intercede for human need until the Lord whispers to us that he has another purpose in hand. This, I believe, is an appropriate Pentecostal understanding of our responsibility regarding the engagement with human suffering.[77]

Last Words: Tasks for Further Reflection

This essay builds on the assumption that suffering—however diversely it is understood in these two traditions—may be a viable candidate for a proper interfaith and missionary encounter with (*Theravada*) Buddhism. Having outlined the two respective views of suffering and causes behind it, I have attempted to contrast the visions of liberation and suggest several tasks for Renewal Theology to facilitate a proper missionary response.

I have several topics for further reflection in my mind; some of them are such that intentionally I had to leave out to make the discussion more manageable; others are offshoots from this reflection. Let me just list them in no order of importance and thus issue an invitation for continuing mutual reflection grouped under two subheadings, first Christian and then Buddhist. From the Christian Renewal side I would be interested in knowing more about these issues, among others:

- What would it mean to Renewal Theology as a whole and the Pentecostal version thereof if the topic of suffering were included in the substructure of that tradition in a more integral and robust way? Would that move affect the stress on faith-based optimism and the mentality of overcoming?
- What might be some of the aspects of the wider Renewal Theology framework that were not present in the Pentecostal form of that tradition? Are there any significant areas or themes missing?
- What are some of the ways the Renewal/Pentecostal approach to an interfaith missionary encounter with Buddhism differs from that of other Christian traditions?
- Would the inclusion of the Liberationist task affect significantly this interfaith encounter in the framework of how suffering and liberation might play their roles?
- What are some of the lessons we (as outsiders to the Thai *Theravada* milieu) would learn from Thai Christians in terms of our own tackling the problem of suffering?

From the Buddhist perspective, I wish to gain more insights into these topics, among others:

- How would reflection on and interfaith encounter take place in other Buddhist contexts, particularly with regard to *Mahayana* traditions? Would some of the themes be differently interpreted, particularly those having to do with the possibility of "redemptive suffering" and "healing suffering"?
- Consequently, would a Pure Land context move the two traditions, Christian and Buddhist, even closer to each other—if there is, as is often assumed, a notion of "grace" available in that version of Buddhism?
- Are there valuable lessons that *Theravada* Buddhists may teach Christians when it comes to suffering and liberation?

May the conversation continue . . .

Notes

1. I would like to acknowledge my indebtedness to the work of my Thai student Satanun Boonyakiat, who recently finished an excellent doctoral dissertation titled, "A Christian Theology of Suffering in the Context of Theravada Buddhism in Thailand" (PhD dissertation, Fuller Theological Seminary, 2009). During the process of mentoring

(with Professor Bill Dyrness), I had an opportunity to revisit many experiences and ideas springing from the years that I spent in Thailand in firsthand contact with *Theravada* Buddhism.

2. Among the many divisions in Buddhism in Cambodia, Laos, Myanmar, Sri Lanka, and Thailand , the two main ones (besides with *Vajrayana, Zen,* and Pure Land) are *Theravada* and *Mahayana.* About 95 percent of Thais consider themselves Buddhists, and the remaining minorities consists of Muslims (by far the largest one) and Christians (as well Hindus, mainly immigrants from India). For a succinct introduction to Thai Buddhism, see, e.g., Karuna Kusalasaya, *Buddhism in Thailand: Its Past and Its Present* (Bangkok: Mental Health Publishing House, 2001).

3. *Dhammacakkappavattana Sutta* 11 (*Samyutta Nikāya* 56.11, in *Access to Insight* [ATI], http://www.accesstoinsight.org/tipitaka/index.html); I also add the standard Pali Text Society [PTS] reference: S v 420. I have replaced the English translation "suffering" (in other renderings "pain" or "stress" or similar) with *dukkha.*

4. Similarly to the notion of *dukkha,* the term *tanhā* ("craving" or "desire") used by Buddha is a multifaceted concept. It is customary to divide it into three meanings: craving for sensual pleasures, craving for existence, and craving for non-existence (which means the longing to avoid unpleasant conditions or situations such as when a person does not want to grow old).

5. See *Paticca-samuppada-vibhanga Sutta: Analysis of Dependent Co-arising* (*Samuyttanikāya Nikaya* 12.2, ATI; PTS: S ii 2) for the famous analysis of Gautama concerning the idea of "Dependent Origination" which names ignorance as the genesis of the cycle of actions and dispositions which ultimately lead to suffering, and identifies "complete abandoning of ignorance" as the way out of it.

6. *Kamma* ("the law of reaping and sowing") has two sides in the Buddhist analysis: on the one hand the "bad" *kamma* which consists of "unskillful" actions and attitudes such as greed or hatred, and on the other hand the "good" *kamma* which consists of "skillful" actions and attitudes such as non-greed, non-hatred, and non-delusion. Good *kamma* produces good while bad *kamma* bad effects and results. Ven. Phra Dammapitaka (P.A. Payutto), *Dictionary of Buddhism* (Bangkok: Mahachulalong-kornrajavidyala University, 2003), 60.

7. Saeng Chandngarm, *Arriyasatsee [The Four Noble Truths]* (Bangkok: Sangsan Books, 2001), 9-14. According to this leading Thai Buddhist scholar, even other cardinal beliefs such as Dependent Origination and Threefold Training (in morality, mentality, and wisdom) are dependent on the core (pp. 39-40).

8. I am well aware of the fact that current anthropological discourse doesn't endorse the use of the term "animism." Yet, I can hardly find a more suitable term to describe the religious phenomenology of, say, Thailand. It is of course one of the great ironies of the folk religious transformation that all living faiths, not excluding parts of Christianity, tend to shift focus on "animistic" practices, rituals, and rites. This orientation is all the more astonishing with regard to *Theravada,* a form of Buddhism, the most "orthodox" and most non-theistic doctrinally!

9. Boonyakiat, "A Christian Theology of Suffering in the Context of Theravada Buddhism," 3.

10. Walpola Rahula, *What the Buddha Taught: Revised and Expanded Edition with Texts from* Suttas *and* Dhammapada, 2nd ed. (New York: Grove Press, 1974), 16n2.

11. Here there is an interesting parallel between *dukkha* and the idea of "vanity" in Ecclesiastes. It would be an interesting line of investigation to pursue that comparison. For starters, see Daniel F. Polish, "The Buddha as a Lens for Reading *Koheleth*/Ecclesiastes," *Journal of Ecumenical Studies* 43:3 (2008): 370-82.

12. See further, Rahula, *What the Buddha Taught*, ch. 2.

13. See, e.g., *Anana Sutta: Debtless* (*Anguttara Nikāya* 4.62, ATI; PTS: A ii 69).

14. See further, *Samyutta Nikāya* 22.59, ATI (PTS S iii 66).

15. Venerable Phra Dhammapitaka (P.A. Payutto), *Tri-Luk* (*Three Characteristics of Existence*) (Bangkok: Buddhadhamma Foundation, 2004), 23-24.

16. An insightful illustration of these two types of suffering is the following: built-in suffering is like a family member whereas the miscellaneous suffering is like a visiting guest; Pin Muthukan, *Buddha-Sart* (Buddhalogy), vol. 2 (Bangkok: Mahamakut Buddhist University Press, 1992), 16-17.

17. See also the helpful and clear exposition of *dukkha* in Paul O. Ingram [Christian] and David Loy [Buddhist], "The Self and Suffering: A Buddhist-Christian Conversation," *Dialog: A Journal of Theology* 44:1 (2005): 99-100.

18. Boonyakiat, "A Christian Theology of Suffering in the Context of Theravada Buddhism," 70.

19. Ibid., 77.

20. Ibid., 3-4. Well-known in Buddhist tradition is Gautama's refusal to tackle the metaphysical questions of the ultimate origins of evil; instead, the Buddha wanted to turn attention to the "practical" task of dealing with suffering in order to be released from it. For the classic story of the man wounded with an arrow thickly smeared with poison which makes this point, see *Cula-Malunkyovada Sutta: The Shorter Instructions to Malunkya* (*Majjhima Nikāya* 63, ATI; PTS: M i 426).

21. Jay McDaniel makes the important observation that even though it is often assumed "that the appropriate aim of dialogue is an identification of similar concerns..., contrary to expectations talk between Buddhists and Christians may also lead in different directions." In other words, what each religion means with the alleged shared concern or theme may not be the same. Jay McDaniel, "The God of the Oppressed and the God Who is Empty," *Journal of Ecumenical Studies* 22:4 (1985): 689. Whereas in contemporary interfaith encounters there is often a felt need to both minimize the differences and also highlight the alleged convergences between religions—in order to boost the dialogue— some informed observers make the healthy remark that an honest acknowledgment of the differences may be the key to a fruitful exchange. Malcom David Eckel speaks of the encounter of the world's religions in terms of "the maxim that opposites attract" and remarks that "nowhere does this simple truism seem more readily confirmed than in the encounter between Buddhism and Christianity.... In some ways it is hard to imagine two more unlikely candidates for the deep sense of communication and communion conveyed by the term 'dialogue'"; Malcolm David Eckel, "Perspectives on the Buddhist-Christian Dialogue," in Donald S. Lopez Jr. and Steven C. Rockefeller, eds., *The Christ and the Boddhisattava* (Albany: State University of New York Press, 1987), 43.

22. As said, this presentation does not give an opportunity to even begin to tackle the profound and utterly complicated theological questions about the origins of suffering, such as what exactly is the relation of suffering (and which kinds of suffering) to the Fall and sin; whether life before the Fall was "perfect" in the sense that suffering at least in the negative sense was not yet there (as traditional theology has tended to believe); whether there is any kind of Christian answer to the question of the ultimate origins of suffering (say, in relation to the tragic events in the angelic world as traditional theologies have speculated), and so forth.

23. This is not necessarily a statement in support of Augustine's traditional view of evil as the *privatio boni* (privation of goodness) but rather a more general statement based on creation theology.

24. Including the important contributions by Jewish scholarship such as the groundbreaking work of Abraham Heschel on the prophets.

25. See further, Veli-Matti Kärkkäinen, "'Evil, Love and the Left Hand of God': The Contribution of Luther's Theology of the Cross to Evangelical Theology of Evil," *Evangelical Quarterly* 79:4 (2002): 215-34.

26. Again, the whole question of what is the appropriate and theologically consistent way of speaking of a suffering God or God in suffering will not be tackled here.

27. Jürgen Moltmann, *The Trinity and the Kingdom: The Doctrine of God*, trans. Margaret Kohl (San Francisco: Harper & Row, and London: SCM Press, 1981), 22-25.

28. Again, in the words of Moltmann: "A God who cannot suffer is poorer than any man. For a God who is incapable of suffering is a being who cannot be involved. Suffering and injustice do not affect him. . . . But the one who cannot suffer cannot love either. So he is also a loveless being"; Moltmann, *The Crucified God: The Cross of Christ as the Foundation and Criticism of Christian Theology*, trans. Margaret Kohl (London: SCM Press, 1974), 222.

29. Moltmann, *Trinity and the Kingdom*, 23.

30. Another heavy-weight theological debate would engage questions such as what happened on the cross in terms of its salvific effects (so-called atonement theories) and in what ways the cross is related to the whole history of Jesus Christ.

31. See the helpful discussion in Ingram and Loy, "The Self and Suffering," 100-102.

32. "[T]here are, in fact, forms of suffering which belong, in God's intention, to the human condition. Not all of what we experience as suffering is totally absurd, a mistake, an oversight, or the consequence of sin. There is something about a significant portion of suffering through which we pass that belongs to the very foundations of beings— something without which our human being would not and could not be what is meant to be." Douglas John Hall and Wendy Farley, *God and Human Suffering: An Exercise in the Theology of the Cross* (Minneapolis: Augsburg, 1986), 57. This said, one should be very careful of not sanctioning suffering in a way that would thwart attempts to help deliver people from it. An insightful Pentecostal-Charismatic discussion of mistaken notions of suffering (particularly with regard to illness and healing) is Ken Blue, *Authority to Heal* (Downers Grove: InterVarsity Press, 1987), chs. 1 and 2 particularly.

33. Veli-Matti Kärkkäinen, "Theology of the Cross: A Stumbling Block to Pentecostal-Charismatic Spirituality," in Wonsuk Ma and Robert P. Menzies, eds., *The Spirit and Spirituality: Essays in Honour of Russell P. Spittler* (London and New York: T & T Clark International, 2004), 150.

34. It is illustrative of this tendency that neither the recent major missiological treatise on Pentecostalism (Allan Anderson, *Spreading Fires: The Missionary Nature of Early Pentecostalism* [Maryknoll: Orbis Books, 2007]) nor the most important Pentecostal systematic theological presentation (Amos Yong, *The Spirit Poured Out on All Flesh: Pentecostalism and the Possibility of Global Theology* [Grand Rapids: Baker Academic, 2005]) have the term "suffering" in their index or any discussion of the theme.

35. See n33.

36. See Gabriel Reuben Louis, "Response to Dr. Wonsuk Ma's 'Toward an Asian Pentecostal Theology'," *Cyberjournal for Pentecostal-Charismatic Research* 4 (1998) [http://www.pctii.org/cyberj/cyberj4/louis.html]; and Wonsuk Ma, "Toward an Asian Pentecostal Theology," *Cyberjournal for Pentecostal-Charismatic Research* 1 (1997) [http://www.pctii.org/cyberj/cyberj1/wonsuk.html].

37. Louis, "Response to Dr. Wonsuk Ma," n.p.

38. See. e.g., J. Kwabena Asamoah-Gyadu, *African Charismatics: Current Developments within Independent Indigenous Pentecostalism in Ghana* (Leiden: Brill, 2006), 218, 228-32, and Paul Gifford, *Ghana's New Christianity: Pentecostalism in a Globalizing African Economy* (Bloomington and Indianapolis: Indiana University Press, 2004), 50. For an important discussion, see also Richard Burgess, "Nigerian Pentecostal Theology in Global Perspective," *PentecoStudies* 7:2 (2008): 29-63, available online at: http://www.glopent.net/pentecostudies/2008-vol-7/no-2-autumn/burgess-2008.

39. William W. Menzies, "Reflections on Suffering: A Pentecostal Perspective," in Wonsuk Ma and Robert P. Menzies, eds., *The Spirit and Spirituality: Essays in Honour of Russell P. Spittler* (London and New York: T & T Clark International, 2004), 141-49, at 141. See also the important essay by the British Pentecostal biblical scholar who has written extensively on healing, Keith Warrington, "Healing and Suffering in the Bible," *International Review of Mission* 95:376/377 (2006): 154-64.

40. Martin William Mittelstadt, *The Spirit and Suffering in Luke-Acts: Implications for a Pentecostal Pneumatology*, Journal of Pentecostal Theology Supplement Series 26 (London and New York: T & T Clark International, 2004).

41. Samuel Solivan, *The Spirit, Pathos and Liberation: Toward an Hispanic Pentecostal Theology*, Journal of Pentecostal Theology Supplement Series 14 (Sheffield: Sheffield Academic Press, 1998).

42. Isaiah Majo Dau, *Suffering and God: A Theological Reflection on the War in Sudan* (Nairobi: Paulines Publications Africa, 2003).

43. Boonyakiat, "A Christian Theology of Suffering in the Context of Theravada Buddhism," 77-78.

44. In order to understand properly the "necessary" nature of suffering in the Buddhist vision, one must keep in mind the fact that whereas "other religions might ask why there is suffering—as though it should not be there ... the Buddhist simply acknowledges the fact that there is suffering"; indeed, even "karma and samsara do not explain suffering; they are suffering." Whalen W. Lai, "Tillich on Death and Suffering: A Key to Buddho-Christian Dialogue," *Journal of Ecumenical Studies* 28:4 (1991): 574.

45. This is not to argue against the existence of some kind of suffering from the beginning of creation such as loneliness, limitations, temptation, and anxiety as do Hall and Farley (*God and Human Suffering*, ch. 1). Even those kinds of potential for suffering are not ontologically primary in the Buddhist sense. See also the important work by Wendy Farley, *Tragic Vision and Divine Compassion: A Contemporary Theodicy* (Louisville: Westminster John Knox, 1990).

46. Boonyakiat, "A Christian Theology of Suffering in the Context of Theravada Buddhism," ch. 3. See the helpful comparison between Buddhist and Christian notions in Rahula, *What the Buddha Taught*, 32.

47. It is of course true that the Christian idea of reaping and sowing also has next-life implications in terms of choices and actions done in this life having consequences for the afterlife. Yet the radical difference is that in the Christian vision, one only has this one life to make choices and that, according to the Bible, the reaping begins already in this life.

48. Boonyakiat, "A Christian Theology of Suffering in the Context of Theravada Buddhism," 127-28, issues a call for his fellow Thai Christians to see clearly the importance of this point.

49. Ibid., 114.

50. In *Mahayana* Buddhism, the *Boddhisattva*—differently from the *Theravada Arahat* (*ariya-puggala*)—is willing to postpone his own entrance into the *nibbana* to help others reach the goal. Even that, however, is not the function of a "savior" but rather of a

"good neighbor," even when the Boddhisattava may grant his own merit to help the other. Only in Pure Land Buddhism is there a notion of "mercy" and perhaps "salvation" somewhat similar to that in Christianity. For differences between *Mahayana* and *Theravada* in this respect, see John R. Davis, *Poles Apart: Contextualizing the Gospel in Asia* (Bangalore: Theological Book Trust, 1998), 98-104.

51. Boonyakiat, "A Christian Theology of Suffering in the Context of Theravāda Buddhism," 115. Calling Buddhism "atheistic" is not to say that in Buddhism there is no place for divine beings and gods. Yes, there is—even in its original form. The Buddhist worldview locates angels, divinities, divine beings on top of the hierarchy of reality, and Gautama himself—as any of his followers—knew of divine beings; the point in calling Buddhism atheistic is the marginal, in some sense, "counterproductive," role of gods and divinities. Turning to gods in the Buddhist vision means turning away from one's own responsibility to redeem one's self from the predicament of *dukkha*.

52. The Middle Way or The Noble Eightfold Path consists of "right" understanding, thought, speech, action, livelihood, effort, mindfulness, and meditation. This is not a sequence but rather they are simultaneous acts. The various aspects are all interrelated and mutually supportive. For a brief, accurate description, see Rahula, *What the Buddha Taught*, ch. 5.

53. I acknowledge the fact that the term *orthodoxy* is only partially fitting to describe the Buddhist vision based on knowledge and understanding. In its commonsense Christian usage, orthodoxy is of course that: right knowledge and grasping of basic teachings of religion. In its etymology, however, the term of course means something like "right glory," in other words "right worship." While that aspect is foreign to Buddhism (except for the everyday "animistic" form), it accurately describes the ancient Christian vision in which the knowledge of God is both a function of and the result of right prayer and worship as much as a rational act.

54. I have intentionally left out of the consideration the ultimate state of the Buddhist vision of "salvation," namely *nibbana* (*nirvana*), in order to make the discussion more manageable. A reliable, helpful Buddhist reflection can be found in Abe Masao, "Suffering in the Light of Our Time, Our Time in the Light of Suffering," *Eastern Buddhist* 27:2 (1994): 1-13.

55. For this Latino theologian, the term *orthopathos* is the third "leg" of the theological "table" alongside *orthodoxy*, right belief and [*ortho*]*praxis*, proper action or ethics. Building solely on orthodoxy has often led to Christian passivity about the issues of oppression and injustice, whereas focusing on praxis alone "as a critical reflection on action ... remains distant from the very persons it seeks to serve or represent." Consequently, *orthopathos* then positively means, "the type of critical, theological and personal first-hand engagement with the biblical, theological and social reality of suffering and marginalized communities" (Solivan, *The Spirit, Pathos, and Liberation*, 11).

56. That my list here does not include more intentionally the kind of socio-political aspects typical of Liberation theologies is not because I don't consider them important. I just want to keep this discussion more focused and limited.

57. Solivan, *The Spirit, Pathos, and Liberation*, ch. 2

58. A formative work with which Solivan also dialogues widely is that of the Jewish scholar Abraham J. Heschel, *The Prophets* (New York: Harper & Row, 1962).

59. Mittelstadt, *The Spirit and Suffering*, vii. The "Pentecostal neglect" included the standard works on Lucan pneumatology by R. Stronstadt, H. Ervin, J. Shelton, and R. Menzies (Mittelstadt, *The Spirit and Suffering*, 20-28).

60. See further Judith Simmer-Brown, "A Buddhist Response to the Gospel of Luke," *Buddhist-Christian Studies* 16 (1996): 107-09 particularly.

61. One of my students at Fuller Seminary (School of Intercultural Studies), an American missionary to Thailand, recently finished a groundbreaking PhD dissertation on the themes of " face and shame" in Thai culture and its religious, theological, and sociological implications. Part of that discussion is a multidisciplinary theological reflection on how to best speak of atonement in an Asian culture not plagued with the consciousness of guilt and condemnation (as in post-Reformation cultures of the Global North) but rather with shame and the avoidance of not "losing one's face" as the all-embracing cultural norm and motif. For a brief discussion (in anticipation of a published monograph), see Chris Flanders, "Face" and "Shame," in William Dyrness and Veli-Matti Kärkkäinen, eds., *Global Dictionary of Theology* (Downers Grove: InterVarsity Press, 2008), 308-11 and 813-17 respectively.

62. Pope John Paul II, "Letter on the Meaning of Christian Suffering" (http://www.vatican.va/holy_father/john_paul_ii/apost_letters/documents/hf_jp-ii_apl_11021984_salvifici-doloris_en.html), §1. See also the thoughtful reflections on Christian and Buddhist views of suffering and its meaning in Thomas Ryan, "Gethsemani II: Catholic and Buddhist Monastics Focus on Suffering," *Buddhist-Christian Studies* 24 (2004): 249-51.

63. Pope John Paul II, "Letter," §3.

64. Ibid., §23, among others.

65. In a most helpful and theologically grounded analysis of forms of suffering, Dau distinguishes the following types of sufferings which he sees presented in the biblical narrative: suffering as a consequence of sin, suffering as a corrective and disciplinary measure, suffering as a test of faith or faithfulness, suffering as a direct result of being followers of Christ, and innocent suffering (Dau, *Suffering and God*, ch. 5).

66. Dau, *Suffering and God*, 59-61. He says that was not always the case. Indeed, in the past suffering people not only did not look at the church as the community for suffering people but rather as something different and foreign. Nowadays, happily enough, "the church . . . has become the centre for social solidarity, ritual and healing" (*Suffering and God*, 60).

67. Mittelstadt, *The Spirit and Suffering*, vii.

68. Ibid., 8.

69. Dau, *Suffering and God*, 185-90.

70. Boonyakiat, "A Christian Theology of Suffering in the Context of Theravāda Buddhism," 92. The concept of "integrative suffering" is from Hall and Farley, *God and Human Suffering*, 54-62.

71. Boonyakiat, "A Christian Theology of Suffering in the Context of Theravada Buddhism," 101.

72. David Yonggi Cho, *When I am Weak, Then I Am Strong: A Sermon Series*, vol. 3 (Seoul: Logos Company, 2003), 72.

73. Ibid., 72.

74. V.-M. Kärkkäinen, "March Forward to Hope: Yonggi Cho's Pentecostal Theology of Hope," *PNEUMA: The Journal of the Society for Pentecostal Studies* 28:2 (2006): 258.

75. This general principle holds even when one takes into consideration the Buddhist tradition of the extraordinary compassion of Gautama towards not only all sentient beings but also all other beings, and of the fact that in *Mahayana* history, Gautama is known not only as the teacher of wisdom but also as a magical healer and miracle worker, including passing through walls, flying, and walking on water. The

Mahayana tradition also knows of self-sacrificial acts of healing and alleviation of other people's pain such as the story of Vimalakīrti. A virtuous *Boddhisattava*, he made himself sick and in the presence of Sākyamuni (Gautama) and his disciples explained that the reason why there is sickness is because of ignorance and thirst for existence. In order to help fellow men and women realize this, he tied his own healing to the healing of the others. See *Vimalakīrti Nirdeśa Sutra* 5.6-7 (trans., Robert A. F. Thurman, copyright 1976, The Pennsylvania State University; http://www2.kenyon.edu/Depts/Religion/Fac/Adler/ Reln260/Vimalakirti.htm (accessed October 12, 2009).

76. Again, I am informed enough of the complicated and complex state of affairs in the Buddhist capacity—or lack thereof—to respond to social concern both generally and in terms of the *Theravada* tradition. Any informed observer knows that while Western, particularly American-based (*Mahayana*) Buddhism, is anxious to highlight the capacity of that religion to elicit a proper response to social needs, it also is the case that in most *Theravada* lands (and in many *Mahayana* regions) there simply is not much record of acts of "redemptive suffering." Many personal conversations with (Thai *Theravada*) Buddhists, including monks and other informed mentors, have simply strengthened in my mind the conviction that in the mainline, that religious tradition is by and large focused on one's own capacities to facilitate liberation. (Ironically, a few blocks from my house in Temple City—a predominantly Asian populated area of the greater Los Angeles area—there is the headquarters of a non-profit [*Mahayana*] Buddhist organization of social concern!)

77. Menzies, "Reflections on Suffering," 149.

Chapter 5

Theologies of Religious Pluralism: Pneumatological Foundations and Conversion in India

Kirsteen Kim

In late summer 2008, news began to filter out of India about the widespread violence against Christians in the state of Orissa. According to Christian Solidarity Worldwide, between August and October 2008, religiously motivated violence spread across fourteen districts of Orissa and led to widespread devastation.[1] 315 villages were affected, 4,640 Christian houses were burnt, 54,000 Christians were left homeless, there were seventy deaths and another fifty people were missing and presumed dead (of the dead, six were Protestant pastors and one a Catholic priest), 18,000 Christians were injured, two women (including a nun) were gang-raped, at least 149 churches were destroyed, and thirteen Christian schools and colleges were damaged.[2] Chris Morris, who reported the story for the BBC, described an "anti-Christian pogrom" sparked by the murder of a Hindu leader which was blamed on Christians.[3] Most of the violence took place in the district of Kandhamal where desecrated churches were seen with the saffron flags of the nationalists flying over them, and reporters witnessed the burning of Bibles and forced conversions to Hinduism.[4]

However, although most Christian reports focused simply on the explicitly religious Hindu violence against Christians, the anti-Christian feeling in Kandhamal is not without social reasons. The explicitly religious rioting was preceded by serious communal clashes during Christmas 2007.[5] Kandhamal is targeted by Maoist (Naxalite) insurgents who are a threat to the social fabric and especially to its traditional leaders, high caste Hindus. The majority of the Kandha (Kond) are *Adivasis* or tribal people, and the rest are Pana, otherwise known as *Dalits* or outcastes, who have turned in large numbers to Christianity in recent years. The violence was sparked by the assassination of a Hindu religious and nationalist leader who had been campaigning against conversion. Hindu nationalists put the blame on Christians. In fact, Maoists later claimed responsibility but since the nationalists see the Christians in league with Maoists, this makes little practical difference. Liberation theologians in particular share in common with the Maoists the concern for, and language of, socio-economic liberation. Another important factor is that the Pana have prospered as Christians, and the Hindu nationalists have fueled the suspicion that Christian missionaries, backed by foreign funds, have exploited the illiteracy and poverty of the Pana to induce them to convert. Roman Catholic and Baptist missionaries have worked in the region for many years but more recently neo-Pentecostal groups have entered, and have been accused of exacerbating the situation by using more aggressive tactics. The tribal Kandhas, who like the Panas until recently followed their own local religion, have come under the influence of the Hindu activists, who are also funded by foreign funds from non-resident Indians, and have largely embraced their intolerant Hinduism. They feel exploited by the Panas who hold more economic and political power.

Since Swami Vivekananda spoke at the World's Parliament of Religions in 1893,[6] Hinduism has been regarded in the West as a tolerant religion, and India as a success story of inter-religious harmony. India has been the main laboratory for the development of theologies of religious pluralism and the practice of inter-faith dialogue. The truth, however, is far more complex. Theologies of dialogue have been developed in the face of aggressive forms of Hinduism which have been growing in India since independence, and which attempt to block conversion of Hindus to other religions. In the interests of peace between religions, theologies of pluralism emphasize the wider work of the Spirit among people of all religions. In so doing they down-play, even call into question, the Great Commission, the specific association of the Holy Spirit with the Spirit of Christ, and the call for conversion. Yet most Indian Christians are converts, or descendents of converts, who thus find their Christian identity undermined by their fellow Christians. Most are *Dalits*, whose forebears turned away from Hinduism in hope of freedom from their outcaste status. They experience the Holy Spirit not as uniting them with Hindus but as bringing liberation from caste oppression; and their leaders reject dialogue with Brahminical Hindus. This paper will introduce the controversy about conversion in India and examine the pneumatological foundations of Indian theologies of religious pluralism, and of *Dalit* spirituality, in search of a mission theology of the Holy Spirit which both affirms religious plurality and is also obedient to the Great Commission.

The Great Commission, Indian Christianity, and the Question of Conversion

For many, the Great Commission, especially in its Matthean version,[7] is understood to mean the explicit conversion of "non-Christians to the Christian faith." Often this religious agenda has been co-opted as part of political programs of imperial expansion or used to further economic globalization. As such, and even for purely religious reasons, Christian conversion campaigns are often perceived as threatening to those of other faiths and militate against harmonious relations between faith communities. The question of conversion lies at the heart of interreligious relations, especially in the context of democracy where political power is awarded to the group with the largest numbers of people. Nowhere is conversion from one religion to another more controversial than in India.

The British rulers of India defined each person as a member of a particular religious community—Hindu, Muslim, Christian, Sikh, Buddhist, Jain, etc.—and allowed these communities to have different "personal laws" or legal systems concerning matters such as marriage and inheritance. This system continued after independence in 1947. Changing religion in India therefore is not a personal matter but implies leaving one's birth community and joining another. Since the colonial period, when there were mass conversions to Christianity among lower caste groups and *Dalits* (formerly known as outcastes or untouchables), Hindus have felt threatened by Christian evangelism. They perceive it to be backed by Western power and funds and to unfairly target vulnerable members of the society. Such feelings have fueled the growth of *Hindutva*, a form Hindu nationalism, the premise of which is that to be Indian is to be Hindu.[8]

Conversions out of Hinduism have provoked furious debate and even violence in India's recent history. Sebastian C. H. Kim relates a series of occasions since independence in 1947 in which the topic of conversion has come to the fore in public debate, one of which is the passing of the first "Freedom of Religion" bills.[9] These are commonly referred to as "anti-conversion bills" because they are promoted by some leaders of the majority Hindu community to prevent conversions to other religions, particularly Christianity, which might be "by the use of force or inducement or by fraudulent means."[10] Those who promote "Freedom of Religion" bills argue that Hindu freedom to practice their traditional religion is under attack by Christian calls for conversion, which they suggest have ulterior motives of extending Christian or Western power and undermining Hindu society.[11] Their understanding of "freedom of religion" is not—as it is for the Christian community—the freedom to propagate the faith but freedom for the masses to practice Hinduism without aggressive proselytizing by other faiths.[12]

The violence in 2008 in the state of Orissa was among the most serious incidents to date. Perhaps it is not coincidental that it was in Orissa that the first "Freedom of religion" bill was passed in 1967. The law states that "Conversion in its very process involves an act of undermining another faith. The process becomes all the more objectionable when this is brought about by recourse to methods like force, fraud, material inducement and exploitation of one's poverty, simplicity and ignorance."[13] It was followed by the passing of a similar bill in Madhya Pradesh the following year. Another anti-conversion law was passed in Arunachal Pradesh in 1978. The movement to ban conversion has accelerated especially since 2002. Currently seven states have similar legislation in place.[14] Apart from prohibiting conversions for any ulterior motive, each law also imposes legal formalities, which are expensive, for converts and for those conducting "ceremonies" for conversion.[15] Christian Solidarity Worldwide identifies several concerns about the legislation: (1) far from reducing inter-religious tension, "Freedom of religion" bills more often act as a pretext for attacks on Christians; (2) they place insurmountable obstacles in the way of an individual's "freedom to change his religion or belief" which is defined as a human right; (3) they place limits on a wide variety of legitimate religious activities because they may be construed as attempts to convert; (4) the laws do not apply equally to all religions but favor Hinduism; (5) what is called "re-conversion" to Hinduism is not included in the legislation (on the grounds that all Indians are originally Hindus); (6) the penal provisions are disproportionately harsh, especially if *Dalits* and tribal peoples are converted, the prevention of which seems to be their main aim. The bills are promoted mainly by the Hindu nationalist BJP political party and seem to be directed at keeping the poor and socially disadvantaged—especially *Dalits*—within the fold of the system of caste; that is, within the very system which disadvantages them.[16]

Each situation is complex and the Orissa case is an extreme one, but Christians in independent India have felt vulnerable to Hindu nationalism and to accusations that they are the result of conversions associated with colonialist or neo-colonialist designs on India. It is in the context of this powerful myth, and their minority status, that Indian Christians today must witness, interpret the Great Commission, and develop their theology of religious pluralism.

The Universal Spirit: Theologies of Religious Pluralism

It is largely in India, or with an Indian multireligious model in mind, that the practice of interfaith dialogue has been developed, and it is reflection on Indian realities particularly which has stimulated theologies of religious pluralism. Interfaith dialogue was promoted by the World Council of Churches under the leadership of South Indian Methodist theologian Stanley J. Samartha, who was appointed to lead the unit on dialogue in 1971. The World Council of Churches' *Guidelines for Dialogue* (1979), drafted by Samartha and reworked at various levels in the Council, clearly had the Indian situation in mind. They set the need for dialogue in the context of the contribution of the Christian community to the wider multireligious community, of power relations, and of disruption of communities by religious tensions.[17] In the context of the World Council of

Churches, theology of dialogue became for many conceptually a natural extension of ecumenism between churches to a "wider ecumenism" of religions.

Samartha's dialogical approach was opposed by some prominent mission leaders, mostly Western evangelicals, supported by the Barthian theology applied to mission by the Dutch missiologist Hendrik Kraemer, which emphasized the discontinuity between Christianity and the negatively defined "non-Christian religions," and stressed the need for conversion.[18] Samartha saw such "exclusivism" as a remnant of colonialism, which was unjust and untenable in the post-colonial era.[19] And he regarded the proselytism to which it led as de-stabilizing of society.[20] Due to the tension between the two groups in the World Council of Churches, dialogue was developed separately from mission "in order to explore … ways [other than explicit confession of Christ] of making plain the intentions of Christian witness and service."[21] *Guidelines for Dialogue* is primarily a practical handbook but it hints at a theological foundation that "God… is the creator of all things and of all humankind" and gives life to all, and at the significance of the Triune unity of God for inter-religious harmony.[22] The document suggests that dialogue is possible because Christ's work is mediated to the world through the wider work of the Spirit.[23] Samartha himself made the pneumatological foundation for dialogue explicit in his work, as have some other theologians of dialogue such as the Roman Catholics Paul Knitter and Jacques Dupuis.[24] In this section we will outline Samartha's pneumatology of dialogue, which was foundational to what was established in the late twentieth century as the ecumenical approach to inter-religious relations.

Samartha began his research with a study of what he called "the unbound Christ," whom he believed was discernible in the attitudes and actions of "our neighbors of other faiths." This led him to posit that the boundaries of the Christian church extended to include an "unbaptised *koinonia*" of Christ-like people in other religions. In the face of the danger of "communalism" (or sectarianism), Samartha urged integration between the different communities of India and encouraged Christians to participate in local affairs and national life so that there was "traffic across the boundaries" between Hindu, Muslim, Christian and other communities. As Paul Knitter later pointed out, Samartha's thought gradually changed its focus from "the unbound Christ" to the wider movement of the Holy Spirit.[25] Samartha found no clear statement in Scripture regarding the relationship between the Holy Spirit and people of other faiths[26] but two verses from John's Gospel became especially significant for his view that the essence of the Spirit is "boundless freedom"[27]: John 3:8, "The wind blows where it chooses, and you hear the sound of it, but you do not know where it comes from or where it goes. So it is with everyone who is born of the Spirit," and John 16:13, "When the Spirit of truth comes, he will guide you into all the truth; for he will not speak on his own, but will speak whatever he hears, and he will declare to you the things that are to come." These he used to justify his view that the Holy Spirit cannot be confined to the Christian church but is present in and among all the communities of India. His exegesis of John 16:13 was directly challenged by Lesslie Newbigin,[28] who emphasized the distinctive and counter-cultural nature of the Christian community, and therefore the need for conversion, in his mission in India, and later back in the UK. Samartha was confident that "truth" in John 16:13 includes the truth of other religions,[29] whereas Newbigin argued the opposite because "the Holy Spirit does not lead past, or beyond, or away from Jesus."[30] Samartha regarded his own position as "inclusive" and therefore positive for communal relations, and regarded Newbigin's as "exclusive" and harmful to communal harmony.

Theologically, Samartha supported his understanding that the Holy Spirit may be present where Christ is not explicitly named in two main ways. First, he drew on the "Spiritual Presence" theology of his mentor Paul Tillich and associated the Spirit with life, truth, and creativity. He used this to challenge the salvation-historical approach of Karl Barth which he sees as limiting the work of the Spirit to Israel and then the church. He regarded Barth's views, mediated to missiology by Hendrik Kraemer, as claiming the Spirit exclusively for a particular brand of Evangelical Christianity.[31] He questioned whether Barth's approach is tenable or relevant in religiously plural societies and accused him of "imprisoning" the Spirit "within the steel and concrete structures of Western dogma and a permanent Atlantic Charter."[32] Second, he turned to the Orthodox theological tradition which stresses the procession of the Holy Spirit from the Father, rather than from Jesus Christ, because he feared that, unless God is understood to deal directly (by the action of his Holy Spirit in history) with all people, "the heritage of people other than the Western Judaeo-Christian" becomes "subservient to the mainstream of salvation history."[33] Samartha drew on the Orthodox theology of George Khodr, who so emphasized the distinctive personhood of Word and Spirit that he surmised there was a certain "hypostatic independence" between them. He saw the Spirit and Christ were two distinct missions (or sendings) of God which did not always overlap. It was possible for these "two hands of the Father" not always to be involved in what the other was doing.[34]

There are parallels between the non-dualist philosophy of Hinduism, known as *advaita*, and the concept of the Spirit in Christian theology, as has already been pointed out. This is true of John's Gospel, particularly, where the Spirit is portrayed as the one who brings about the unity of Father and Son and the oneness of the believers in Christ. So Samartha described the Spirit as the *advaita*, the Spirit of oneness.[35] Without identifying the two, he finds in the "unitive vision" of *advaita* the same qualities conducive to dialogue and harmonious living which he found in the Holy Spirit.[36] For Samartha, the Spirit, or *advaita*, is the Spirit of dialogue, which creates the openness to cross over to the shore of another's experience that is necessary for interfaith understanding. Wherever this attitude is to be found, he suggested, the Spirit is at work. In this way, Samartha attempted to establish dialogue on a pneumatological foundation both for Hindus and for Christians. However, in reaching out to Hindus in this way, Samartha alienated the mass of Indian Christians, and particularly *Dalits*, who experienced the unifying power of Hinduism as oppression.

The Encounter of Spirits:
Dalit Spirituality, Indian Pentecostalism, and Other Religions

The "freedom of religion" bills targeted particularly the Indian communities known as *Dalits*. The communities of India are traditionally described in terms of caste, a highly complex and continually evolving system of inherited social status.[37] Conceptually outside this system, but defined by it, are the "outcastes" or "untouchables," who were—and often still are—treated in a sub-human way because they were traditionally regarded as polluted by birth and defiled by occupations such as sweeping, tanning leather, and carrying night soil. "*Dalit*" is the self-designation of this group, which is not homogeneous but divided into many different communities. Meaning "broken" or "downtrodden," the term recognizes the continuing suffering and humiliation these people undergo daily at the hands of higher castes that they are expected to serve. *Dalits* represent about fifteen percent of the Indian population and are overwhelmingly found in rural areas, where they are usually landless and excluded from access to even the most basic amenities, such as village wells. Economic poverty is not identical with caste status but affects the low and outcastes disproportionately. The constitution of the modern state of India does not recognize caste and provides for positive discrimination on behalf of lower and outcastes in the form of welfare benefits and quotas through a system which is probably unparalleled in any other country. However, the ancient caste system continues to be supported by certain forms of Hinduism, and discrimination on grounds of birth blocks the social mobility of many, even in the thriving economy of contemporary India. Since the 1970s *Dalits* have faced increasing violence from caste Hindus as they have actively campaigned for their human rights.[38] In a similar position outside the caste system are tribal communities—about five to seven percent of the total population. Furthermore, on the grounds that Islam and Christianity, having been introduced into India from elsewhere, are free from caste, *Dalit* converts to these religions are not eligible for the compensatory benefits enjoyed by *Dalits* of other faiths. Contemporary *Dalit* Christians therefore face double discrimination in Indian society. Christian social activists in India have long campaigned on their behalf.

Many *Dalit* communities have attempted to solve the problems of their outcaste status by "Sanskritisation," or becoming Hindus in faith and claiming a position in the caste hierarchy. M. N. Srinivas, who coined the term, described Sanskritisation as an evolutionary process rather than a conversion.[39] *Hindutva* activists actively encourage it, and euphemistically describe it as a "home-coming" (*shuddhi*) to the Hindu fold. Other *Dalits*, partly in protest at caste oppression, have converted to other major religions. The famous *Dalit* leader B. R. Ambedkar, who championed their cause during the nationalist movement and in newly independent India, vowed that he would not die a Hindu and actively sought an alternative religion. He encouraged the idea that the most effective way to protest caste oppression was for *Dalits* to convert to other religions. This is necessary, he argued, both for material gain and for spiritual growth; because only conversion out of Hinduism could bring equality and dignity.[40] Conversion (out of Hinduism) therefore became a political device to press for improvement in social status.[41] Christian missionaries hoped Ambedkar would convert to Christianity, and there were many mass conversions of *Dalit* communities during the colonial period.[42] However finally, in 1956, Ambedkar and a large group of followers opted publically for Buddhism. Buddhism not only repudiates caste but is regarded as an Indian religion because it originated in the subcontinent. It is treated more favorably in law than Islam and Christianity.

Christian churches vary in their attitude to caste. Over their nearly 2000-year history in India, the Syrian Orthodox community has integrated into the caste system, and they believe themselves to be among the higher castes; Syrian churches do not include *Dalits* and there is much resistance to attempts by some to reach out to them. To the anger of many *Dalits* and their supporters, the Roman Catholic Church has accommodated to caste by providing separate cups for different communities at the Eucharist. Protestant churches have made strong statements against caste and draw most of their membership from *Dalit* communities who converted en masse, but in practice local congregations tend to be caste-based. Some church leaders and theologians are from *Dalit* backgrounds but not in proportion to *Dalit* numbers.[43]

As part of the *Dalit* affirmation of their identity and campaigns for human rights, *Dalit* Christians have developed *Dalit* theology.[44] *Dalit* theology draws on the thought of Ambedkar as well as Christian sources. Ambedkar held human dignity at the centre of his thought and ruthlessly exposed the injustices of Indian society, and the way in which it received religious sanction from Hinduism and, to an extent, Christianity. His program to "educate, agitate and organize" has been taken up by *Dalit* theologians who challenge both government and religious leaders and refuse to conform to the expectations of caste.[45] *Dalit* Theology was found to be necessary because what is known as Indian Christian Theology was done by people from higher castes and lacked empathy with *Dalit* Christians.[46] *Dalit* experience was not considered and *Dalits* were not encouraged to do theology.[47] Even liberation theologians were criticized for on the one hand denying the specific *Dalit* identity defined by the caste system under the socio-economic category of "the poor,"[48] and on the other hand heightening caste consciousness to the detriment of *Dalit* freedom.[49] "The real problem of *Dalits* is not caste" but "their right to be human on their native Indian soil."[50] Current *Dalit* activism therefore focuses on the human rights of *Dalits* and the repudiation of caste. Indian Christian theology is accused of continuing the Brahminic or priestly tradition, which affirmed caste, in its efforts to inculturate Christian theology. Theologians uncritically appropriated Hindu myths and symbols which disparaged and insulted *Dalits*, and were used to justify their oppression.[51] Furthermore, *Dalit* theologians complained, Indian Christian theologians were leaders in the ecumenical movement's attempts to build up interfaith relations, without considering questions of justice.[52] Theologians like Stanley Samartha, whose ancestors were caste Hindus, expressed appreciation for aspects of Brahminic spirituality while criticising the majority of Indian Christians for failing to take a dialogical approach to their "neighbours of other faiths." Samartha deplored what he described as the "exclusive" attitudes of the mass of Indian Christians.[53] *Dalit* theologians, who represent people threatened daily by Brahminic Hindus, strongly criticise the dialogue theology of Samartha and others, and refuse to dialogue with Hindus unless and until they explicitly reject the caste system.[54]

Self-conscious *Dalit* Theology has been developed by academic theologians in dialogue with other Third World theologians through the networks of the older churches of the colonial era or before.[55] *Dalit* Theology was initiated in the late 1980s by A. P. Nirmal as a liberation theology *of* the *Dalits* rather than *for* them. Nirmal insisted that no one outside the *Dalit* community could appreciate the depth of suffering of this community except Jesus Christ. Jesus, he argued, was himself a *Dalit*. The evidence for this was that Jesus was of lowly birth, and as the *Dalits* are born to serve the higher castes, Jesus was the servant/slave of all (Mark 10:45; John 13). He was "despised and rejected" (Isa 53:2ff) and, like the *Dalits* who are sweepers, he cleaned the temple (Luke 19:45-48). Nirmal therefore conceived the incarnation as God's identification with suffering humanity and regarded the example of Jesus Christ as affirming *Dalit* identity and dignity. He saw the resurrection as a vindication of suffering, and salvation as participation in the risen Christ's messianic movement, campaigning for *Dalit* human and civil rights.[56]

However, other *Dalit* theologians complain that affirming *Dalits* for their humble servitude, by comparison with Jesus Christ, does not challenge the status quo and even encourages "passive acceptance of their religiously imposed inferiority." In this way, "pathos-based Christology" can lead to "masochistic resignation" and *Dalit* theology does not deal with the problem of the internalization of inferiority and a slave mentality by *Dalits*.[57] Therefore contemporary *Dalit* Theology is not only concerned to reinterpret the Bible in the light of *Dalit* realities but also to take seriously *Dalit* conceptions of God from their own myths and motifs.[58] Previously dismissed as "animism," "idolatry" or "superstition," *Dalit* religion is now a focus of scholarly interest and is gaining acceptability as "indigenous" or "primal" spirituality.[59] Before the encounter with the major religions, modernity, and urban life, *Dalit* religion was a folk or local religion concerned with solving the problems of everyday life by interaction with the spirit-world which they believed surrounded them.[60] Some *Dalit* communities, such as the Satnamis of Chhattisgarh and the Chuhra of Punjab, also maintained and developed their own traditions of gods—often goddesses—and gurus, distinct from the Hindu mainstream. Each *Dalit* group had its own traditions but most groups absorbed aspects of the major religions, generally Hinduism but also Islam where that was dominant. *Dalits*—in Andhra Pradesh for example—were attracted by Hindu reform movements, both *Bhakti* (devotional) movements, which were egalitarian in nature, and neo-Vedantic movements such as the Ramakrishna Mission, which advocated social reform.[61] However they all rejected the Hindu view that their status was caused by their actions in a previous life; they tended to attribute it to a "primordial injustice or subsequent historical change."[62]

In general, *Dalit* religion is not concerned with the transcendent or meta-cosmic but is engaged with cosmic forces and spiritual powers which impinge on the local community. *Dalit* theologians therefore do not share the vision of oneness of advaitic philosophy, which Samartha used to portray Hinduism as inclined toward unity. Theirs is a world of many spirits rather than one universal Spirit. The liberation theological approach of *Dalit* Theology incorporates a "spirituality of combat" which recognizes divided interests and adversarial powers and, like other liberation theologies, engages in spiritual conflict. Even though modern medicine and science removes the traditional fear of demons, the biblical language of exorcism and spiritual conflict can be applied theologically to the economic powers of oppression, political authorities, and social marginalization.[63]

In the post-colonial period, Pentecostal churches are growing rapidly in India, especially South India, against an otherwise downward trend.[64] Many of these are Indian-led, and some were in existence as independence movements during the colonial period when leadership of other churches was still bound up with their founding mission societies.[65] Pentecostalism is being embraced disproportionately by *Dalit* communities, such as the Pana in Orissa, as we saw at the start of this chapter. However, the origins by caste of South Indian Pentecostal churches show little difference to those of the established churches.[66] Although in early Pentecostalism in Kerala, South India from the 1920s, the radical Pentecostal message that God gives gifts impartially led to fellowship across caste boundaries, this has not lasted.[67] In his extensive study of South Indian Pentecostalism, Michael Bergunder shows how the oldest and largest movement, the Indian Pentecostal Church (IPC), like many other Indian churches, is dominated by people of Syrian Christian descent, who regard themselves as high caste, although predominantly *Dalit* in membership. In general *Dalit* leadership in Pentecostal churches is less than twenty percent. Unable in this situation to significantly influence church policy, *Dalits* have founded their own *Dalit*-led Pentecostal churches. These, however are greatly disadvantaged, financially and in terms of contacts, compared to the IPC.[68]

The main reason advanced for the growth of Pentecostalism worldwide is that it engages with beliefs in a world of many spirits, which is the framework for popular forms of religion the world over.[69] As Bergunder has observed in South India, Pentecostals attribute the causes of the misfortune from which they are delivered to evil spirits in much the same way as believers in popular or folk Hinduism do. Popular Christianity has accommodated to these beliefs, rarely taken seriously by European missionaries, and this helps to account for the attraction of Pentecostalism.[70] As Allan Anderson points out, early Pentecostal missionaries had an advantage over many other missionaries in that they "acknowledged all these various forces as real problems to be overcome, and not as ignorant superstitions from which people simply needed enlightenment."[71] At the same time, they also felt a strong alienation from the other religions of India, as most missionaries did, but which was in their case heightened by their background of a marginalized social and religious context in the West.[72] Combined with the Fundamentalist tendencies of their Evangelical theology, this resulted in a very negative appraisal of other religions, a great deal of "religious intolerance and bigoted ignorance,"[73] and a confrontational approach which amounted to perpetual spiritual warfare.[74]

This is not to suggest that spiritual warfare, or worse, fear of the spirit-world, is at the center of the concern of Pentecostal churches. If it is so, then these churches would be dualistic and not properly defined as Christian because the Christian confession is that Jesus Christ has triumphed over the rulers and authorities (Col 2:15) and the Holy Spirit, by definition, is above the cosmic world of the spirits. The heart of Pentecostal spirituality is a celebration of the outpouring of the Holy Spirit and the healing, blessing and gifting which results from that.[75] Pentecostals may utilize Evangelical-Fundamentalist exclusive theologies but theirs is primarily an experiential not a cognitive faith.[76] If this is so then Pentecostals need not necessarily hold an exclusivist theology of religions, and indeed leading Pentecostal and charismatic theologians today have advocated inclusive or dialogical approaches to other faiths.[77]

For practical reasons also, it is difficult for Indian Pentecostals to perpetuate the negative stance toward other faiths common among foreign missionaries. Aggressive evangelism aimed at the Hindu community poses considerable risks for local Christians, and so most evangelists target the Christian community. Antagonizing the dominant Hindu majority is dangerous, as the Orissa situation shows, and in order to survive, Christian communities, especially *Dalit* communities, need majority Hindu support.[78] In the long run, Pentecostals in India, like the other Christian communities, need to find a mode of peaceful co-existence with Hindus. But although leading missiologists in various denominations advocate inculturation or contextualization of the Gospel in order to be faithful to the Great Commission, this can also be counter-productive in India in the context of *Hindutva*. Roman Catholic theologians of inculturation who have attempted to live out their Christian faith in a more Indian way have been criticized by militant Hindus for aping Hinduism. Vandana Mataji, for example, who adopting the saffron robes of a holy person, set up an ashram or Hindu-style religious community, and described Jesus Christ as the Supreme Guru (*Satguru*), was accused of duping people into following Christianity under the guise of Hinduism.[79] Pentecostals who have related their faith constructively to Hindu beliefs have used forms of fulfillment theology, and are similarly susceptible to Hindu criticism. Oneness Pentecostal evangelist Paulaseer Lawrie founded an ashram—a form of Hindu religious community—and drew on the teachings of Hindu scriptures to prove his own divine calling.[80] Sadhu Chellappa styles himself as a Hindu holy man and urges seekers after God to welcome Christian truth that (quoting John 8:32). However, his earlier attempts to convince Hindus that their scriptures pointed to Christ led to violent reaction from militant Hindus.[81] Christians are caught between the Scylla of foreignness and the Charybdis of disingenuousness.

The Holy Spirit in the World:
Religious Plurality and the Great Commission

In this section, I wish to draw several conclusions from the foregoing discussion about fulfilling the Great Commission in the context of religious pluralism.

First, Christians need to beware of the cooption of Christian theology and mission in India by caste interest. On the one hand, the dominance of Hindu thought and the threat to the Christian community of militant forms of Hinduism mean that Indian Christianity is always in danger of losing its distinctiveness and becoming Sanskritized. It is in danger of further oppressing *Dalits* by cooperation with spirit of *Hindutva*. If it loses its prophetic edge and particular message, then Christianity has little to offer India. On the other hand, Christianity is also in danger of cooption by *Dalit* liberation movements, which may seek to use Christianity as a means to communal power and in a violent way which is incompatible with the Spirit of Christ. In particular, some Pentecostal churches, it is clear, have also succumbed to caste discrimination. There is a danger that Pentecostal leaders from a caste background betray the interests of their majority *Dalit* congregations.

Second, the interface between Pentecostalism and popular Hinduism or *Dalit* religion challenges theologies of religions such as Samartha's which deal only with the major world religions.[82] T. Swami Raju argues that such folk religion has great potential for inter-religious relations. He gives the example of the "Vira Cult of Palnad" which he regards as "one of the best examples for dialogue and multi-faith relations from subaltern perspective."[83] The festivals of this and other popular cults, he points out, are inclusive and not clericalized. Indeed it is the *Dalits* who organize and officiate on such occasions. Through festivals, folk religion crosses religious boundaries, while also maintaining the integrity of each cult. Raju therefore regards them as a form of dialogue and a basis for a fresh approach to theology of religions.[84] Pentecostal celebrations in India are similarly able to attract people from a range of religious backgrounds and castes. Pentecostal theologians in India may therefore be in a good position to develop a new theology of religions utilizing this insight.

Third, Pentecostal theology has the potential to develop a theology of religions which embraces religious plurality but steers a course between monistic and dualistic theologies of the Holy Spirit. A pluralist view that assumes all religions are manifestations of the same Spirit is neither true to the Christian gospel nor truly pluralist.[85] In the Indian context it will be seen as an adaptation of non-dualist philosophy (*advaita*), which *Dalit* theologians perceive serves the interests of the dominant castes and encourages the absorption of other communities under the Hindu canopy. *Hindutva* tactics should cause Christians who aggressively claim India for Christ to ask whether Christianity is a mirror image of *Hindutva*, declaring that everyone in India should be Christian. Such an attitude is incompatible with the Spirit of Christ who is given freely and not imposed.

When criticized that his affirmation of *advaita* was tantamount to embracing Hinduism, Samartha was adamant that he was proposing only that

Christians adopt the "unitive vision" of *advaita*, not the Hindu religion itself. Although his theology emphasized unity and oneness, Samartha also developed a theology of discernment. He made it clear that he did not advocate unquestioning cooperation with other faiths or "indiscriminate acceptance" of all new movements as works of the Spirit but "critical engagement" with other perspectives. Samartha's method of discernment, which he pointed out, is a dialogical activity in itself, proceeded by recognizing what he regarded as scriptural "signs" of the Spirit: life, which he associates with creativity; order, which is linked to truth; and community, which has to do with sharing.[86] Theology of discernment presupposes that spiritual reality is not monistic and that it is possible for the Spirit to be absent as well as present.[87] It also requires the development of criteria for discernment of the Spirit. Samartha worked with a generic understanding of the Spirit as life, but for Christians the criteria for discernment must also be Christological.[88] This distinction is crucial since it affirms the distinctive contribution of Christian faith in the context of religious plurality, while also affirming other faiths and their right to discern the spirits by different criteria. In his desire to overcome the barriers separating Christians from their neighbors of other faiths, Samartha suggested that what was essential to Christian faith was also held in other faiths, and that what was not shared was not essential.[89] This is most certainly not *Dalit* experience, and to suggest it undermines their conversion.

Theology of discernment comes naturally to Pentecostal theology because one of the gifts of the Spirit listed in 1 Corinthians 12 is the gift of "discernment of spirits" (12:10). This expression presupposes a plural universe with a multiplicity of spirits, a spirit-world. However, the pre-eminence of the Holy Spirit and belief in the victory of Jesus Christ on the Cross prevent Pentecostalism from descending into dualism, as we saw above. A. P. Nirmal suggested that *Dalit* theology would also develop a distinctive pneumatology. From a *Dalit* perspective the Holy Spirit is the life-giver who revives the dry bones (Ezek. 37) and also the Comforter in suffering (John 14:16, etc.). The Holy Spirit is specifically the Spirit of Jesus Christ, whose power was "doing good and healing all that were oppressed" (Acts 10:38). Furthermore, Nirmal suggested, the Spirit descends on *Dalits* without waiting for their baptism because, like Jesus, the Spirit is on their side.[90]

Finally, Pentecostals and all Christians in India are challenged to fulfill the Great Commission. The Great Commission is to "make disciples of all nations"—or of "the whole inhabited earth"—and this consists of two activities: baptizing and teaching (Matt. 28:18-20). The tensions between Christians and the *Hindutva* movements we have examined mean that baptism in India is seen as a divisive and political act of severing of links with one community to join the Christian one. Where "freedom of religion" legislation is in place, both those baptized and those who baptize are accountable to the courts. Therefore the call for conversion is highly problematic in many parts of India. Taking baptism in the name of the Father, Son, and Holy Spirit is costly in terms of personal relationships and livelihood. Nevertheless, the Christian call for conversion is liberating, and should be affirmed, despite its political incorrectness, while being sensitive to the political context of *Dalits*. *Dalit* theologians generally adopt a post-colonial view that colonial missionary activity further contributed to the slave mentality of *Dalit* communities.[91] However, in a study of two communities in Andhra Pradesh, Samuel Jayakumar shows how, even in the straightjacket of colonial Christianity, the proclamation of the gospel and the presence of expatriate missionaries awakened the consciousness of *Dalits* and transformed their thinking to believe that "life is meaningful and that it is possible to change one's quality of life."[92] Christianity therefore was a first step in liberating *Dalits* from the oppressive culture, customs, and behavior forced on them by caste Hindus. Furthermore, "conversion to Christ minimized caste disabilities among the outcaste believers and brought solidarity among the castes."[93] *Dalit* communities, and others, who choose to convert offer a brave challenge to *Hindutva* attempts to control the religious freedom of others. Jesus Christ has promised to be with them in spirit "to the end of the age."

The second activity is "teaching them to obey everything that I have commanded you." In the context of Matthew's Gospel, the teaching of Jesus Christ has a very specific ethical content. Matthew's Gospel includes the Sermon on the Mount and repeated injunctions to consider "the little ones." Dhyanchand Carr has expounded Matthew's Gospel in the context of *Dalit* Theology. He argues that, far from spiritualizing the option for the poor, Matthew's concern for the "poor in spirit" (5:3) expresses "the destitution of the spirit consequent upon the loss of human dignity and freedom arising from being marginalized, ostracized or stigmatized" that characterizes the *Dalit* condition.[94] "The lost sheep of the house of Israel" for whom Jesus was primarily concerned (10:5-6; 15:24) are the harassed and helpless sheep without a shepherd (9:36).[95] The baptized community—in India and elsewhere—are taught to care for "the little ones" (11:11; 18:6, 10, 14; 10:42) or "the least of these" (18:5; 25:40, 45).

Notes

1. For an overview of these issues, see Christian Solidarity Worldwide, "Briefing: Aftermath of Anti-Christian Violence in Orissa State" (June 2009), http://dynamic.csw.org.uk/article.asp?t=report&id=108&search.

2. All India Christian Council (2009), "Orissa Anti-Christian Attacks 2008," http://indianchristians.in/news/content/view/2332/45/.

3. Chris Morris, "Christians under Attack in India," British Broadcasting Corporation [BBC] (October 14, 2008), http://news.bbc.co.uk/2/hi/south_asia/7670747.stm; see in addition, "Fear and Fundamentalism in India," BBC (October 14, 2008), http://news.bbc.co.uk/2/hi/programmes/from_our_own_correspondent/7672228.stm.

4. Discussed in an article by the Christian Solidarity Worldwide, "Briefing"; Ed Beaven, "Anti-Christian Violence in Orissa," *Church Times* (November 14, 2008), http://www.churchtimes.co.uk/content.asp?id=66248. At the meeting of the Commission for World Mission and Evangelism meeting in Bangalore in October 2009, I heard first-hand reports of the violence and the wider Christian response.

5. Somini Sengupta, "Hindu Threat to Christians: Convert or Flee," *New York Times* (October 12, 2008), http://www.nytimes.com/2008/10/13/world/asia/13india.html?_r=1;

see also Jajati Karan, "Caste, Tribe, Conversion Make Orissa District Volatile," *CNN-IBN* (December 30, 2007), http://ibnlive.in.com/news/caste-tribe-conversion-make-orissa-district-volatile/55272-3.html; for further discussion, consult the article by Rhys Blakely, "Extremists Stoke the Fires of Persecution: Hindus and Christians Are at Each Other's Throats in Orissa, One of India's Poorest States," *The Times* (October 17, 2008), http://www.timesonline.co.uk/tol/comment/faith/article4964742.ece, and see also by Angana Chatterji, "It's Still Religion, Stupid," *Indian Express* (August 7, 2009), http://www.indianexpress.com/news/its-still-religion-stupid/369086/2. Other discussions are available at http://en.wikipedia.org/wiki/Religious_violence_in_Orissa and http://kuidina.blogspot.com/2009_04_01_archive.html.

6. Marcus Braybrooke, *Pilgrimage of Hope: One Hundred Years of Global Interfaith Dialogue* (London: SCM Press, 1992).

7. Matt. 28: 18-20 (NRSV): "And Jesus came and said to them, 'All authority in heaven and on earth has been given to me. Go therefore and make disciples of all nations, baptizing them in the name of the Father and of the Son and of the Holy Spirit, and teaching them to obey everything that I have commanded you. And remember, I am with you always, to the end of the age.'"

8. For background see Christophe Jaffrolet, *The Hindu Nationalist Movement in India* (New Delhi: Viking, 1996).

9. Sebastian, C. H. Kim, *In Search of Identity: Debates on Religious Conversion in India* (Oxford: Oxford University Press, 2003).

10. Quoted in Kim, *In Search of Identity*, 76.

11. Arun Shourie, *Missionaries in India: Continuities, Changes, Dilemmas* (New Delhi: ASA Publications, 1994).

12. Kim, *In Search of Identity*, 186.

13. Quoted in Kim, *In Search of Identity*, 76.

14. See further the discussion available in the All India Christian Council, "Laws and Policies" (2009), http://indianchristians.in/news/content/view/1432/118/.

15. As discussed in the article by the Christian Solidarity Worldwide, "Briefing," 2, http://dynamic.csw.org.uk/article.asp?t=report&id=3.

16. Christian Solidarity Worldwide, "Briefing," 2-3.

17. World Council of Churches, *Guidelines for Dialogue* (Geneva: WCC, 1979), 1-2.

18. Hendrik Kraemer, *The Christian Message in a Non-Christian World* (London: Edinburgh House, 1938).

19. Stanley J. Samartha, *One Christ—Many Religions: Toward a Revised Christology* (Maryknoll: Orbis Books, 1991), 2-3, 32-37, 84-85, 96-98, 101, 146.

20. Samartha, *One Christ—Many Religions*, 98-103; see also Stanley J. Samartha, *Between Two Cultures: Ecumenical Ministry in a Pluralist World* (Geneva: WCC, 1996), 138-39.

21. World Council of Churches, *Guidelines for Dialogue*, 3.

22. Ibid.

23. Ibid., 7-8, 12, and 13.

24. Paul F. Knitter, *One Earth, Many Religions: Multifaith Dialogue and Global Responsibility* (Maryknoll: Orbis Books, 1995); Jacques Dupuis, *Toward a Christian Theology of Religious Pluralism* (Maryknoll: Orbis Books, 1997).

25. Paul F. Knitter, "Stanley Samartha's *One Christ—Many Religions*: Plaudits and Problems," *Current Dialogue* 21 (December 1991) 25-30, at 29; Stanley J. Samartha, "In Search of a Revised Christology: A Response to Paul Knitter," *Current Dialogue* 21 (December 1991): 30-37, at 34.

26. Stanley J. Samartha, *Courage for Dialogue: Ecumenical Issues in Inter-religious Relationships* (Geneva: WCC, 1981), 66, 72.

27. Ibid., 73-74.

28. David M. Paton, ed., *Breaking Barriers: Nairobi 1975* (Geneva: WCC, 1976), 70.

29. Stanley J. Samartha, "The Promise of the Spirit," in Stanley J. Samartha, *The Pilgrim Christ: Sermons, Poems and Bible Studies* (Bangalore: ATC, 1994), 43-49, esp. 47-48.

30. Lesslie Newbigin, *The Light Has Come: An Exposition of the Fourth Gospel* (Edinburgh: Handsel, 1982), 216-17.

31. Samartha, *Courage for Dialogue*, 67-71.

32. Ibid., 63-64.

33. Ibid., 80.

34. Stanley J. Samartha, "The Holy Spirit and People of Various Faiths, Cultures and Ideologies," in Dow Kirkpatrick, ed., *The Holy Spirit* (Nashville: Tidings, 1974), 20-39. The view of Khodr that there are two distinct missions of Son and Spirit has been refuted by Orthodox theologian John Zizioulas, who argues that Son and Spirit should be regarded as cooperating in the one mission of God. See John D. Zizioulas, *Being as Communion: Studies in Personhood and the Church* (Crestwood: St Vladimir's Seminary Press, 1985), 124-29.

35. Samartha, *One Christ—Many Religions*, 83.

36. Ibid., 110-11.

37. See Ishita Banerjee-Dube, ed., *Caste in History* (Delhi: Oxford University Press, 2008).

38. For details of the treatment of Dalits in contemporary India, see National Campaign on Dalit Human Rights, http://www.ncdhr.org.in/, and International Dalit Solidarity Network, http://www.idsn.org/.

39. M. N. Srinivas, *Social Change in Modern India* (Berkeley: University of California Press, 1966).

40. B. R. Ambedkar, "Why Conversion?" reproduced in Joseph D'Souza, *Dalit Freedom: Now and Forever* (Centennial, Colo.: Dalit Freedom Network, 2004), 109-23.

41. Pradip Kumar Sethi, "Conversion as a Device," in Ambrose Pinto, ed., *Dalits: Assertion for Identity* (Delhi: Indian Social Institute, 1999), 158-59.

42. John C. B. Webster, *The Dalit Christians: A History*, 2nd ed. (Delhi: ISPCK, 1994).

43. Duncan B. Forrester, *Caste and Christianity: Attitudes and Policies on Caste of Anglo-Saxon Protestant Missions in India* (London: Curzon Press, 1980); Michael Bergunder, *The South Indian Pentecostal Movement in the Twentieth Century* (Grand Rapids: William B. Eerdmans Publishing Company, 2008), 17, 234.

44. V. Devasahayam, ed., *Frontiers of Dalit Theology* (Delhi: ISPCK/Gurukul, 1997); John Parratt, "Recent Writing on Dalit Theology: A Bibliographical Essay," *International Review of Mission* 83:329 (1994): 329-37.

45. John C.B. Webster, *Religion and Dalit Liberation: An Examination of Perspectives* (Delhi: Manohar, 2002), 65-73.

46. James Massey, "Ingredients for a Dalit Theology," in James Massey, ed., *Indigenous People: Dalits—Dalit Issues in Today's Theological Debate* (Delhi: ISPCK, 1998), 338-43, esp. 339-40.

47. Webster, *Religion and Dalit Liberation*, 62.

48. V. Devasahayam, "Doing Dalit Theology: Basic Assumptions," in V. Devasahayam, ed., *Frontiers of Dalit Theology* (Delhi: ISPCK, 1997), 270-82, at 274-75.

49. Kothapalli Wilson, "A Dalit Theology of Human Self-Development," in James Massey, ed., *Indigenous People: Dalits—Dalit Issues in Today's Theological Debate* (Delhi: ISPCK, 1998), 267-76, at 269-70.

50. Wilson, "A Dalit Theology of Human Self-Development." See also "A Charter of Dalit Human Rights" at http://www.hrsolidarity.net/mainfile.php/1999vol09no03/817/.

51. A. M. Abraham Ayrookuzhiel, "Dalit Theology: A Movement of Counter-Culture," in James Massey, ed., *Indigenous People: Dalits—Dalit Issues in Today's Theological Debate* (Delhi: ISPCK, 1998), 250-66; Wilson, "A Dalit Theology of Human Self-Development," 270; Franklyn J. Balasundaram, "Dalit Theology and Other Theologies," in V. Devasahayam, ed., *Frontiers of Dalit Theology* (Delhi: ISPCK, 1997), 253-69, at 259-60.

52. A. P. Nirmal, "Towards a Christian Dalit Theology," in Arvind P. Nirmal, ed., *A Reader in Dalit Theology* (Madras: Gurukul Lutheran Theological College and Research Institute, 1988), 53-70.

53. See, for example, Stanley J. Samartha, "The Quest for Salvation and the Dialogue between Religions," *International Review of Mission* 62:228 (1968): 424-432, at 429.

54. I. John Mohan Razu, ed., *Struggle for Human Rights: Towards a New Humanity. Theological and Ethical Perspectives* (Nagpur: National Council of Churches of India, 2001).

55. Kirsteen Kim, "India," in John Parratt, ed., *Introduction to Third World Theologies* (Cambridge: Cambridge University Press, 2004), 44-73.

56. Nirmal, "Towards a Christian Dalit Theology."

57. Peniel Jesusdason Rufus Rajkumar, "Rethinking Dalit Theology from the Perspective of Dalithos," *Rethinking Mission* (June 2006), available at http://www.rethinkingmission.org.uk/.

58. For example, V. Devasahayam, *Outside the Camp: Biblical Studies in Dalit Perspective* (Chennai: Gurukul Theological College and Research Centre, 1998); Ayrookuzhiel, "Dalit Theology"; Sathianathan Clarke, *Dalits and Christianity: Subaltern Religion and Liberation Theology in India* (Delhi: Oxford University Press, 1999).

59. Webster, *Religion and Dalit Liberation*. Studies include Webster, *The Dalit Christians*; Chad M. Bauman, *Christian Identity and Dalit Religion in Hindu India, 1868-1947* (Grand Rapids: William B. Eerdmans Publishing Company, 2008); Saurabh Dube, *Untouchable Pasts: Religion, Identity, and Power among a Central Indian Community, 1780-1950* (Albany: State University of New York Press, 1998); Clarke, *Dalits and Christianity*; James Elisha, "Liberation Motifs in Dalit Religion," *Bangalore Theological Forum* 34:2 (2002): 78-88.

60. See Bauman, *Christian Identity and Dalit Religion in Hindu India*, 41.

61. T. Swami Raju, "Subaltern Movements: Insights for Inter-Faith Dialogue," paper presented to the conference on "Christian Mission among Other Faiths," United Theological College in Bangalore, India, July 17-19, 2009; available at http://www.edinburgh2010.org/.

62. Webster, *Religion and Dalit Liberation*, 24-52.

63. For example: M. M. Thomas, "The Holy Spirit and the Spirituality for Political Struggles," *Ecumenical Review* 42:3/4 (1990): 216-24; Walter Wink, *Engaging the Powers: Discernment and Resistance in a World of Domination* (Minneapolis: Fortress Press, 1992); Samuel Rayan, "Spirituality for Inter-faith Social Action," in Xavier Irudayaraj, ed., *Liberation and Dialogue* (Bangalore: Claretian Publications, 1989), 64-73.

64. Bergunder, *The South Indian Pentecostal Movement in the Twentieth Century*, 18.

65. Roger E. Hedlund, "Indigenous Pentecostalism in India," in Allan Anderson and Edmund Tang, eds., *Asian and Pentecostal: The Charismatic Face of Christianity in Asia* (Oxford: Regnum, 2005), 215-44, at 217.

66. Bergunder, *The South Indian Pentecostal Movement in the Twentieth Century*, 234.

67. Amos Yong, *The Spirit Poured Out on All Flesh: Pentecostalism and the Possibility of Global Theology* (Grand Rapids: Baker Academic, 2005), 56-57.

68. Bergunder, *The South Indian Pentecostal Movement in the Twentieth Century*, 29-30, 45, 53-57, 234, 252.

69. Allan H. Anderson, "Pentecostalism in India and China in the Early Twentieth Century and Inter-religious Relations," in David Westerlund, ed., *Global Pentecostalism: Encounters with Other Religious Traditions* (London: I. B. Taurus, 2009), 117-36, at 131.

70. Bergunder, *The South Indian Pentecostal Movement in the Twentieth Century*, 123-27.

71. Anderson, "Pentecostalism in India and China," 131.

72. Ibid., 125.

73. Ibid., 126.

74. Ibid., 128.

75. Allan H. Anderson, *An Introduction to Pentecostalism* (Cambridge: Cambridge University Press, 2004), 187-92.

76. Cf. Bergunder, *The South Indian Pentecostal Movement in the Twentieth Century*, 128.

77. Amos Yong, *Beyond the Impasse: Toward a Pneumatological Theology of Religions* (Grand Rapids: Baker Academic, 2003); Clark H. Pinnock, *A Wideness in God's Mercy: The Finality of Jesus Christ in a World of Religions* (Grand Rapids: Zondervan, 1992); Clark H. Pinnock, *Flame of Love: A Theology of the Holy Spirit* (Downers Grove: InterVarsity Press, 1996).

78. Cf. Asonzeh F.-K. Ukah, "Contesting God: Nigerian Pentecostals and Their Relations with Islam and Muslims," in David Westerlund, ed., *Global Pentecostalism: Encounters with Other Religious Traditions* (London: I. B. Taurus, 2009), 93-114.

79. Vandana Mataji, for example, who adopting the saffron robes of a holy person, set up an ashram or Hindu-style religious community, and described Jesus Christ as the Supreme Guru (*Satguru*), was accused of duping people into following Christianity under the guise of Hinduism. See Kirsteen Kim, *Mission in the Spirit: the Holy Spirit in Indian Christian theologies* (Delhi: ISPCK, 2003), 109-17.

80. Bergunder, *The South Indian Pentecostal Movement in the Twentieth Century*, 117-18, 281-82; see also http://www.lawrieministries.net/.

81. Ibid., 108, 261-62; see also http://www.agniministries.org/.

82. Cf. Amos Yong, "Spirit Possession, the Living, and the Dead: A Review Essay and Response from a Pentecostal Perspective," in *Dharma Deepika: A South Asian Journal of Missiological Research* 8:2 (2004): 77-88.

83. Raju, "Subaltern Movements," 11.

84. Ibid.; T. Swami Raju, *Vira Cult in Folk Religion of Guntur District: A Dalit Perspective* (Delhi: ISPCK, 2005).

85. Cf. Gavin D'Costa, ed., *Christian Uniqueness Reconsidered: The Myth of a Pluralistic Theology of Religions* (Maryknoll: Orbis Books, 1990).

86. Samartha, *Courage for Dialogue*, 73-74.

87. Yong, *The Spirit Poured Out on All Flesh*, 250-53.

88. Kirsteen Kim, *The Holy Spirit in the World: A Global Conversation* (Maryknoll: Orbis Books, 2007), 164-69; Yong, *The Spirit Poured Out on All Flesh*, 256.

89. Samartha, *One Christ—Many Religions.*

90. Nirmal, "Towards a Christian Dalit Theology," 69-70.

91. Samuel Jayakumar, *Dalit Consciousness and Christian Conversion: Historical Resources for a Contemporary Debate* (Chennai: Mission Educational Books, 1999), 364-65.

92. Ibid., 286.

93. Ibid., 319.

94. Dhyanchand Carr, "Dalit Theology is Biblical and It Makes the Gospel Relevant," in Arvind P. Nirmal, ed., *A Reader in Dalit Theology* (Madras: Gurukul Lutheran Theological College and Research Institute, 1990), 71-84, esp. 77.

95. Ibid., 77.

Chapter 6

Renewal, Christian Mission, and Encounter with the Other: Pentecostal-Type Movements Meeting Islam in Ghana and Nigeria

Cephas N. Omenyo

Christian and Muslim have been encountering each other in Africa for many centuries, but now do so in increasingly complex ways. Regrettably religious conflicts between people in these religious traditions have become part of the Nigerian scene over the last two plus decades. Ghana, too, has experienced some incidents of religious tensions and unrest. Christians and Muslims in Africa often live in segregated communities; sometimes they enjoy the services of one another, share common culture, borrow from each other, and even convert to each other's religion. Of course, they have also often competed and collided with each other. In some cases they are flexible, making it possible for the two to cooperate on common projects, while other times they are rigid to the extent of seeing each other as enemies.

The historic or mainline churches (Catholic and Protestant) have sought formal dialogue with Muslims, while invariably Pentecostal-type or renewal movements who are more radical and enthusiastic in their evangelization endeavors tend to be less diplomatic and sensitive. The Pentecostal-type movements usually adopt an exclusivist approach to salvation. Furthermore, they demonize the others, particularly Muslims whom they perceive as being a major obstacle to their proselytizing endeavors. Similarly, some Islamic preachers also adopt such attitudes to Christians. These attitudes on both sides coupled with religious polemics result in tensions, misunderstandings, quarrel, and violence.

This chapter looks at these rather complex relationships in Ghana and Nigeria in particular, identifies the evangelistic styles and methods of the renewal groups, and makes recommendations as to how renewal Christians can best address this issue in their missionary efforts. Better understanding of religious encounters will arguably help to prevent future suspicions, apprehensions, and clashes.

Islam in Ghana

Islam arrived in West Africa as early as the eighth century when Islamic traders from North Africa transmitted the religion initially among the ruling classes, followed by their fellow traders in commercial towns and later in the rural settings.[1] The advent of Islam in Ghana was during the fourteenth century, predating Christianity. Muslim traders, mainly the trading enterprises of Wangara Muslims, constituted the main "missionary group" who together with their clerics (called *malam* or *alfa*) were successful in converting a significant numbers of indigenous people, particularly the traditional rulers, to Islam through their mystic practices.

The Islamic influence on the Akans, particularly the Ashanti monarchy between the fifteenth and eighteenth centuries, has been profound. Yet this influence has not occurred without resistance. In his history of Islam in Ghana, Patrick Ryan observes: "When Muslim influence in the fifth Asantehene, Osei Kwame, struck the queen mother, Konadu Yaadom, as excessive, she launched a 'destoolment' campaign that led to his deposition in 1798. Twenty-two years later, Dupuis, the British envoy to Kumasi, was told that Konadu Yaadom and her allies among the kingmakers resented Osei Kwame's attachment to the Moslems, and, as it is said, his inclination to establish the Koranic law for the civil code."[2]

It is important to note that the world view of Africans (particularly Ghanaians and Nigerians) among whom Muslims work is one that is inhabited by physical and metaphysical beings and forces such as the Supreme Being, angels, Satan, ancestors, witchcraft, and animals. As a result a major attraction of the Ashantis of Ghana to Islam is the use of amulets that are produced by *malams*. Amulets are made with small leather pouches that contain verses from the Qur'an which are believed to protect the user or are thought capable of harming one's enemies. Ashanti rulers and warriors wore smock (*batakari*)[3] which have several amulets sewn on them. These smocks, which are closely associated with *malams*, are believed to have magical powers, capable even of protecting users from the effects of bullets.

Islam spread mainly from Northern Ghana southwards to Kumasi, the capital of the Ashanti state, in the eighteenth century.[4] The spread continued to the coastal towns, particularly among Gas and Fantis. Generally, Muslim communities in the south are located in the "Zongos," which are quarters found on the outskirts of large towns.[5]

Muslims in Ghana generally belong to two major groups, the Sunni and the Ahmadiyyah. Traditionally, Sunni Muslims adhere to one of the four schools of Islamic jurisprudence (*sharia*), namely, the Maliki, Hanafi, Hanbali and Shafi. The majority of Ghanaian Muslims identify with the Maliki. It is noteworthy that "Sufism," a term used to refer to Islamic mysticism, has profoundly influenced this school.[6]

Contemporary Islam in Ghana attracts to its fold people from all classes: intellectuals, businessmen and women, politicians, and government officials. Islam has also been accorded recognition, as evident in the establishment of an Islamic Education Unit that supervises the English/Arabic schools in Ghana and in parliamentary approval of two statutory Muslim holidays, the Eid-ul-Fitr and Eid-ul-Adha, which passed in 1996.

After Ghana gained independence in 1957, other forms of Islamic movements from the Middle East have become influential. These movements have promoted the hajj (pilgrimage to Mekka), donated funds for the construction of Muslim schools and mosques, and supported Muslim NGOs committed to the promotion of education, agriculture, and health, and to the provision of social amenities in Islamic communities.

The population census held in 1970 and 2000 in Ghana summarizes religious affiliation as follows:

TABLE 1
Percentage of Adherents of Major Religious Groups in Ghana in 1970 and 2000

Religious Affiliation	% adherents 1970	% Adherents 2000	% increase/ decrease
Christian	52.65	69.0	+16.35
Muslim	13.92	15.6	+1.68
African indigenous religions	21.61	8.5	-13.11
Other or no religions	11.82	6.9	-4.92

Sources: Ghana's 1970 Population Census conducted by the Ghana Statistical Service and "Selected Social Characteristics of Population by Region, Preliminary figures from the 2000 Population Census conducted by Ghana Statistical Service.

What the figures in the table above mean is that Muslims increased by only 1.68 percent between 1970 and 2000. To be fair we should add that The Coalition of Muslim Associations vehemently disputed the figures of the 2000 Census, claiming a figure that puts Muslims between 30 and 45 percent of a population of about 21 million.[7] Be it as it may, Islamic resurgence in Ghana is an undisputable fact. Their increase in public space is visibly acknowledged. Furthermore, there is evidence that some Christians are being won over to Islam in Ghana.[8]

Christianity in Ghana

Arguably "Ghana's ethos is recognizably Christian."[9] Contemporary Christianity in Ghana is largely shaped by its current renewal as a non-Western religion.[10] The table above makes it evident that Christianity has increased significantly recently from 52.65 percent of the population in 1970 to 69 percent in 2000, gaining primarily from members of indigenous religious traditions.

There is an enormous variety of churches in Ghana due to rapid proliferation of new churches and schisms in some of the older churches. Therefore, in order to get a fair view of Christianity in Ghana we must delineate the major strands of churches. The following typology takes into accounts both historical and theological categories represented in Ghana:

a. mainline or historic churches
b. African independent churches
c. classical Pentecostal churches
d. neo-Evangelical or mission-related churches
e. neo-Pentecostal and charismatic churches.

For the purpose of this essay we shall single out three major strands for a little more discussion, namely, mainline or historic churches, classical Pentecostal churches, and neo-Pentecostal and charismatic churches.

Conventional academic portrayals of the mainline or historic churches describe them as the older and generally larger churches instituted as the result of European missionary endeavors in Ghana during the nineteenth century. These churches are modeled on the pattern of Western Christianity, although they are fast departing from their Western parent churches and adopting African as well as Pentecostal features. Among churches so defined are the following: The Presbyterian Church of Ghana (180 years), The Methodist Church Ghana (173 years), the Evangelical Presbyterian Church (161 years), the Roman Catholic (120 years), The African Methodist Episcopal Zion Church (110 years), The Baptist Church (about 105 years), and the Anglican Church (103 years). Together they claim over 38 percent of Ghana's population.

All the mainline Protestant churches are members of the Christian Council of Ghana (CCG), which was formed in 1929 as a fellowship of churches. Currently the Council has fourteen member churches and two affiliated organizations. Internationally, it is linked to the World Council of Churches (WCC); continentally, to the All African Conference of Churches (AACC).

The Catholic Church is the largest single denomination in Ghana with 16.6 percent of the population. The various dioceses are autonomous, but the bishops meet together at the Bishops' Conference at least once a year. The activities of the Bishops' Conference are coordinated by the National Catholic Secretariat, which facilitates the Catholic Bishops' Conference of Ghana. The Catholic

Church and the Christian Council of Ghana enjoy a good working relationship. They have on a number of occasions issued joint pastoral letters and memoranda addressing sensitive national issues.

The Classical Pentecostal churches in Ghana trace their history to the Faith Tabernacle Church, which started in 1917 and later gave birth to the Christ Apostolic Church, The Church of Pentecost, and the Apostolic Church, Ghana. The Assemblies of God Church and the Four Square Gospel Church also belong to this genre. Today over one hundred and ninety seven Classical Pentecostal churches have joined together to form The Ghana Pentecostal Council (GPC). Apart from their emphasis on the fact that Christians must manifest the various gifts of the Holy Sprit with speaking in tongues as a sign, a major feature of the Classical Pentecostal churches, particularly the Church of Pentecost, is their immense zeal for mission and evangelism. They hold open air evangelistic campaigns as well as engage in house to house evangelism and produce radio broadcasts and television programs.

The neo-Pentecostal Churches appeared on the Ghanaian religious landscape in the late 1970s. They are distinguished from the Classical Pentecostal Churches by features such as their predominantly youthful membership, their use of the English Language, their adoption of American Pentecostal worship styles in terms of music, preaching, etc. These movements emerged on the Ghanaian scene during the period of the harsh economic recession in the 1970s and 1980s, a situation which perhaps led them to emphasize prosperity in their sermons and prayer sessions.[11] The influence of these churches is quite immense. Apart from their emphasis on healing, deliverance, and prosperity, and their goal-oriented attitudes which make them attractive to the youth, they are dynamic and aggressive in their use of the media as well as in their evangelistic outreaches. Furthermore, they employ modern church growth techniques in their missionary and evangelistic endeavors. Indeed the current phenomenal growth of Christianity in sub-Saharan Africa is largely attributed to the strong evangelistic drive of these new Pentecostal and charismatic churches.

The Nigerian Situation

Modern Nigeria dates back to 1914 when the British Protectorates of Northern and Southern Nigeria were joined. The Federal status was achieved in 1954, after which Nigeria gained independence from British colonial rule in 1960 and became a federal parliamentary republic in 1979. Nigeria is a highly multi ethnic nation with more than 200 different language groups spread throughout the country. The dominant ethnic groups are the Hausa, Igbo (Ibo), and Yoruba—all three combined constitute over 60 percent of the population.

The demographic character of Nigeria is crucial for understanding the religious conflicts in this nation. It is estimated that the Federal Republic of Nigeria has a population of over 120 million. But because the religious ethos of

Nigeria is so highly politicized, getting official figures is problematic.[12] Both Christians and Muslims claim over 50 percent of the population. Objectively, it is believed that each of the two major religions claim a minimum of 40 percent of the population. Nevertheless, what is obvious is among the three predominant language groups, Hausas are largely Muslims, while Ibos are mainly Christians, with Yorubas having a mixed community of Christians and Muslims in almost equal numbers. The fact that in Nigeria religion and ethnicity are intertwined lends itself to a situation where, generally speaking, any conflict between an Ibo and Hausa and vice versa is seen as a conflict between a Christian and a Muslim. A typical example is the conflict in Kaduna where there were reprisal killings of Hausa in Abba in the south-east when Ibos were informed that some of their kinsmen had been killed in Kaduna by the Hausas. Clearly, a combination of ethnic and religious concerns has led to conflicts.

On the political scene, the North has dominated the national political leadership by producing six heads of state during the past forty years of Nigeria as an independent nation. Unfortunately, in this country, Christianity and Islam have reinforced ethnic antagonisms in a very pronounced way.

The first successful attempts to evangelize Nigeria date back to the nineteenth century. Successful mission in Northern Nigeria, began around 1900 with the opening of the first mission station in a village near Zaria by the Church Missionary Society (CMS).

The British colonial administration pursued a pro-Islamic policy in Nigeria. This policy disallowed the spread of Christianity and missionary activities in most parts of northern Nigeria which resulted in part in the laying of the foundation of contemporary religious conflicts.

Today in Nigeria, besides the Catholic Church and the mainstream Protestant churches, there are a variety of Pentecostal, neo-Pentecostal, and Charismatic churches. Indeed the upsurge of Pentecostal and charismatic churches in Nigeria is the single major religious revival in Nigeria.

Cases of Christian-Muslim relations and Conflicts in Ghana and Nigeria

Conflicts in Ghana

Generally, Christians and Muslims have coexisted peacefully in Ghana. There are several cases where members of one extended family is made up adherents of traditional religion, Islam, and Christianity, but have coexisted harmoniously. Members come together during family occasions such as marriages, outdooring of new babies, and funerals, without any tension. Once those concerned agree as to the religious tradition to use in the ceremony all the others, irrespective of their religious inclinations, come on board. Nevertheless what sometimes brings tension is when children of particular nuclear families convert, particularly from

Islam to Christianity; depending on the temperament of the parents that could give rise to a major crisis. Oftentimes such converted children are given the option to renounce Christianity or be disowned. Those who choose to remain Christians are often banished from their parental homes and ostracized by Muslim relations. This trend has led to the formation of the Converted Muslims Christian Ministries (CMCM) in Ghana with the following aims:

> Winning Muslim souls for Christ wherever they are found; ensuring that Muslim converts remain and abide in the Christian faith through fellowship and teaching; training and equipping Muslim converts with sound biblical teaching and relevant Qur'anic instructions towards effective Muslim evangelism (mission); organizing fervent and constant prayer meetings on behalf of convert's parents, relatives, friends and all Muslims in general for their ultimate salvation in Jesus Christ.[13]

As Elom Dovlo and Alfred Asanta comment regarding the CMCM, "These…aims show that the thrust of the Fellowship in becoming a Ministry was redefined to go beyond the protection and building up of Muslim converts to include the active evangelization to Muslims."[14]

Conflicts in Nigeria

In most West African countries, Muslims and Christians have coexisted peacefully with a high degree of mutual acceptance, except in Nigeria, particularly northern Nigeria. Indeed the southern part of Nigeria enjoys relative inter-religious peace and harmony while the North experiences a lot of both intra- and inter-religious conflicts.[15] Since the 1980s it is estimated that more than twenty major crises have occurred in Nigeria. Most of the crises often begin as a result of some social, ethnic, or political misunderstanding and soon assume religious dimensions. Indeed there is no monocausality in these conflicts due to the multifaceted nature of life in Northern Nigeria.

However, in the wake of the debate on *sharia* with its attendant problems, all other causal factors in the conflict have been subsumed under the religious factor. Indeed during such crises not only lives have been lost (Christians and Muslim fall victims), but property, particularly churches and mosques, has also been burnt. Cleary, major conflicts in northern Nigeria in recent history (since the 1980s) such as Kano (1980), Maiduguri (1982), Yola (1984), Gomb (1985), and Kaduna (1987), were largely attributable to religious causes.[16] Yet Amos Yong documents some encouraging reports about how some Muslim neighbors have rescued some Christians from attacks from other Muslims and vice versa:

> While these were dark days for interreligious relations in Nigeria, there have also been some signs of hope in Muslim neighbors protecting and saving Christians and vice versa. One Christian testified, "An old

Muslim man took me into his house where I stayed until 6:30 p.m....," while two elderly Christian men said they "managed to escape and were saved by a Muslim acquaintance who hid them, along with eight women and two young men, in his house close to the church premises," Other Muslims warned Christians in advance of potential attacks, or gave their Christian neighbors Muslim headscarves enabling their escape from rioting areas; some even risked their own lives in the face of threatening fellow-Muslim attackers. That many on both sides have been preserved from harm and death by neighbors, friends, and total strangers from the other faith shows that interreligious relations, even in Nigeria, have not been marked solely by violence.[17]

This development is indicative of the fact that the situation in Nigeria is not completely a dismal one. It also confirms the hypothesis that when Nigerians are left on their own (without external influences), they are capable of living harmoniously as Christians and Muslims.

For all intents and purposes no other issue has caused northern Nigeria so much distress as what has come to be known as the *sharia* crisis.[18] Critical analysis of the situation may reveal that the introduction of *sharia* in 1999 was not motivated by religious piety, but it was meant to serve the parochial interest of some politicians who are neither clerics nor pious. With the introduction of *sharia* Christians entertain the fear of the Islamization or "shariazation" of Nigeria much as Muslims also fear that Christianity could dominate the Nigerian state. Christians see *sharia* as a complete violation of the constitutional provision that describes Nigeria as a secular state. The fear and suspicion of Christians heightened when former President Ibrahim Babangida pushed for Nigeria to be converted from observer status to a full member of the Organization of Islamic Conference in 1986. Many Christians saw this development as a calculated sequel to and indeed execution of the Islamization of Nigeria program which was started during the rule of General Murtala Muhammed in 1975.

Efforts by Mainline Christians to Dialogue with Muslims

Ghana

For a long time, the mainline churches in Ghana had no missionary strategy to reach Muslims, thus typifying William Miller's statement that "the adherents of Islam have been more neglected by missionaries of the Gospel than any other people."[19] Mainline churches partly blame this attitude on the colonial administrators who had a definite plan to close off the predominantly Muslim areas of West Africa (particularly Northern parts of Ghana and Nigeria) to

Christian missionaries.[20] The mainline churches have consciously adopted a policy of dialogue and coexistence with Muslims, which makes it appear that they are indifferent in sharing the Gospel with Muslims.[21]

The International Missionary Council meeting in 1957 in Accra, Ghana, noted among other things the lack of sustained reflection on the relationship between Christianity and Islam.[22] At the All African Conference of Churches meeting in Ibadan, Nigeria, the following year, this concern was re-visited, leading to the establishment of the Islam in Africa Project (IAP) in 1959, renamed as Project for Christian Muslim Relations in Africa in 1987, and as Program for Christian Muslim Relations in Africa (PROCMURA) in 2003. The PROCMURA was established with the aim of educating Christians to witness to Muslims in a spirit of mutual respect and love, rather than in a spirit of confrontation and combat. Another of its aims was to get the church to come to a deeper understanding of its Muslim neighbors and the religion of Islam. As part of the project, the Christian Council of Ghana (CCG) appointed a Dutch specialist on Islam, Rev. Roelf Kuitse, as a consultant. He was based in Yendi, the capital of a major northern Ghana ethnic kingdom, Dagbon, and a predominantly Islamic centre. The CCG sought to use the project as a means to fulfill its mission to Muslims by equipping Christians to witness to Muslims in a non-confrontational manner through the organization of seminars and retreats for church leaders. The project also adopted the use of booklets, tracts, and audio-visual aids in this mission.

Essentially, the mainline churches adopted a mission strategy emphasizing a gentle person-to-person approach to evangelism, a method which employs dialogue with Muslims. Of course this is the approach that missionaries should have used in reaching out to people of African Indigenous Religion rather than the monologue which characterized missionary activities in most parts of Africa, particularly during the nineteenth century.

The Roman Catholic Church in Ghana's approach to mission among Muslims is similar to that of the mainline Protestant churches. Indeed Vatican II recommended a dialogical approach to mission to Muslims as stated in *Nostra Aetate*: "Although in the course of the centuries many quarrels and hostilities have arisen between Christians and Muslims, this most sacred Synod urges all to forget the past and to strive sincerely for mutual understanding. On behalf of all mankind, let them make common cause of safeguarding and fostering social justice, moral values, peace and freedom."[23]

In northern Ghana, the Roman Catholic Church has made a tremendous impact in their dialogue with Muslims. In 1991 they formed an Inter-Religious Dialogue Committee (IRDC) which seeks to promote peace, encourage cooperation, and enhance religious freedom. The IRDC focuses more on youth, who oftentimes are noted for their intolerance and radicalism on ethnic and religious issues. Later, in December 1995, Catholic Christians and Muslims held an interreligious prayer meeting to promote harmonious coexistence between adherents of the two religions.[24]

Consequently most African Episcopal conferences (particularly in Ghana and Nigeria) were challenged to feature missions among Muslims prominently in their scheme of things. They also have devoted substantial resources to train personnel, publish materials, and actively participate in dialogue programs with Muslims, sometimes in concert with PROCMURA.[25]

Nigeria

One major venue through which the mainline churches in Nigeria are dealing with the unhealthy religious crises is the Nigerian Inter-Religious Council (NIREC), which is co-chaired by the Sultan of Sokoto, the head of Muslims in Nigeria, and the president of the Christian Association of Nigeria. The Council meets regularly and makes efforts to lower religious tension and inspire new and healthy relationships between Muslim and Christians.

The Roman Catholic Archbishop of Jos, the Most Ignatius A. Kaigama, who is highly positive about the potential of the NIREC to broker peace in northern Nigeria, has said the following about some of the efforts and achievements of the Council:

> We have seen encouraging gestures such as the building of mosques being facilitated by Christian Governors as in Abia, Akwa Ibom, Benue States etc. areas considered to be predominantly Christian. In a similar vein, the Christian Association of Nigeria National Youth Wing gave an award of Excellence and Exemplary Leadership to Alhaji Danjuma Goje, the Muslim Governor of Gombe State in recognition of his kind and generous disposition to Christians in his state. The very swift condemnation of the Boko Haran sect that its philosophy and practice are not in consonance with the teaching of Islam by prominent Muslim groups and individuals could be attributed to the NIREC influence. There is increasing efforts of many Muslim/Christian NGOs in peace building and conflict resolution. I know well of the Catholic Bishops Conference of Nigeria which has a special Committee on Christian/Muslim relations and uses the apparatus of the Justice, Peace and Development commission to foster greater collaboration with Muslims. Recently, the Conference of Women Religious held seminars and workshops on inter-religious issues, just as Islam is now part of the curriculum in seminaries and many religious houses of formation. The interfaith Mediation Centre in Kaduna jointly founded and directed by Pastor James Wuye and Imam Muhammad Ashafa, who were both leaders of religious militant groups, offer a faith based approach to peace building through the use of non-violent methods.[26]

Pointing further to the positive working relationship with the Emir of Wase in Plateau State who spearheaded a successful peace initiative, the Archbishop noted:

The Emir of Kanam Alhaji Mohammadu Muazu Babangida, impressed by the positive and constructive engagement by the Emir and I, asked if he could join us, and now he is our partner in the search for peace. About two months ago I got a phone call from him asking for the establishment of a Catholic parish in his Emirate. I created not only a parish in the Muslim dominated area but also appointed a parish priest...Immediately after the November 2008 crisis some men, women and youths representing a group called the Dynamic Women and Youth Negotiators for Peace with a membership of about three thousand made up of Christians and Muslims came to my office to tell me how they have resolved to work together and never to allow religious differences make them fight each other. They wanted my moral support and to be their patron. [27]

The mainline churches and the Roman Catholic Church know the realities on the ground in northern Nigeria and demand that all Christians to live in peace with Muslims and to promote peace efforts in order to forestall future crises.

Emergence of Evangelical and Charismatic Renewal Movements in Ghana and Nigeria and Their Evangelistic Efforts among Muslim Communities

One of the most remarkable and significant developments of Christianity in both Ghana and Nigeria beginning in the 1970s was the advent of Evangelical para-church Christian fellowships, particularly in colleges and universities.[28] Examples are the Scripture Union (SU), Ghana Fellowship of Evangelical Students (GHAFES), and Fellowship of Christian Students (FCS), mainly in Nigeria. A radical experience of "new birth" underlined the self-consciousness of these movements, including the insistence that every Christian must know the exact date when this experience took place.[29] This emphasis produces egocentric tendencies resulting in religious elitism even among Christians.[30] For instance renewalists admonish their members not to get married to non-members of the movements since they were not committed Christians. All non-Christians religious groups, particularly Islam and traditional religion, are highly demonized and targeted by evangelistic endeavors.

In part for this reason, the renewal movements have also been noted for their keen sense of mission and evangelism. They have actively organized several mission and evangelistic revivals and outreaches. Matthews Ojo has noted the following trends in universities in Northern Nigeria:

Evangelistic activities were the major avenues for spreading the renewal, and by 1973 more than ten charismatic organizations established by graduates have emerged from the evangelistic aspirations of the revival.... The charismatic renewal spread gradually over the country, and by 1973 it had already spread to educations institutions in Northern Nigeria, with the Fellowship of Christian Students (FCS) groups in the Ahmadu Bellow University, Zaria, and in the University of Jos. During such programs they invited people to make definite personal commitment to Jesus Christ.[31]

Converts to these movements became leaders of neo-Pentecostal and Charismatic churches that emerged in both Nigeria and Ghana in the 1970s and the 1980s. This development constituted a major turning point in the history of Christianity in these countries, manifesting enthusiastic spirituality and vigorous Christian life, features which have been sustained until the present. Churches that have emerged since (in the last two decades) have taken on the character of their mother movements particularly in the area of radical evangelism. They have employed methods such as open air crusades, house-to-house and person-to-person witnessing, and the use of the media (particularly the radio, television, literature, and audio visual aids) in their evangelistic programs.

Pentecostal-Type Christianity and
Its Implications for Christian-Muslim Relations

Intensification of Christian-Muslim Stresses

A careful observer can establish a positive correlation between the insurgence of Pentecostal-type movements and increase of Christian-Muslim tensions in both Ghana and Nigeria in particular. The upsurge of Pentecostalism in Northern Nigeria is a major contributory factor to the militancy in contemporary Islam in that region. Ogbu Kalu notes that, "Commentators connect the violent response of incensed Muslims in the last two decades with the implosion of Pentecostal-charismatic spirituality. Since the mid 1970s, charismatic evangelical activities have intensified in the northern regions that had been preserved Muslim enclaves."[32] Beyond this, "Equally crucial is the fact that from the mid-1970s, charismatic Christianity flooded the northern regions after the civil war. This period of rapid expansion coincided with the rise of youthful radical Islam. University students from the south who went for National Youth Service Corps in the north, established vigorous evangelical programs that differed from the muted, accommodationist, quarantined forms of Christian presence symbolized by the mission churches located in enclaves known as 'strangers' quarters."[33]

Pentecostal and charismatic Christians in Ghana and Nigeria perceive Islam as a major threat and see it as their missionary duty to check its growth. They, therefore, engage Muslims in intemperate and provocative religious polemics in their open-air crusades and radio programs.[34] There are cases where Pentecostal-type movements are alleged to have publicly desecrated the Qur'an and burnt it, and defiled mosques to demonstrate that Islam is not worth belonging to. Similarly, there are cases where Muslim fundamentalists have been hostile to Pentecostal and Charismatic groups.[35]

Charismatic Influence on Mainline Churches

It is significant to note that in both Ghana and Nigeria, charismatic phenomena immensely influenced the mainline churches to the extent that it has moved from the fringes to the centre in those churches.[36] Vibrant Charismatic movements have been established in all the mainline churches in both countries. The charismatization of the mainline churches also meant that those churches acquired new spirituality and resources which made them evangelize vigorously like Pentecostals. These evangelistic activities covered people of other religions, especially Muslims. Kalu writes: "Christian resurgence through charismaticism has enabled the mainline churches to become keenly aware of Islamic efforts to capture the public space. When a Muslim military leader surreptitiously registered Nigeria as a member of the Organization of Islamic Countries in 1986, the uproar mobilized by the Christian Association of Nigeria forces its withdrawal."[37]

The charismatic ethos has also influenced the Christian Association of Nigeria (CAN), an association which hitherto has been committed to the promotion of peaceful coexistence with Muslims. This has had implications for CAN's commitment to dialogue with Muslims since the charismatic influence has led mainline and historic churches to adopt more aggressive evangelistic methods in their mission to Muslims. The Pentecostalization of the mainline churches means that even the posture of the mainline churches regarding Christian-Muslim relationship is gradually changing in the sense that some mainline churches themselves are behaving like the Pentecostal-type churches in their relationship with Muslims. Such developments give credence to the belief that Pentecostal spirituality is increasingly becoming the characteristic spirituality of African Christianity.

Power Evangelism and Demonstration of the Charisma

The proliferation of Pentecostal-type movements brings in its trail emphases on healing and deliverance. A number of healing and deliverance centers and camps have been established. Such centers host large numbers of clientele who approach the ministers for assistance. An interesting development is that the clients cut across churches and all religions represented in Ghana. For instance the present writer has observed instances where the Grace Presbyterian Deliverance Ministry attracts a number of Muslims to its ministry and there are testimonies of some of them getting healed and delivered. As a result some become Christians.

The international evangelist, Reinhard Bonnke, conducts outreaches in Africa which attract thousands of people. In 1986 when he visited Tamale, a predominantly Muslim city in Northern Ghana, tens of thousands of people (including Muslims) gathered to listen to him. During his ministry of healing most of the people who were healed were Muslims. A similar crusade held in Kano city, Nigeria, attracted over a million people who filled the Race Course night after night for one week. Bonnke dispatched vans to convey lame people from the streets to the crusade grounds and it is reported many claimed to be healed and many Muslims converted to Christianity. When it was planned to bring him back to Kano in 1991, some Muslim rioters vehemently protested that the posters which advertised the crusade desecrated the walls of the city and angrily burnt churches. These activities succeeded in preventing Bonnke's return to Kano.

High Profiling of Converted Muslims

What has become fashionable among charismatic movements in both Ghana and Nigeria is giving a high profile to converted Muslims by making them keynote speakers in churches, open air crusades, and on both radio and television programs. Their testimonies, flavored with their knowledge of both the Qur'an and the Bible and coupled with their experiences in both religions, are convincing to other Muslims and effective in urging conversion to Christianity. In Nigeria, people like Shaba Adams, an Islamic scholar who converted in the late 1970s, and Pastor El-Isa Buba, who confessed to leading armed bands to kill Christians, are popular speakers at charismatic gatherings.

In Ghana in the 1980s, there was an upsurge of Christian missions by converted Muslims specifically targeted at Muslims. At typical example is the role that Rockybell Adatura, an evangelical and charismatic convert from Islam, plays in mission to Muslims. His strategy was to engage in public debates with Muslim leaders in Accra, the capital city, and other key cities in Ghana, and to use such debates to convince Muslims about Christ and win them over to Christianity. Indeed he was employed by the Christian Council of Ghana in 1984. However the CCG saw his confrontational approach as too radical and inconsistent with its non-confrontational policy.

Another example from Ghana is the Converted Muslims Christian Ministries (CMCM), founded by Rev. Ahmed Agyei. Rev. Agyei was banished by his parents and ostracized by Muslim friends and family for several months. This bitter experience led him to form this ministry which brought together converted Muslims in similar situations.[38] The CMCM which is charismatic in orientation has adopted a variety of mission strategies: open air crusades which sometimes sparked violence; person-to-person evangelism and workshops that follow up with converts; literature media such as Agyei's book, *The Comforter: Muhammed or the Holy Spirit?*, which has influential in the conversion of Muslims to Christianity; and an audio visual media ministry which also sparked controversy from the Muslim camp.[39] Dovlo and Asante observe regarding the impact on Muslims of a CMCM radio broadcast:

> In 1997 when it started its broadcasts, the Muslim community complained to Garden City Radio about Christians preaching on the station and quoting from the Qur'an. According to the General Secretary of CMCM, Rev. Ibrahim Muhammed, at a meeting called on May 14, 1997, between Christian and Muslim groups that preach on the station, it was agreed that a ban be placed on the use of the Qur'an by Christians, and the Bible by Muslims on Garden City Radio until the issue could be properly addressed. The General Secretary explained that the use of the electronic method media proved very effective in evangelism among Muslims. It has a wide coverage and many listeners, since it is broadcast in Twi. He claimed that within three months of its inception, about twenty Muslims have converted and are now attending Straightway Chapel in Kumasi and the number has been on the increase. He also claims that they have letters from other Muslims who have converted and are attending other churches.[40]

The CMCM has morphed into a charismatic-oriented church, Straightway Chapel, with the first congregation starting in Kumasi in 1989. Straightway Chapel has designed a logo: "the Cross with a dove descending from the Cross with the *kalmia* (word) in its mouth to the Crescent, the symbol of Islam. They explain that the dove is bringing the message of the Cross to the Muslim world."[41] The logo is a conscious attempt to use Islamic imagery to contextualize the Gospel to Muslims. As at 2003, Straightway Chapel in Kumasi reported a membership of 450, and it has several branches across the country.

While most educated Muslims do not see anything wrong with CMCM's radio broadcast some are very worried about the approach employed by the ministry. Sheikh Ishaak Ibrahim Nuamah, a leading Muslim radio and television preacher in Ghana, in the introduction to his book, *Islam: The Misunderstood Religion in Ghana*, writes:

> Of late, we have been witnesses to instances of incessant derogatory verbal attacks on Islam and Muslims in Ghana by some Evangelical groups in Christendom. Without mincing words, we are greatly shocked by these unwanted developments in view of the fact that Ghana, has for years, been regarded as a land of peace, civilization and hospitality despite the existence of multi-faceted religious dogmas.... Upon analyzing these attacks, it became quite conspicuous that they are part of a cunning but failure-bound strategy aimed at swaying Muslims away from the noble religion of Islam. This strategy finds expression in the following approaches. a) Driving Muslims towards worldly pleasures; b) Wrong analyzing of [sic] Qur'anic quotations through the following methods: misrepresentation, misinterpretation, employing the

art of creativity; c) Casting of insinuations at Islam and Muslims; d) Attacking the personality of the Holy Prophet Mohammed (P.B.U.H); e) Using some Qur'anic quotations to support their fabricated stand of Jesus.[42]

Kalu underscores the fact that the use of the electronic media by Pentecostal-type moments has intensified rivalry over the appropriation of the modern media as propaganda, thus exacerbating competition in the religious market in Nigeria. Muslims try to counter the use of the electronic media by the Pentecostal-type movement in Nigeria by imitating their propagation techniques such as the use of television, radio, and audio cassettes. The invasion of Muslim vendors at motor parks and public places with cassettes blaring Muslim songs and sermons explains the easy resort to violence.

Demonization of Islam

Pentecostals, charismatics, and renewalists are very much aware that Islam serves as an alternative or complementary source of spiritual protection for many people, including some who attend church services on Sunday. However Pentecostals have demonized both African indigenous religions and Islam. Both are the subject of many of renewalist sermons, teachings, and songs. A chorus sung by Pentecostal-type churches in Ghana says: *It is God who grants healing, I will not go to Muslim Spiritualist, I will not go to a Traditional healer, It is God who grants healing.*[43] Pentecostals equate Islam with a religion of Satan. Yet they recognize the attraction of Islam because it is a common knowledge that *malams* offer viable resolutions to life's crises. However, they strongly believe that Muslims in general, particularly *malams*, are agents of Satan. Therefore contacting *malams* opens up a "demonic door-way" that exposes people to the Devil and his machineries. Pentecostals therefore see it as their responsibility to warn Muslims and other people about the demonic character of *malams*.

Furthermore, there is a growing trend among Pentecostals that constructs the Islamic religion as an enemy, using satanic metaphors. As Matthews Ojo notes, "Such expression as 'religion of the bondwoman', 'the religion of force and violence', 'the slaves', 'the spirit of anti-Christ', etc., become prominent terms used widely by Pentecostals to describe Islam."[44] Pentecostals depict Islam as an illegitimate religion which does not deserve following. Kalu has also observed that Pentecostals portray Islam "as the illegitimate religion of the bondwoman. As Ishmael's descendants constitute a threat to the children of Isaac, so does Islam constitute a threat to Christians."[45] This kind of biblical hermeneutic convinces some Muslims to abandon their religion while reinforcing the stand of Christians.

The introduction of *sharia* in parts of Northern Nigeria was perceived by Pentecostals as a satanic attack against Nigeria in her quest for peace and unity. Pentecostals therefore interpret it as an issue for spiritual warfare against demons assigned to invade Nigeria as well as its demon-infested political structures. Thus the introduction of the *sharia* reinforced the conspiracy theory held by some Pentecostals that Muslims have a grand design to make Africa a Muslim continent, a subject which featured prominently during the 7th International Ministers and Christian Leadership Conference and Prayer Retreat at Port Harcourt in 2003.[46]

Conclusions

Ghanaians and Nigerians will for a long time to come live with religious diversity. In the words of Johnson Mbillah, General Coordinator of the Program for Christian Muslim Relations in Africa:

> Whatever the case, religious diversity has become the lot of the human race. God-given freedom allows free human beings to choose the religious path they wish to tread; the churches in Africa and like elsewhere therefore, cannot be impatient with the religious diversity around them since arguably, religious variety will remain the lot of the human race until the end of time. A credible question for the churches to ask therefore, is not how to eradicate religious diversity (for that will mean attempting to eradicate the God-given freedom of human beings) but how to constructively relate with religious diversity.[47]

Pentecostals in Ghana and Nigeria should reckon with the differences between them and people of other faiths, particularly Muslims, and learn to live with such differences in harmony. This is the reality of the context in which God has called Pentecostals to do mission. Indeed, the ability to coexist harmoniously with people of other faiths is a missionary task.

Pentecostal-type Christians like all Christians are given the mandate to preach the Gospel as a matter of urgency in the multireligious context in which they find themselves. They may not fully resolve the complex nature of this mission in the midst of other religions. However, that does not negate the rightful place of their witness to the Gospel. The responsibility of Christians with regards to the Gospel in a pluralistic world is to bear witness to Jesus Christ with the deepest conviction and live out the Christian faith in the most concrete way possible.[48]

The non-aggressive posture adopted by the mainline churches over the years with regard to ministry to Muslims has succeeded in brokering peace among Christians and Muslims in Ghana and Nigeria to the extent of the Emir of Kanam Alhaji Mohammadu Muazu Babangida requesting a Catholic parish be established in his Emirate and Christian Governors in Abia, Akwa Ibom, and Benue States facilitating the building of mosques, all in pursuance of peace, harmony and stability. These initiatives are praiseworthy. Nevertheless the approach of mainline churches blurs its ministry to Muslims. In fact Pentecostals perceive mainline churches as having no ministry to Muslims.

The non-confrontational approach to mission adopted by the mainline churches is seen by Pentecostal-type movements as watering down the Gospel of Jesus Christ among non-Christians. They in turn adopt an extreme negative attitude towards Islam and Muslims. This exclusivist and hostile posture towards Muslims sometimes result in religious polemics and, eventually, in violence. Clearly Muslims have been very uncomfortable about the approach adopted by Pentecostal-type renewal groups which they see as insulting. This development, of course adversely affects the gains the mainline churches have made in their attempt to dialogue with people of other faiths.

Pentecostal-type movements should accept the religious diversity of their context. They should acknowledge the fact that conflict and consensus must be factored into the equation of religious understanding in their milieu and learn the language of dialogue without which there would be no peace and harmony for mission activity. Their use of a religious lens in reading all kinds of social realities, thus demonizing Islam for instance, could wreck havoc for their countries, particularly in the case of Nigeria.

The approach to mission by Pentecostal-type movements that has proven to attract relatively minimal conflicts is the manifestation of charismata and power evangelism, especially healing. This method attracts people of other faiths, and should be emphasized by Pentecostals. After all that is the essence of Pentecostal-type movements and that is their specialty. This non-confrontational approach Pentecostals and charismatics could be a useful tool for doing mission among Muslims. This approach may not avoid the legitimate offense of the gospel, but this is in fact an integral part of the cost Christians must pay in their genuine encounter with the "other."

Notes

1. See Peter Clarke, *West Africa and Islam: A Study of Religious Development from the 8th to the 20th Century* (London: Edward Arnold, 1982), vi.

2. Patrick Ryan, "Islam in Ghana: Its Major Influences and the Situation Today," *Orita* 28 (1996):73. He refers to Ivor Wilks, *Asante in the Nineteenth Century: The Structure and Evolution of a Political Order* (Cambridge: Cambridge University Press, 1975), 245, and Timothy Garrard, *Akan Weights and the Gold Trade* (London: Longman, 1980), 24-25.

3. Big Northern traditional smock formerly associated with citizens from Northern Ghana and formerly worn by traditional priests who "bought" deities from Northern Ghana.

4. Ivor Wilks, *The Northern Factor in Ashanti History* (Legon: Institute of African Studies, 1961); Patrick Ryan, "Ariande Auf Naxos: Islam and Politics in a Religiously Pluralistic African Society," *Journal of Religion in Africa* 26:3 (1996): 314-16.

5. Deborah Pellow, "Muslim Segmentation: Cohesion and Divisiveness in Accra," *Journal of Modern African Studies* 23:3 (1985): 419-44; Enid Schildkrout, *People of the*

Zongo: The Transformation of Ethnic identities in Ghana (Cambridge and New York: Cambridge University Press, 1978).

6. See paper presented by Haj. Mumuni Sulemana, at seminar on "Christian-Muslim Relations in Ghana," held at the University of Ghana on the August 5, 2000.

7. The Coalition of Muslim Associations held a press conference on January 9, 2002, attributing the figures in table 1 to the website of the Central Intelligence Agency of the United States of America.

8. See Elom Dovlo and Alfred Ofosu Asante, "Reinterpreting the Straight Path: Ghanaian Muslim Converts in Mission to Muslims," *Exchange: A Journal of Missiological and Ecumenical Research* 32:3 (2003): 214-38.

9. Paul Gifford, *African Christianity: Its Public Role* (London: Hurst, 1998), 110.

10. See Kwame Bediako, *Christianity in Africa: The Renewal of a Non-Western Religion* (Edinburgh: Edinburgh University Press, and Maryknoll: Orbis Books, 1995), ix.

11. See Elom Dovlo, "A Comparative Overview of Independent Churches and Charismatic Ministries in Ghana," *Trinity Journal of Church and Theology* 2 (1992): 55-73; Paul Gifford, "Ghana's Charismatic Churches," *Journal of Religion in Africa* 24 (1994): 241-65; Gerrie ter Haar, "Standing up for Jesus: A Survey of New Developments in Christianity in Ghana," *Exchange: A Journal of Missiological and Ecumenical Research* 23 (1994): 221-40.

12. The Federal Government of Nigeria has been sensitive about the explosive nature of religion and ethnicity so it consciously decided to be silent on it during the last national census.

13. See Dovlo and Asante, "Reinterpreting the Straight Path," 226.

14. Ibid.

15. See Rotgak I. Gofwen, *Religious Conflicts in Northern Nigeria and Nation Building: The Throes of Two Decades 1980-2000* (Kaduna: Human Rights Monitor, 2004), 65-67, for the list of major conflicts associated with religion. See also the article by Ismail Omipidian, "Why North is on Fire," *Sunday Sun* (August 2, 2009): 4.

16. See Amos Yong, *Hospitality and the Other: Pentecost, Christian Practices, and the Neighbor* (Maryknoll: Orbis Books, 2008), 17-18, for a more exhaustive list of Christian-Muslim conflicts in Northern Nigeria between 1980 and 2004.

17. Ibid., 19.

18. Matthew Kukah, *Human Rights in Nigeria: Hopes and Hindrances* (Aachen: Missio, 2003), 19.

19. William M. Miller, *A Christian's Response to Islam* (Nutley: Presbyterian and Reformed Publishing Co., 1977), 8; Andrew N. Potter, "Evangelicalism, Islam and Millennial Expectations in the Nineteenth Century," *International Bulletin of Missionary Research* 24:3 (2000): 111-18, points out the emphasis mainline churches put on dialogue with Muslims.

20. Lissi Rasmussen, *Christian-Muslim Relations in Africa: The cases of Northern Nigeria and Tanzania Compared* (London: British Academic Press, 1993), 16-21; Mervyn Hiskett, *Development of Islam in West Africa* (London: Longman Group Ltd. 1982), 381.

21. See James Anquandah, *Together we Sow and Reap: The First Fifty Years of the Christian Council of Ghana* (Accra: Asempa Publishers, 1979).

22. For details see www.procmura-prica.org.

23. As cited in Maurice Borrmans, *Guidelines for Dialogue between Christians and Muslims* (New York: Paulist Press, 1990), 2.

24. Dovlo and Asante, "Reinterpreting the Straight Path," 221.

25. Examples are the Association of Episcopal Conference of Anglophone West Africa (AECAWA) publications: Joseph Kenny, *West Africa and Islam: History, Beliefs, Practices and Christian Attitudes—What Every Catholic Should Know* (Takoradi, Nigeria: AECAWA/Nativity Prints, 2000), and *Islam and Christianity in Dialogue* (Jos, Nigeria: Imico Books, and Cape Coast, Ghana: Mfantsiman Press, 1987).

26. Most Rev. Ignatius A. Kaigama, Archbishop of Jos, "My Experience of Christian/Muslim Relations in Jos and Nigeria," paper presented by at the conference organized by CAFOD (the official overseas development and relief agency of the Catholic Church in England and Wales) and Heythrop College, London, October 28, 2009.

27. Ibid.

28. See Matthews A. Ojo, "Pentecostal Movements, Islam and the Contest for Public Space in Northern Nigeria," *Islam and Christian-Muslim Relations* 18:2 (2007): 179.

29. Cephas N. Omenyo, "Pentecostal-Type Renewal and Disharmony in Ghanaian Christianity," in David Westerlund, ed., *Global Pentecostalism: Encounters with other Religious Traditions* (London and New York: I. B. Tauris, 2009), 64.

30. Omenyo, "Pentecostal-Type Renewal and Disharmony in Ghanaian Christianity," 66.

31. Ojo, "Pentecostal Movements," 179.

32. Ogbu Kalu, *African Pentecostalism: An Introduction* (Oxford and New York: Oxford University Press, 2008), 240.

33. Ogbu U. Kalu, "Sharia and Islam in Nigerian Pentecostal Rhetoric, 1970-2003," *PNEUMA: The Journal of the Society for Pentecostal Studies* 26:2 (2004): 252-53.

34. Ryan, "Islam and Ghana," 84.

35. For instance see *The Ghanaian Times* of December 5, 1995, where it was reported that a groups of Muslims forced two foreign Christian evangelists and their Ghanaian hosts to abandon a preaching campaign in Tamale, the capital of the Northern Region of Ghana.

36. See Cephas N. Omenyo, *Pentecost Outside Pentecostalism: A Study of the Development of Charismatic Renewal in the Mainline Churches in Ghana* (Zoetermeer: Boekencentrum, 2006).

37. Kalu, *African Pentecostalism*, 240.

38. Dovlo and Asante, "Reinterpreting the Straight Path," 226.

39. Ibid., 235-36.

40. Ibid., 230.

41. Ibid., 231.

42. Sheikh Ishaak Ibrahim Nuamah, *Islam: The Misunderstood Religion in Ghana* (Kumasi, Ghana: Islamic Social Centre, n.d.), quoted in Dovlo and Asante, "Reinterpreting the Straight Path," 234-35.

43. Omenyo, *Pentecost Outside Pentecostalism*, 33.

44. Ojo, "Pentecostal Movements," 186.

45. Kalu, "Sharia and Islam in Nigerian Pentecostal Rhetoric," 256.

46. Ibid., 259.

47. Johnson Mbillah, "African Churches and Interfaith Relations, Food for Thought," in Johnson A. Mbillah and John A. Chesworth, eds., *From the Cross to the Crescent* (Nairobi: Programme for Christian-Muslim Relations in Africa, 2004), 3-4.

48. See also S. Wesley Ariarajah, *Not Without My Neighbour: Issues in Interfaith Relations* (Geneva: WCC, 1999), 111.

Conclusion

From Demonization to Kin-domization: The Witness of the Spirit and the Renewal of Missions in a Pluralistic World

Amos Yong

This concluding chapter builds upon the previous chapters, but goes beyond them to attempt to adjudicate the urgent missiological questions. We hope to chart the way forward to viable theological views regarding interreligious interaction in the twenty-first century, especially as these might enable the renewal and re-invigoration of mission in the present pluralistic age. To do so, we begin by confronting squarely the discourses of demonization so prevalent in renewal circles.[1] The question is this: how do we eliminate such demonological modes of engagement but yet not lapse into a non-discerning relativism about the diversity of religions? The central and longest part of these concluding pages will suggest, in dialogue with the author of the book of Acts and my colleagues in the preceding chapters, precisely such an anti-demonization set of strategies for renewal missiology that enables honest but yet respectful engagement with religious others in a pluralistic world. The emergent result, I proffer, is a "kin-domization" model that counters the discursive rhetoric of demonization and does so by anticipating the formation of the new people of God beyond the historical divisions that have separated humankind. Such is the eschatological community that is reflected in the miracle of human communication manifested in the Day of Pentecost narrative, and that is unfolded subsequently in the relationality and mutuality of the apostolic encounter with those in other faiths.

Demonization and the Religious Other: The Challenge for Renewal Missiology

Renewalists have always presumed a demonology from their plain reading of the Bible. While this is neither the time nor the place to undertake a critical analysis of such ideas,[2] it is important to note that renewal demonology resonates with and maps onto much of the cosmological intuitions of populations in the global South. Hence practices like exorcism, deliverance, and spiritual warfare are prominent in certain renewal circles, even if these are certainly not limited to such circles. When enacted vis-à-vis the interreligious encounter, however such demonological discursive practices are problematic, in some cases, lethal.

For example, one potentially explosive form of renewalist engagement with the pluralistic public square of late modernity involves the political demonization of the opposition party or opposing candidate that is from the "other" religious tradition. Given the dualistic framework of much of renewal cosmology, Jesus' words, "Whoever is not with me is against me" (Luke 11:23),[3] lend themselves to the conclusion that the non-Christian option receives its mandate, empowerment, and agenda from the prince of darkness himself.[4] Yet this can be taken even further, as when the rhetoric and cosmology of demonization is extended to provide theological legitimation for egregious political and military activity. The most prominent example concerns the Sandinista government of Ríos Montt in Guatemala in the early 1980s.[5] Montt, at that time, had testified of a Pentecostal conversion, and submitted himself under the spiritual advisement of a neopentecostal church. In response to the accusations of human rights atrocities committed against the indigenous people of Guatemala by Montt's army, Verbo Church pastors said: "The Army doesn't massacre the Indians. It massacres demons, the Indians are demon possessed; they are communists. We hold Brother Efraín Ríos Montt like King David of the Old Testament. He is the king of the New Testament."[6] At a broader level, as this quotation suggests, such reasoning also serves as theological justification for international military operations, whether in the past against Muslim infidels (during the crusades) or against the advance of communism and socialism (during the Cold War era) or in the present at the vanguard of American-led forays into the Muslim-dominated Middle Eastern arena.[7] At this point the lines between the American renewal movement and the conservative Christian "right" become blurred. Unfortunately, renewalists have, in general, supported such political agendas with their own distinctive theological rationales rather than prophetically protested against these developments.

Cephas Omenyo's chapter on renewal in West Africa also is suggestive for understanding how renewal demonology engages with a pluralistic world with violent consequences, even when not specifically sanctioned by the political powers that be. The Nigerian case especially invites further comment.[8] The emergence of renewal churches and Christians in Nigeria during the last thirty years has complicated an already hotly contested interreligious arena. Besides revitalizing Christianity in general in terms of competing for the allegiance of the Christian faithful with historic Protestant and Roman Catholic churches in Nigeria, renewalists have also aggressively engaged the interreligious arena. On the one hand, they have picked up on earlier missionary polemics against African traditional religions, to the point of being very concerned that even the retrieval of African culture—e.g., such as that which occurred at FESTAC 1977 (the 2nd World Black and African Festival of Arts and Culture)—was and would be "an open door to the demonic" in terms of re-instilling the covenants with the indigenous religious traditions and their spiritual entities.[9] On the other hand, renewalists are not only countering the Islamization of Nigeria, but have sought to do so by evangelizing both the nation and, as seen in renowned evangelist Reinhard Bonnke's "Africa for Christ" crusades, the entire continent.[10]

For our purposes, it is important to note not just the fact of the renewalist commitment to mission and evangelism, but the tactics and, especially, rhetoric that is often employed. The inflammatory nature of renewalist modes of evangelization can be identified at multiple levels. First, renewal "political theology" is based not on political action but on fasting, prayer, spiritual warfare, and even exorcism and deliverance ministries against the principalities, powers, and covenants of the heavenly realms.[11] Following from this, second, there is the consistent demonization not only of African religions but also of Islam in renewalist literature. For renewalists, Ishmael is outside the covenant, born out of the Abraham's lack of faith to Hagar "the bondwoman" (cf. Gal. 4:22-31), Mohammad is not a prophet but an epileptic and womanizer, and Allah is not the supreme God but one of 360 in the Ka'abah of pre-Islamic Arabia; hence, Islam is idolatry, Muslims are caught up "in Satan's bondage," and renewalists reject as demonic core Islamic symbols such as the moon, the star and Islamic rituals.[12] Third, and perhaps most provocative in terms of its practical effects, renewalists have employed the full range of media and technology in their evangelism campaigns—loud speaker public address systems, cassettes, videos, CDs, DVD, radio, TV, the internet—all of which not only clearly publicize the renewalist understanding of other religions but also generate new forms of interreligious animosity and hostility.[13] Of course, such defamatory literature and media communications are also now being produced by Muslims, with the resulting intensification of interreligious "hate" rhetoric further destabilizing the region rather than providing a platform for building a harmonious multifaith Nigeria.[14] Partly as a result of such developments within the socio-political and economic backdrop of an otherwise extremely contested Christian-Muslim public space, there has been a series of tragic and violent conflicts particularly in the Muslim-dominated regions of northern Nigeria.[15]

In her chapter, Kirsteen Kim also calls attention to the violence attending some of the interreligious interactions in the South Asian context. The enactment of martyrdom in the name of religion and in the call for liberation and emancipation highlight the potential that the rhetoric of demonization can play in such extreme political environments. On the one hand, the martyrs are resisting the oppressiveness under which they and their peoples are burdened, and such situations of injustice certainly must be called demonic. On the other hand, the radical acts of martyrdom also surely should be interpreted as a manifestation of the demonic character of reality that must be otherwise opposed with the full range of non-violent means of resistance (instead of passive resignation at the hands of violent perpetrators). Renewalists find themselves across this spectrum of responses, and not infrequently engage in their own theological analyses of the demonic character of their political experiences.

As people of the book, like most other Protestant Christians, renewalists believe their notions about the demonic are scripturally grounded. The biblical categories that divide the light from the darkness, the good from evil, and the children of God from the children of the devil, are certainly present across the pages of especially the New Testament.[16] Missiologically and practically, this leads to an understanding that only believers in Christ (i.e., converts) are children of light, while all others (i.e., non-converts) remain as children of darkness.[17] With regard to the interfaith encounter, then, a similar theme emerges: only followers of Christ are the children of God, while people of other false religions should only be evangelized, if not engaged with other more forceful strategies of missionization and even Christianization.

To be sure, few if any contemporary texts in renewal missiology either utilize this rhetoric of demonization or advocate their corollary missional practices. However the problem persists at least at the following two levels: 1) in the popular arena, lay renewalists continue to imbibe a remnant mentality that situates themselves over and against those not within their own group amidst an apocalyptic understanding of the impending eschatological conflagration between the forces of light and of darkness, and 2) even among the ecclesiastical hierarchy, many of whom are involved in organizing, mobilizing, and securing funding for mission projects and ventures, the dualistic worldview of the New Testament narratives implicitly informs the renewal self-understanding of having to engage in spiritual warfare "against the rulers, against the authorities, against the cosmic powers of this present darkness, against the spiritual forces of evil in the heavenly places" (Eph. 6:12). These renewal demonologies need to be critically interrogated, especially for the purposes of constructing a more plausible and viable theology of mission in a religiously plural world.

The Missiology of Renewal and The Renewal of Missiology: Apostolic Insights in a Pluralistic World

In this section I sketch a renewal missiology that simultaneously serves to renew the Christian mission in a pluralistic twenty-first century. Such a renewal, I proffer, proceeds less from a polemical demonization of religious others than it does from a respectful, even deferential posture, toward them, albeit one informed deeply by theological convictions rather than merely driven by pragmatic or politically correct concerns. In order to accomplish this objective, I want to bring the perspectives registered by the authors in this book into dialogue with Luke, especially his narrative of the earliest or apostolic Christian encounter with religious diversity in the book of Acts.[18] On the one hand, I recognize that there is a dualistic strain even in Acts which accents evangelistic urgency precisely to turn people "from darkness to light and from the power of Satan to God" (Act 26:18), even as I also realize that Paul confronts Elymas, the shaman on the island of Cyprus, as a "son of the devil, [an] enemy of all righteousness, full of all deceit and villainy" (Acts 13:10), and that he later exorcises evil spirits from the Jewish sons of Sceva (Acts 19:13-16). On the other hand, I believe that this strategy of demonization is neither dominant in the Acts narrative nor that it best describes the early Christian encounter with those in other religions. In the following, I focus on five occasions of the apostolic interaction with people of other faiths, highlighting especially the practical dimensions of such encounters.[19] This will set the stage for the discussion in the final section when we turn to draw some overarching theological and missiological conclusions. We proceed in reverse, arguing from the end of Acts to the beginning of the book, only because I think the salient issues are most observable by proceeding in this light.[20]

Acts 28

The first part of this chapter describes the encounter between Paul and his travel companions with the Maltese islanders, which Luke identifies (in the original Greek) as βαρβαροι, transliterated as "barbarians" (Acts 28:2, 4). Three observations are especially noteworthy vis-à-vis a renewal missiology in a pluralistic world. First, there is no explicit reference to the proclamation of the *kerygma* in this passage. This means neither that such did not occur nor that there were no conversions to Christ (although the text is equally silent about that as well). Second, Paul and his comrades are repeatedly described in this passage as having received the hospitality of the barbarian islanders (Acts 28:2, 7, 10). Third, whereas elsewhere in Acts the apostles had resisted obeisance from those who thought them deserving of gestures usually reserved for deity or had strongly corrected misapprehensions by pagans about their divinity (i.e., Acts 10:25-26, 14:11-18), in this case, there is no noted response to the islanders thinking that Paul, because he had escaped death expected from a snakebite, was divine (Acts 28:3-6). This indicates that while often Christians find themselves as hosts of people in other faiths—an important set of interreligious practices— equally important but often neglected is a theological self-understanding that involves consideration of how to be guests in the presence of religious others. The combined missiological effect of this passage should not be underestimated. While there are certainly occasions for overt proclamation of the gospel,

Christians need to be sensitive to their missional contexts and, especially when being guests of those in other faiths, need to interact with their hosts in ways that are respectful of their traditions. This does not undermine the variegated expressions of the Christian mission, in the Maltese case, involving the ministry of healing the sick (Acts 28:8-9).

What I find remarkable is that whereas much of the history of Christian missions has demonized pagans and barbarians of the world, in this text, Paul and his fellow missionaries receive the generosity of their Maltese hosts instead. There is no indication of any suspicion regarding the islanders and their gifts. There is an authentic mutuality: the hosts opened up their homes and gave of their possessions to the visitors and the latter ministered healing to the former in turn. Although it may have been that Paul and his friends simply found themselves as guests of these barbarians because of the shipwreck and hence cannot be said to ever have intended to engage in the formal evangelization of the island, these developments highlight the importance of being ready, as Christians, to be hosted by those in other faiths. In fact, in a globally shrinking world of massive immigration, exile, and refugee experiences, more often than not we find ourselves cast in the presence of religious others never having asked to be put in those situations. So even in stable societies, Christians need to pause and ask themselves: how often do we put ourselves in the position of being invited over as guests of folk in other religions? There is a form of relationality and neighborliness that Paul manifests in his encounter with the Maltese pagans that should model for us the character of the missionary posture which anticipates the coming of the Day of the Lord in which the hostilities between human beings will be no more.

Further, the value of Luke's discussion of Paul's shipwreck on Malta is especially lifted up in light of Clifton Clarke's urging that we take non-Western and non-Enlightenment epistemologies, traditions, and perspectives into account. Clarke's focus is on the African continent, in particular on the import of African worldviews, use of symbolisms, and cultural orality. The Lukan missiology of guests would invite further consideration of how to defer to local norms and ways of knowing in articulating and living out the Christian faith. Such a call for contextualization, however, is not limited to what occurs only in the global South, as in Clarke's example. Rather, I would suggest that the contextualization of the gospel of Christ is a universal phenomenon and obligation, one that begins and is reflected in the apostolic experience itself. In this case, then, other religious traditions are not just "objects" to be overcome, but realities to be respected, carefully engaged, and even received as guests in certain contexts. To be sure, on some occasions, the proper Christian response is a discerning rejection of that local reality; on other occasions, however, what Walter Hollenweger calls a theologically responsible syncretism is the appropriate result, one that involves the enrichment of the gospel by the local cultural forms, even as the latter are critically transformed and even in some respects redeemed in light of the power of the Spirit.[21]

Acts 19

The riot in Ephesus described in the last half of Acts 19 is the occasion that provides us with another glimpse of how the early Christians encountered other religions. In this case, the economy of Ephesus was being shaken by the growth and expansion of the messianic community. Not only had conversions to Christ resulted in the rejection of the magical practices that had been prominent in that community, but the local economy had also suffered in the process since sales of the silver shrines of Artemis had plummeted. Part of the accusation by the craftsmen, intended to rile up the crowd in defense of Artemis and against Paul and his missionary friends, was that "Paul has persuaded and drawn away a considerable number of people by saying that gods made with hands are not gods" (Acts 19:26). Yet the response of the city clerk, intended to quiet the mob, was equally straightforward: "You have brought these men here who are neither temple-robbers nor blasphemers of our goddess" (Acts 19:37). On the one hand, the accusations of the craftsmen may have been true in some respect—after all, Paul had said elsewhere that, "no idol in the world really exists" (1 Cor. 8:4); on the other hand, it is also clear that the clerk's insistence that more formal charges be brought to try the missionaries never materialized, and in that sense, the apostles were vindicated as having been deferential, or at least non-blasphemous, in their approaches to the cult of Artemis. Rather than demonizing Artemis or its cult, the Christian mission to Ephesus appears to have been conducted with respect vis-à-vis the pagan deities.

Renewalists have a good deal to learn about being respectful of the beliefs and even practices of those in other faiths from this account. On the one hand, public expressions of faith in Christ are by no means out of order, as the burning books devoted to magical practices attests (Acts 19:18-19). On the other hand, such practices can and did, in this case, occur quite apart from irreverent polemics against other religious traditions and their practices, doctrines, and even deities. For purposes of thinking theologically and missionally about the religions, the task of negative apologetics—being against or tearing down the religious others' beliefs and practices—is less important than is a positive witness to the transformative power of the gospel. Our goal is not to exacerbate interreligious enmities but to be sufficiently deferential in order to establish dialogical relationships with those in other faiths.

Further, Steven Studebaker's claim that the religions are culturally situated is also pertinent vis-à-vis this account of what transpired at Ephesus. Studebaker's argument is that insofar as the religions are constituted at least in part by wider cultural realities, to that same extent the universal presence and activity of the Spirit in such wider cultural domains suggests the presence and activity of the Spirit in the religions as well. The Acts narrative acknowledges the complex and interrelated nature of religion and economics at Ephesus. Not only does religion, especially its conversion dynamics, have an economic dimension, but economics also has religious implications and consequences. In short, any theology of religions, such as that proposed by Studebaker, must be consistent with theological reflection on the various domains that comprise human life, including not only the economic but also the social and the political, among others.[22]

Acts 17

Luke's discussion of Paul at the Areopagus has, of course, been consistently mined for missiological insights. Here, let me make only the following observations before bringing the discussion into dialogue with the proposals of Richie and Kärkkäinen. First, Luke repeatedly highlights Paul's dialogical approach. Thus the word διελεγετο translated into English as "argued" (Acts 17:17) can also be translated as "dialogued" as it includes both the disputative and conversational character of Paul's exchanges with the Athenians. Second, as perennially noted, Paul enters into the discussion with the Epicurean and Stoic thinkers on their own philosophical territory, quoting from their own poets and authorities (Acts 17: 28). Most importantly for our purposes, however, is that Paul articulates an inclusive theology, cosmology, and anthropology, one that does not divide the world between "us" and "them" but which suggests that the unknown god of the Athenians was the God of Jesus Christ, and that emphasizes the one world (Acts 17:24, 26) and the common humanity between himself and his heathen interlocutors (Acts 17:25, 27). From this Paul approvingly quotes from the pagan sources, "*we* are God's offspring" (Acts 17:29, my italics), in a way which binds him and his interlocutors together. Paul thus begins with the theological and anthropological common ground: humankind remains one family, all of us in some sense being children of the one God.

All of this is consistent with our preceding deliberations from Acts 19 and 28, including Clarke's advocacy of contextualization of local traditions, even if in this case, St. Paul engages with what later has emerged as being part of the dominant philosophical tradition of the Western world. As important, rather than mocking the Athenians, deprecating their idolatry, or demonizing their theological ideas, Paul's approach to the religious traditions of the Athenians is to treat their beliefs and practices with respect, albeit firmly also suggesting alternate ways of understanding these realities as well. Hence witness is borne through the Spirit regarding the possibility of overcoming the estrangement that divides family members from each other.

What, then, are the implications of this Lukan passage for the contemporary interreligious encounter? I see at least two lines of convergences with the proposals made in this book. First, Richie's advocacy of an inclusivist approach to the religions deserves comment in light of these developments at the Areopagus. For Richie, theological inclusivism is pneumatologically expansive but christologically tethered, ecclesiologically connected, and missionally driven. Such an inclusivist vision is, arguably, Lukan and Pauline, at least as refracted in this text. The inclusive theology, cosmology, and anthropology recorded as proclaimed to the Athenian philosophers nevertheless neither presumed a chasm between synagogue (where the believers gathered) and marketplace (Acts 17:17) nor neglected the judgment of God appointed through the man who was raised from the dead (Acts 17:31). It is precisely such an inclusivist dynamic that allows for open and honest but also respectful encounter between the religions. Without common ground, there would be no possibility of encounter; but without differences, there would be nothing to discuss.[23]

Kärkkäinen's chapter presents a clear example of how the interreligious dialogue can proceed in light of Paul's dialogical strategy. First, Kärkkäinen proceeds carefully and contextually, focused on the South East Asian Theravadan Buddhist contexts, and thus is mindful about Theravadan Buddhists, texts, concerns, and issues. His chapter is a model of respectful and deferential engagement with the religious other at least initially on its own terms, rather than by imposing a Christian interpretive framework.[24] Second, such serious interaction with local voices and perspectives is not then left to its own, but taken up within the response of the gospel. What I mean here is that Theravadan Buddhist concerns call forth a renewal response, but one that heeds the insights of the former. What emerges is a renewal theology of suffering, a theme not otherwise given much attention by renewalists because of a triumphalism that usually overlooks (at best) or suppresses (at worst) such realities. But, finally, the result nevertheless allows the gospel to speak forth, albeit this time within the resonances of the South East Asian Theravadan Buddhist self-understanding. Thus Buddhist *apatheia* encounters, informs, and is transformed by renewal *orthopathos* in the process. Hence here we have a genuine dialogue, one that unfolds as a theologically responsible syncretism, on the one hand taking up the indigenous religious concerns but on the other hand enabling the good news of divine, redemptive, integrative, and healing aspects of suffering to be registered in local idiom. In the process, Christians and Buddhists learn how to meet each other potentially as equals, at least in their common humanity, and even perhaps in anticipation of the eschatological community that will be full of surprises for both sides.[25]

Acts 8-7

The expansion of the gospel into Samaria as recounted in Acts 8 is not often viewed as an interreligious encounter.[26] While the narrative is dominated by the apostolic interaction with Simon the magician, we need first to emphasize that the antagonism between Jews and Samaritans was so palpable—i.e., John mentions that "Jews do not share things in common with Samaritans" (John 4:9)—that they can be considered to have inhabited, by the time of the first century, two distinct religious traditions. In fact, things had so degenerated between Jews and Samaritans that the former had already begun to engage in the rhetorical demonization of the latter; thus does John record the Jewish leadership's polemic against Jesus: "you are a Samaritan and have a demon" (John 8:48)! Yet Philip, when driven out of Jerusalem by persecution, did not (perhaps unlike the other deacons and leaders) avoid Samaria. More pointedly, Philip did not evade Simon, well known as a powerful religious leader (Acts

8:10-11), but fairly engaged his world.

I suggest, however, that there is more involved in the mission to Samaria than simply the miraculous signs and wonders among the Samaritans and their conversion, as important as these are. Rather when it is understood that Jews and Samaritans had different theological self-understandings, and that within these theological schemes the place of worship of the one true God was centrally important and served as a dividing theological line—with Jews worshipping at Jerusalem and Samaritans at Mount Gerizim (John 4:20-22)—then Stephen's speech before the Sanhedrin illuminates how the mission to Samaria helped transform the early Jewish messianic theology as well. This was related to Stephen, as a Hellenist Jew, coming to see that the Jewish insistence on localizing the presence and activity of God in the temple at Jerusalem reflected a parochial theological viewpoint. Instead, God did not dwell in local temples, nor was God's domain geographically or regionally limited (Acts 7:48-49).

It was this radical theological revisioning that made it possible, I suggest, for Philip, another Hellenist, to venture out into Samaria, in contrast with the other Judean apostolic leaders who stayed put in Jerusalem (Acts 8:1) perhaps because they had long held more conservative or classical Jewish views that restricted the sphere of God's operations. It was also this thorough theological reconstruction that enabled Philip both to preach Christ, not just a place, and to insist that the apostles come up to Samaria rather than that the converted Samaritans go down to Jerusalem. Put more strongly, might it be more appropriately suggested that it was precisely the possibility if not the actuality of the gospel in Samaritan dress, shorn of its Jerusalemite centeredness and presuppositions, that inspired Stephen's own theological transformation and, eventually and unfortunately, brought about his martyrdom? Is it possible to see that whereas the Jews had rejected as demonic the Samaritan idea of worship at Mount Gerizim, it was precisely the Samaritan intuition about true worship not being bound to Jerusalem that was central to the Hellenistic Jewish-Christian insight into the universal scope of the presence and activity of the God of Jesus Christ, and which motivated the expansion of the Christian mission beyond the confines of Judea toward Samaria initially and then later to the ends of the earth?

Again, these insights highlight the importance of the proposals of Clifton Clarke and Veli-Matti Kärkkäinen regarding allowing the perspectives and voices of religious others to be heard on their terms. What are the possibilities for the effective and powerful witness of the gospel when spoken according to the terms, categories, idioms, and commitments of the world's religious traditions? My suggestion is that just as Samaritan theology, deemed demonic by traditional Jews, can be understood to have provided a critical perspective on the received Jewish theological understanding, so also can the religious traditions of the world, similarly demonized as were the Samaritans from the Jewish point of view, provide critical but no less helpful perspectives for understanding the gospel amidst the pluralistic realities of the twenty-first century. If this is the case, the religions are less demonic realities to be overcome—without denying that there are demonic elements in all religious traditions, including within institutional Christianity itself—than they are invitations to understand the potentiality of the gospel to transform the world. People in other faiths, then, are also less opponents or enemies to be overcome (or destroyed!), but may be potential friends, even family members, if our hearts might first be converted to them.[27]

Acts 6

Going back behind Philip's mission to Samaria and Stephen's speech and martyrdom, we come upon the series of events which drew them both together initially. We meet both Philip and Stephen first as Hellenists, probably from Asia Minor (Acts 6:5). They had somehow been drawn into Judea, with their families and many others, it appears, and gotten caught up in the new messianic movement. What emerged given the explosion of this new movement was, literally, an intercultural phenomenon. If we follow Studebaker's assertion regarding the overlapping of religion and culture, then this sequence of developments demands closer scrutiny vis-à-vis the interreligious encounter.

What we see is that all intercultural encounters are fraught with pitfalls. The Hebraic Jewish widows and the Hellenistic Jewish widows first could not work things out. The emergent conflicts were no doubt felt and interpreted by some as of demonic provenance. The details are sketchy about where the disagreements lie,[28] but I suggest that there were not only linguistic barriers, cultural differences, and economic disparities but also theological dissonances, and these are no doubt sometimes understood spiritually and, hence, in terms of the demon. The last aspect, the religious and theological dimension, unfolded in the opposition to the Hellenistic deaconship of Stephen by other Hellenists with very traditional Jewish commitments (Acts 6:9-10). This was a particularly contentious issue, even demonic, especially when viewed in light of the end of the story which saw the martyrdom of Stephen. But even such highly polemical encounters have a redemptive dimension, and since I have already commented on the potential such intercultural encounters have for the cross-fertilization and transformation of theological understandings, I will say no more about this matter here.

What I want to highlight in this passage, however, is that which is lifted up when read in the context of Kirsteen Kim's discussion of Dalit Christianity in India. As Kim notes in her chapter, renewal Christianity has taken root among the Dalits, even if the results have been mixed. While in many cases, Dalits have experienced uplift as a result of conversion to Christianity, in just as many other cases, the older oppressions and prejudices have re-surfaced within renewal churches.[29] So, on the one hand, renewal Christianity has contributed in some respects to the liberation of the untouchables in India, but on the other hand, renewal churches have also not been immune to being co-opted by the forces of oppression operating at the cultural, political, social, and economic levels. Luke's report in Acts 6 challenges renewalists to follow through with the egalitarian commitments at the heart of the Pentecost narrative—which levels out the hierarchicalism between men and women, old and young, and slave and free (Acts 2:17-18)—and put minorities in charge! Who the minorities are will vary from context to context, whether considered numerically, demographically, culturally, economically, socially, or even theologically.

In the Judean context, the minorities were the Hellenists from the surrounding Mediterranean world. Some might argue in hindsight that this may have been a mistake, that to put Hellenists in charge of food distribution to both Hellenistic and Hebraic widows was to just ask for further divisiveness, resulting in the failed experiment of what some have considered as an early Christian form of communism. I will debate neither the merits nor demerits of such possibilities. More important for our purposes, however, are the intercultural and interreligious implications for the formation of ecclesial communities and for Christian witness, mission, and evangelization. This early messianic community had the potential to model the relationality and mutuality of the coming Day of Lord in ways that invited deference to the leadership and even authority of those initially outside the community of faith. In short, putting minorities in charge not only invites a letting go of power, an elevation of the other, a respectful interface, and a meaningful interdependence, but also expresses a willingness to allow the identity of the community to be transformed by the influx of outside differences. This had the potential to transform the inequalities of the first century Palestinian world, even as it still holds forth possibilities today for accomplishing the rectification of injustices that plague not only Dalit communities in the South Asian continent but all people everywhere.

Mission & Kin-domization:
Pentecost and Mission in a Pluralistic World

Our overarching goal in this concluding chapter in particular and in this volume as a whole has been to suggest how renewal Christianity can continue to engage in the missionary task in a religiously plural world but do so in a manner that neither comprises its core theological convictions on the one hand nor undermines the gospel's capacity to bear witness on the other. More particularly, such an objective is even more urgent given the tendency in renewal missionary and evangelistic practice to demonize the religious other. I have attempted in the preceding to craft a renewal missiology by identifying non-demonization beliefs and practices among the Spirit empowered experiences of the early messianic believers. With these final remarks, then, I want to make three broad theological claims for a renewal missiology in a pluralistic world, all informed by the apostolic practices that highlight and allowed for interreligious engagement rather than demonization.

First, our considerations of the book of Acts suggest a renewal missiology as an extension of the Day of Pentecost narrative in which many different tongues and languages were involved in "speaking about God's deeds of power"

(Acts 2:11). Analogically, whereas the many tongues denoted the many languages and cultures around the Mediterranean world gathered in Jerusalem for the celebration of the Feast Day of Pentecost, in today's pluralistic world, the many cultures of the religions of the world are also potentially conduits for the Spirit's presence and activity in revealing the mystery of Christ and manifesting the wondrous works of God. By extrapolating from what I have suggested in the preceding, renewal approaches to the other religious traditions and to the interreligious encounter should be contextually discerned, taking into consideration the particularities and distinctives of each cultural-religious situation, and being informed by and transform them in turn.[30] This does not lead to any bland universalism since the cross-cultural comprehension and cross-linguistic communication on the Day of Pentecost enabled only a declaration of the wondrous works of God (Acts 2:11), not necessarily resulting in the salvation of all speakers and hearers. Similarly, my minimal claim is that the outpouring of the Spirit makes possible the kin-ship of those who have otherwise been estranged linguistically, culturally, and even religiously, although this in turn certainly has implications for mission and for the eschatological renewal of all creation.

Second, such a dynamic renewal missiology continuously stretches the boundaries of the church and its self-understanding precisely by its poly-contextual set of interactions with its surroundings. Historically, such a project was understood in terms of Christianization, and involved the conversion of the world to the lordship of Christ. The complex interdependence of church, culture, and the political, however, resulted just as often, if not more often, in the transformation of the world according to the image of the missionary and its sending culture than into the image of Christ. In short, Christianization became Westernization because of its complicity with the fortunes of Christendom, with the result that the church became accommodated to the world. Further the Christianization project retained power in the hands of the few at the center— wherever that was ecclesially, politically, and socio-economically—thus simultaneously disempowering those at the margins. It is thus that in our post-Western world, we must get behind Christianization or go beyond it.[31] This involves a rejection of the colonial model of missions and a retrieval and renewal of the apostolic practices instead.[32] From the perspective of the interreligious encounter, what is required is deferentiality toward the religious other that does devolve into an uncritical acquiescence to the other. Urgently needed is the cultivation of a spiritual discernment that is capable of building bridges with people of other faiths but yet is wary of the demonic realities that threaten all with sincere faith. This involves the turn to the religious other that enables us to understand them first on their own terms, rather than an a priori demonization of the other before we have had a chance to get to know them.

Third, then, the call to mission and witness involves, as we have seen with Stephen in the apostolic era and in countless other examples delineated by Kim and Omenyo, the call to martyrdom (Acts 1:8). What Kärkkäinen calls a theology of suffering is simultaneously an *orthopathos* that manifests the suffering love of God for a dying world, a world that includes people of all faiths and even those of no faith. Christian witness may involve, in our pluralistic context, less the capacity to talk louder and do more to Christianize the world than the capacity to defer to others and receive from them, even to the point of death. The renewal of the Spirit may be liberative for the marginalized, but at the expense of our own lives; but even in these cases, our martyrdom is for the glory of God and on behalf of our fellow human beings, motivated by the hope that death sows the seeds of later reconciliation between humanity and with God. While such an approach may render us vulnerable to the demonic realities of the world, it also has the capacity to undermine the demonic expressions in our own faith and equip us with the weapons of the gospel of peace instead.

This common humanity, testified to by St. Paul on the Areopagus means that rather than a demonization of the (religious) other, we must move beyond the failed task of Christianization and work for the kin-domization of the gospel of Christ, with others, even across religious lines, to the level that is possible.[33] Remember that the author of the book of Acts himself records Jesus addressing the impossibility of salvation: "What is impossible for mortals is possible for God[!]" (Luke 18:27). The miracle of Pentecost was precisely the impossible relationality and mutuality of human diversity caught up in the Spirit's redemptive work: the redemption of the pluralism of human tongues inaugurated on that Day initiated a kin-dom movement which stretched from Jerusalem to Judea to Samaria and still yet aspires to reach the ends of the earth. It is that same Spirit's work that enables human interaction, dialogue, and comprehension across the many differences that otherwise separates us. As we have seen in the book of Acts, the Pentecost outpouring brought about a kinship of Hebrews and Hellenists (as fraught as that was with challenges), empowered Hellenistic messianic ventures into Samaria, inspired Paul's affirmation of pagan insights regarding the common humanity that joined him together with his interlocutors, and enabled mutual interactions with the barbarians at Malta, etc. Such relational approaches to religious others, following in the footsteps of the apostolic community, can be found stretching across the last two millennia of Christian history through to the present. So if Jews and Gentiles who were before aliens and strangers to one another are now in effect kin, joined together in Christ and by his Spirit (Eph. 2:12-13), is it possible that there may be a form of relationality and mutuality between Christians and those of other faiths, one that heralds and anticipates the kin-dom? I am certainly aware that there is a type of kinship that can be found within the ecclesial community when those who acknowledge Christ as Lord gather the eucharistic table that is not available to Christian encounters with those in other faiths. At the same time, does not eating together across religious lines or the mutuality of being guests or hosts vis-à-vis those in other religious traditions also signify the acknowledgment of our common humanity and open up a level of kinship that in turn can be a sign of the eschatological redemption to come?

Thus it is that the goal of such Spirit-enabled encounter cannot be merely the expansion of the church as an institution—that is in part what it means to say that we live in a post-Christian world—but must be the dawning of the kin-dom of God proclaimed by Jesus the Messiah. It is also in this sense that I urge viewing the interreligious encounter as an occasion for the manifestation of the kin-dom, an opportunity to do the works of the kin-dom, and as an opening for the coming of the kin-dom. This is the Spirit's invitation to inhabit the kin-dom beyond the superficial boundaries of race, class, gender, culture, ethnicity, and perhaps even religion. It is the work of the Spirit to bring about the redemption of all people and even to enable peoples from many tribes, tongues, and languages and their kings and leaders to bring their riches, purified of all things unholy by the glory of Christ, into the new heavens and new earth (Rev. 21:24, 26), the kin-dom that is now here somehow, but that is also yet to come.[34]

Notes

1. My use of "renewal" and its cognates in what follows is inclusive of classical Pentecostalism, neo-Pentecostalism, the charismatic movement, and those from other related revival and revitalization movements in the Euro-American West and across the global South that feature charismatic spirituality and phenomenology.

2. I provide such a critical account partly in ch. 4 of my *In the Days of Caesar: Pentecostalism and Political Theology* (Grand Rapids and Cambridge, UK: William B. Eerdmans Publishing Company, 2010).

3. Unless otherwise noted, all scriptural quotations are from the New Revised Standard Version of the Bible (available at http://bible.oremus.org/), copyright © 1989 by the Division of Christian Education of the National Council of the Churches of Christ in the U.S.A., and are used by permission. All rights reserved.

4. Birgit Meyer, "The Power of Money: Politics, Occult Forces, and Pentecostalism in Ghana," *African Studies Review* 41:3 (1998): 15-37, esp. 32-33.

5. I present an overview of the issues in my *The Spirit Poured Out on All Flesh: Pentecostalism and the Possibility of Global Theology* (Grand Rapids: Baker Academic, 2005), 35-37. Regretfully, I did not then come out forcefully against the crimes that Montt's government perpetrated against the indigenous people of Guatemala.

6. Sara Diamond, *Spiritual Warfare: The Politics of the Christian Right* (Boston: South End Press, 1989), 166, quoting from *Sectas y religiosidad en America Latina* (October 1984): 23.

7. At the popular level, few pentecostals would question this statement: "The U.S. military machine was God's way of defending the peace so that his message of salvation could be made known. Washington's adversaries around the world therefore continue to be God's adversaries, and evangelizing the world continued to hinge on U.S. power"; see David Stoll, *Is Latin America Turning Protestant? The Politics of Evangelical Growth* (Berkeley: University of California Press, 1990), 67. For an account of the gradual transformation of the Assemblies of God in the USA from a pacifist denomination into one supporting an idolatrous form of nationalism and its accompanying militarism, see Paul Alexander, *Peace to War: Shifting Allegiances in the Assemblies of God*, The C. Henry Smith Series 9 (Telford: Cascadia Publishing House, 2009).

8. This and the next paragraph are adapted from my *Hospitality and the Other: Pentecost, Christian Practices, and the Neighbor* (Maryknoll: Orbis Books, 2008), 25-27.

9. Joseph Thompson, "Rising from the Mediocre to the Miraculous," in C. Peter Wagner and Joseph Thompson, eds., *Out of Africa: How the Spiritual Explosion among Nigerians is Impacting the World* (Ventura: Regal, 2004), 19-36, esp. 26-28. For more

coverage of this issue, see Rosalind I. J. Hackett, "Discourses of Demonization in Africa and Beyond," *Diogenes* 50:3 (2003): 61-75, and the work of Ogbu U. Kalu—i.e., "Estranged Bedfellows? The Demonisation of the Aladura in African Pentecostal Rhetoric," *Missionalia* 28:2/3 (2000): 121-42.

10. Thus the back flap of Timothy O. Olonade, ed., *Battle Cry for the Nations: Rekindling the Flames of World Evangelization* (Jos, Nigeria: CAPRO Media, 1995), announces that this book is designed to mobilize the church to evangelize the "unreached millions" caught up in "idolatry and Islam."

11. Ogbu U. Kalu, *Power, Poverty and Prayer: The Challenges of Poverty and Pluralism in African Christianity, 1960-1996*, Studies in the Intercultural History of Christianity 122 (Frankfurt: Peter Lang, 2000), ch. 5.

12. See Steve Brouwer, Paul Gifford, and Susan D. Rose, *Exporting the American Gospel: Global Christian Fundamentalism* (New York and London: Routledge, 1996), 173-75; Rosalind I. J. Hackett, "Radical Christian Revivalism in Nigeria and Ghana: Recent Patterns of Intolerance and Conflict," in Abdullahi Ahmed An-Na'im, ed., *Proselytization and Communal Self-Determination in Africa* (Maryknoll: Orbis, 1999), 246-67, esp. 252; Rosalind I. J. Hackett, "Managing or Manipulating Religious Conflict in the Nigerian Media," in Jolyon Mitchell and Sophia Marriage, eds., *Mediating Religion: Conversations in Media, Religion and Culture* (London and New York: T and T Clark, 2003), 47-63, esp. 58; Ruth Marshall-Fratani, "Mediating the Global and Local in Nigerian Pentecostalism," in Andre Corten and Ruth Marshall-Fratani, eds., *Between Babel and Pentecost: Transnational Pentecostalism in Africa and Latin America* (Bloomington: Indiana University Press, 2001), 80-105, esp. 102-03; Ogbu U. Kalu, "Sharia and Islam in Nigerian Pentecostal Rhetoric, 1970-2003," *PNEUMA: The Journal of the Society for Pentecostal Studies* 26:2 (2004): 242-61, esp. 256-58; and Matthews A. Ojo, "American Pentecostalism and the Growth of Pentecostal-Charismatic Movements in Nigeria," in R. Drew Smith, ed., *Freedom's Distant Shores: American Protestants and Post-Colonial Alliances with Africa* (Waco: Baylor University Press, 2006), 155-67, esp. 167. The reference to "Satan's bondage" is in Paul Gifford, *The New Crusaders: Christianity and the New Right in Southern Africa*, rev. ed. (London and Concord: Pluto Press, 1991), 111, while the renewalist assertion that Allah is not the supreme God builds on the highly polemical book by a Muslim convert, G. J. O. Moshay, *Who is This Allah?* (Bucks: Dorchester House, 1994).

13. See Rosalind I. J. Hackett, "Devil Bustin' Satellites: How Media Liberalization in Africa Generates Religious Intolerance and Conflict," in Rosalind I. J. Hackett and James H. Smith, eds., *Religious Dimensions of Conflict and Peace in Neoliberal Africa* (Notre Dame: University of Notre Dame Press, in press). Thanks to Prof. Hackett for sending me a draft copy of this paper.

14. Toyin Falola points out that in light of the emerging Muslim literary and media propaganda, some renewalist have sought to rationalize hate crimes in religious terms: "the holy books provide psychological support for all sorts of crimes, including murder"; see Falola, *Violence in Nigeria: The Crisis of Religious Politics and Secular Ideologies* (Rochester: University of Rochester Press, 1998), 264.

15. I detail and discuss these in my *Hospitality and the Other*, 16-19. See also Ruth Marshall, *Political Spiritualities: The Pentecostal Revolution in Nigeria* (Chicago and London: University of Chicago Press, 2009).

16. I have taken up this issue at some length in my article focused on the Gospel of John: "'The Light Shines in the Darkness': Johannine Dualism and the Challenge of Christian Theology of Religions Today," *Journal of Religion* 89:1 (2009): 31-56.

17. This is the gist of Birgit Meyer's analysis that focuses on the Christian mission to convert the heathen by insisting that they do what is indicated in the main title of her by now almost classic essay: "'Make a Complete Break with the Past': Memory and Post-Colonial Modernity in Ghanaian Pentecostalist Discourse," *Journal of Religion on Africa* 28:3 (1998): 316-49.

18. My work has repeatedly focused on the Acts narrative not only because this second Lukan volume has been, historically, the canon-within-the-canon for renewal spirituality and theology, but also because of the renewal restorationist hermeneutic that has consistently sought to enter into the apostolic experience of the earliest Christians. For more on the use of Acts for the purposes of renewal theology, see my *In the Days of Caesar*, ch. 3.1-3.2.

19. My focus on practices derives from my convictions regarding their centrality—over and against more abstract theological or theoretical emphases—for renewal missiology; see my essays, "The Spirit, Christian Practices, and the Religions: Theology of Religions in Pentecostal and Pneumatological Perspective," *Asbury Journal* 62:2 (2007): 5-31, "The Spirit of Hospitality: Pentecostal Perspectives toward a Performative Theology of the Interreligious Encounter," *Missiology: An International Review* 35:1 (2007): 55-73, and "The Inviting Spirit: Pentecostal Beliefs and Practices regarding the Religions Today," in Steven Studebaker, ed., *Defining Issues in Pentecostalism: Classical and Emergent* (Eugene: Wipf & Stock, 2008), 29-44.

20. Those who wish to follow and compare my exegetical arguments in the order that they appear in Acts can consult my *The Spirit and the Public Square: Reflections on the Holy Spirit in Luke-Acts* [working title] (Brewster: Paraclete Press, 2011), chs. 14, 16, 18, 33, 35, and 39.

21. See Walter J. Hollenweger, *Pentecostalism: Origins and Developments Worldwide* (Peabody: Hendrickson, 1997), ch. 11. I address some aspects of the complex issues of culture and syncretism for missiology in my articles, "Culture" and "Syncretism," in John Corrie, ed., *Dictionary of Mission Theology: Evangelical Foundations* (Nottingham and Downers Grove: InterVarsity Press, 2007), 82-87 and 373-76 respectively.

22. For further elaboration of the interconnectedness of these theological domains, see my *Spirit-Word-Community: Theological Hermeneutics in Trinitarian Perspective* (Burlington and Aldershot: Ashgate, and Eugene: Wipf & Stock, 2002), parts II & III.

23. Richie has developed his theology of interreligious dialogue further in his *Speaking by the Spirit: A Pentecostal Model for Interreligious Encounter and Dialogue* (Lexington: Emeth Press, 2010).

24. The importance of this approach is discussed and debated in my co-authored essay with Frank D. Macchia, Ralph Del Colle and Dale T. Irvin, "Christ and Spirit: Dogma, Discernment and Dialogical Theology in a Religiously Plural World," *Journal of Pentecostal Theology* 12:1 (2003): 15-83.

25. My own attempts to engage with Buddhist traditions include the following essays: "Technologies of Liberation: A Comparative Soteriology of Eastern Orthodoxy and Theravada Buddhism," *Dharma Deepika: A South Asian Journal of Missiological Research* 7:1 (2003): 17-60; "The Holy Spirit and the World Religions: On the Christian Discernment of Spirit(s) 'after' Buddhism," *Buddhist-Christian Studies* 24 (2004): 191-207; "Christian and Buddhist Perspectives on Neuropsychology and the Human Person: *Pneuma* and *Pratityasamutpada*," *Zygon: Journal of Religion and Science* 40:1 (2005): 143-65; "The Buddhist-Christian Encounter in the USA: Reflections on Christian Practices," in Ulrich van der Heyden and Andreas Feldtkeller, eds., *Border Crossings:*

Explorations of an Interdisciplinary Historian—Festschrift for Irving Hexham (Stuttgart: Franz Steiner Verlag, 2008), 457-72; "Mind and Life, Religion and Science: The Dalai Lama and the Buddhist-Christian-Science Trilogue," *Buddhist-Christian Studies* 28 (2008): 43-63; and "From Azusa Street to the Bo Tree and Back: Strange Babblings and Interreligious Interpretations in the Pentecostal Encounter with Buddhism," in Veli-Matti Kärkkäinen, ed., *The Spirit in the World: Emerging Pentecostal Theologies in Global Contexts* (Grand Rapids: William B. Eerdmans Publishing Company, 2009), 203-26. Two book length monographs are forthcoming.

26. I treat it as such in my *The Spirit Poured Out on All* Flesh, 241-44.

27. Thus, for example, in Peter's experience conversion on two fronts in his encounter with Cornelius in Acts 9-10: first a conversion that allowed him to enter into the home of an unclean Gentile, and then second, a conversion that allowed him to embrace the Gentile as an equal, despite the fact that this Gentile remained a Gentile rather than becoming a Jew. See Simon S. Maimela, "Practice of Mission and Evangelism," *LWF [Lutheran World Federation] Report* 13-14 (1983): 43-58.

28. A full discussion of all the complex social, historical, cultural, and other issues is Reta Halteman Finger, *Of Widows and Meals: Communal Meals in the Book of Acts* (Grand Rapids and Cambridge, UK: William B. Eerdmans Publishing Company, 2007).

29. I discuss Dalit renewal in my *Spirit Poured Out on All Flesh*, 54-58.

30. I sketch the outlines of such a contextual soteriology in Yong, "Salvation, Society, and the Spirit: Pentecostal Contextualization and Political Theology from Cleveland to Birmingham, from Springfield to Seoul," *Pax Pneuma: The Journal of Pentecostals & Charismatics for Peace & Justice* 5:2 (2009): 22-34.

31. The following summarizes the arguments in my essays, "Many Tongues, Many Practices: Pentecost and Theology of Mission at 2010," in Ogbu U. Kalu, Edmund Kee-Fook Chia, and Peter Vethanayagamony, eds., *Mission after Christendom: Emergent Themes in Contemporary Mission* (Louisville: Westminster John Knox Press, 2010), 43-58, and "The Church and Mission Theology in a Post-Constantinian Era: Soundings from the Anglo-American Frontier," in Akintunde Akinade, ed., *A New Day: Essays on World Christianity in Honor of Lamin Sanneh* (New York: Peter Lang, 2010), forthcoming.

32. See also my "The Missiology of Jamestown: 1607-2007 and Beyond—Toward a Postcolonial Theology of Mission in North America," in Amos Yong and Barbara Brown Zikmund, eds., *Remembering Jamestown: Hard Questions about Christian Mission* (Maryknoll: Orbis Books, 2010), 157-67.

33. My use of "kin-domization" affirms the feminist attempt to avoid perpetuating the sexist, elitist, and hierarchical connotations that have accrued to the classical theological notion of "kingdom"; see Ada María Isasi-Diaz, *Mujerista Theology: A Theology for the Twenty-First Century* (Maryknoll: Orbis Books, 1996), ch. 5, and also Don A. Pittman, "Dialogical Discernment and the 'Kin-dom' of God: On Globalizing Ministries in North America," *Lexington Theological Quarterly* 28:4 (1993): 319-31.

34. Thanks to my graduate assistant, Timothy Lim, my longtime collaborator (in all things related to renewal and theology of religions) Tony Richie, and my co-editor Clifton Clarke, for their comments on a previous draft of this essay.

Contributors

Clifton Clarke (PhD University of Birmingham) is Associate Professor of Global Missions and World Christianity, Regent University School of Divinity, Virginia Beach, Virginia.

Veli-Matti Kärkkäinen (PhD University of Helsinki) is Professor of Systematic Theology, Fuller Theological Seminary, Pasadena, California, and Docent in Ecumenics, University of Helsinki, Helsinki, Finland.

Kirsteen Kim (PhD University of Birmingham) is Associate Senior Lecturer in Theology, Leeds Trinity University College, Leeds, United Kingdom.

Cephas N. Omenyo (PhD University of Utrecht) is Associate Professor, Department for the Study of Religions, and Vice Dean of the Faculty of Arts, University of Ghana, Legon, Ghana.

Tony Richie (DMin Asbury Theological Seminary and PhD London School of Theology) is adjunct professor at Pentecostal Theological Seminary, Cleveland, Tennessee.

Steven M. Studebaker (PhD Marquette University) is Assistant Professor of Systematic and Historical Theology and Howard and Shirley Bentall Chair in Evangelical Thought, McMaster Divinity College, McMaster University, Hamilton, Ontario.

Amos Yong (PhD Boston University) is J. Rodman Williams Professor of Theology, Regent University School of Divinity, Virginia Beach, Virginia.

Index

CPSIA information can be obtained at www.ICGtesting.com
Printed in the USA
BVOW010344160812

297930BV00003B/206/P